Wiyaxayxt/
   Wiyaakaaawn.

wiyáx̣ayx̣t ✳ **as days go by** ✳ wiyáakaaʔawn

Cayuse Sisters

The large basalt pillars on the cover are known as the Cayuse Sisters. Coyote fell in love with three sisters who were building a trap in the river to catch salmon. Always the trickster, Coyote watched them, and at night he would destroy their work. The sisters rebuilt the trap daily, but Coyote would destroy it each time. One morning, Coyote saw the sisters crying. They were starving for fish. Coyote promised to build them a trap if they would become his wives. The sisters consented, and he kept his promise. For many years, Coyote lived happily with the sisters, but after awhile he became jealous of them. Using his supernatural powers, Coyote changed two of his wives into basalt pillars. The third wife he turned into a cave downstream (this cave is now covered by the dammed waters of the Columbia River). He then turned himself into a nearby rock so he could watch over them forever. The photograph above also shows the Sisters, but in the time before the dams, when the Columbia River ran wild.

The person in the foreground on the cover is tribal member Andrew Wildbill (Cayuse/Umatilla/Walla Walla), a young man with ties to the past and to the future in his native community. A beadwork artist, he has also inherited the role of tribal whipman, with the task of keeping order on the ceremonial floor. He is a college student, studying fisheries biology, and plans to return to the reservation to contribute to preservation efforts of critical natural and cultural resources.

•:— ⁎ —:•

wiyáx̣ayx̣t ⁎ as days go by ⁎ wiyáakaaʔawn

Our History, Our Land, and Our People
The Cayuse, Umatilla, and Walla Walla

Edited by Jennifer Karson

Published by Tamástslikt Cultural Institute, Pendleton
& Oregon Historical Society Press, Portland
in association with the University of Washington Press, Seattle and London

•:— ⁎ —:•

13 12 11 10 09 08 07   6 5 4 3 2

Tamástslikt Cultural Institute
72789 Highway 331
Pendleton, Oregon 97801
www.tamastslikt.com

Oregon Historical Society Press
1200 SW Park Avenue
Portland, Oregon 97205-2483
www.ohs.org

In association with
University of Washington Press
PO Box 50096
Seattle, Washington 98145-5096
www.washington.edu/uwpress

Cover and interior design: Jennifer Viviano
Cover photograph: Patrice Hall Walters (Umatilla)

Information on photographs that begin each chapter can be found on page 264.

Library of Congress Cataloging-in-Publication Data
Wiyaxayxt/Wiyaakaa'awn = As days go by: our history, our land, and our people—the Cayuse, Umatilla, and Walla Walla / edited by Jennifer Karson.
    p. cm.
Recollections of the members of the Confederated Tribes of the Umatilla Reservation.
Includes bibliographical references and index.
ISBN: 978-0-295-98623-4 (pbk. : alk. paper)
  1. Indians of North America—Oregon—Interviews. 2. Indians of North America—Washington(State)—Interviews. 3. Oral history—Oregon. 4. Oral history—Washington(State) 5. Oral tradition—Oregon. 6. Oral tradition—Washington (State) 7. Confederated Tribes of the Umatilla Reservation, Oregon—History. I. Karson, Jennifer. II. Confederated Tribes of the Umatilla Reservation, Oregon. III. Tamástslikt Cultural Institute. IV. Title: As days go by. V. Title: Our history, our land, and our people—the Cayuse, Umatilla, and Walla Walla.
E78.O6W59 2006
979.5004´97412—dc22   2006046559

Contributors

PHILLIP E. CASH CASH (Nez Perce/Cayuse) — Ph.D. candidate in the Joint Program in Anthropology and Linguistics, University of Arizona, Tucson. Mr. Cash Cash is engaged in language preservation work among the peoples of the southern Columbia Plateau, studying Nez Perce, Sahaptian, Cayuse, Klamath, Chinook Jargon, and other Oregon languages, and specializing in the digital documentation of these endangered languages.

ROBERTA CONNER (Umatilla/Cayuse/Nez Perce) — Director, Tamástslikt Cultural Institute. Ms. Conner has been director of Tamástslikt, a tribally owned and operated museum/cultural center on the Umatilla Indian Reservation, since 1998. She worked for the U.S. Small Business Administration for thirteen years and is a graduate of the University of Oregon and Willamette University's Atkinson Graduate School of Management.

DEBRA CROSWELL (Cayuse) — Communications Director / Deputy Executive Director, Confederated Tribes of the Umatilla Indian Reservation. Ms. Croswell's responsibilities include public relations and information (including the Tribes' Web site, monthly newspaper, and radio station), legislative and government-to-government affairs, and media relations.

MICHAEL J. FARROW (Cayuse/Umatilla/Walla Walla/Nez Perce/Yakama/Wintun) — Director, Department of Natural Resources, Confederated Tribes of the Umatilla Indian Reservation, until his death in 2004. Mr. Farrow served as a medic in the Vietnam conflict and upon his return to the reservation became a planner for the Tribes, developing the first Comprehensive Plan, a document that has effectively guided the CTUIR tribal development and growth for the past twenty-five years.

DANIEL W. HESTER — Tribal Attorney, Confederated Tribes of the Umatilla Indian Reservation. A graduate of the University of California in 1977 and the University of Oregon Law School in 1981, Mr. Hester has served as tribal attorney for the CTUIR since 1985.

WILLIAM JOHNSON (Cayuse/Walla Walla/Nez Perce) — Chief Judge of the Umatilla Tribal Court, Confederated Tribes of the Umatilla Indian Reservation. Judge Johnson served as tribal attorney and as tribal chair of the Board of Trustees and the General Council. As chief judge since 1988, he is dedicated to family, furthering education, and a career focused on self-determination through judicial administration by and for Indian peoples.

WILLIAM L. LANG — Professor of History, Portland State University. Dr. Lang has written extensively on the history of the Columbia River region, is the former director of the Center for Columbia River History, and is a descendent of Joel Palmer, superintendent of Indian affairs for the Oregon Territories and negotiator at the 1855 Walla Walla Treaty Council.

CHARLES F. LUCE — Mr. Luce was hired as the first attorney for the Confederated Tribes of the Umatilla Indian Reservation in 1947, working on their behalf for fifteen years before moving on to become administrator of the Bonneville Power Administration, undersecretary of the Department of the Interior in the Johnson administration, and CEO of Consolidated Edison, where he retired in 1994.

ANTONE MINTHORN (Cayuse) — Chairman of the Board of Trustees, Confederated Tribes of the Umatilla Indian Reservation. Mr. Minthorn served in the U.S. Marine Corps from 1957 to 1960, went on to attend Gonzaga University, and graduated from Eastern Oregon State College. He previously spent fifteen years as chair of the Tribes' General Council, the voting membership. As tribal chairman from 1997 to 2001 and from 2003 to the present, Mr. Minthorn is the top elected official for the Confederated Tribes of the Umatilla Indian Reservation tribal government.

RONALD J. POND (Umatilla/Palouse) – Director, Plateau Center for American Indian Studies, Washington State University. Dr. Pond, who received his Ph.D. in Interdisciplinary Studies from Washington State University in 2004, is presently serving as interim director of the Plateau Center, and plans to return to teaching as assistant professor at Washington State University at the conclusion of his directorship.

DONALD SAMPSON (Walla Walla/Cayuse/Umatilla) — Executive Director, Confederated Tribes of the Umatilla Indian Reservation. Mr. Sampson has held the executive director position with the Tribes since 2003 and is responsible for more than a thousand employees and a $112 million operating budget. He served as chairman of the Board of Trustees of the CTUIR from 1993 to 1997 and as the executive director of the Columbia River Inter-Tribal Fish Commission from 1998 to 2002.

JOHN DAVID TOVEY, JR. (Cayuse) — Executive Director of the Coquille Indian Tribe from 2002 through early 2006 and Executive Director of the Confederated Tribes of the Umatilla Indian Reservation from 1998 through 2002. Starting in 1986, Mr. Tovey served as director of the Umatilla Tribes' Department of Economic and Community Development, which he initiated. He oversaw all aspects of development of the Wildhorse Resort and Tamástslikt Cultural Institute.

Contents

v   List of Contributors

ix   Foreword, *by Alvin M. Josephy, Jr.*

xi   Preface

xiii   Acknowledgments

xv   As Days Go By — An Introduction, *by Debra Croswell*

3   Tamánwit, *by Thomas Morning Owl*

5   Oral Traditions of the Natítaytma, *by Phillip E. Cash Cash*

23   Early Contact and Incursion, 1700–1850, *by Roberta Conner and William L. Lang*

61   Wars, Treaties, and the Beginning of Reservation Life, *by Antone Minthorn*

93   Through Change and Transition: Treaty Commitments Made and Broken, *by Ronald J. Pond and Daniel W. Hester*

151   The Beginning of Modern Tribal Governance and Enacting Sovereignty, *by Charles F. Luce and William Johnson*

193   Self-Determination and Recovery, *by John David Tovey, Jr. and friends of the late Michael J. Farrow*

239   Other Important Events in Contemporary Tribal History

245   Epilogue: Asserting Sovereignty into the Future, *by Donald Sampson*

253   Index

265   Photographs and Credits

Foreword

A Conversation with Alvin M. Josephy, Jr.

Alvin M. Josephy, Jr., the author of The Nez Perce Indians and the Opening of the Northwest *and many other books on Northwest native history, spoke for many years about Indian people writing their own histories. He was particularly excited about this project. In 2005, during the last summer of his life, in conversations at his home in Joseph, Oregon, and at Tamástslikt Cultural Institute, he commented on the CTUIR tribal history and its importance to Indian and non-Indian people. These are some of his words from those conversations.*

My association with this story begins in 1951 when I was first sent west to research an article for *Time* magazine. I just jumped into the pond. Anytime I took on assignments about writing about Indians later on, I came away thinking that the job should get into the hands of the people themselves. While it is a big story, in one respect, it is not complicated. The Indian people here are just families, and this is their family history. They have coexisted for a long time where the rivers meet, and this has taught them about sharing. To me, it is all one. This book is important; and to tell it, one must pull out the bottom card and throw it away.

One challenge in writing one's own history is that some readers may look for a voluminous encyclopedic work, whereas the true task is to tell the best and fullest historical account from one's own perspective. Another challenge is in understanding how important or significant this particular tribal history is to the national Indian story. Individual tribes may think of themselves in geographic and historic isolation. These three tribes exist in their universe to be sure, and the experiment is in seeing just how they stack up against the national history of Indians.

This project creates an understanding among Indians and non-Indians alike that the Tribes are their own subject matter and that they can benefit from all of the fieldwork and research done in the past. They can also benefit from the elders' insights and remembrances. And together, they can help compile that into a modern picture of the Tribes' people. It is not so much that anybody got it wrong in previous writings; every story can be told in a variety of dimensions. The Tribes simply want to present another perspective. This project will create a place where that can happen more in the future. The Tribes' vision is to be the foremost trusted source of information about themselves, because trust is what Indian people must have in order to be good collaborators.

A great deal has been written about Indians, but nobody has really told this story. In fact, the Cayuse, Umatilla, and Walla Walla people, who today make up the Confederated Tribes of the Umatilla Indian Reservation, are "understudied" in some respects by outside scholars, in comparison to their neighbors the Nez Perce, for instance. The Confederated Tribes consider themselves lucky in this regard. Traditionally, non-Indians are not all that interested in knowing any version of history other than their own. Indian people are very close to their history; but when others sit down and start writing it, it turns out to be the non-Indians' history and not the Indians'. In most cases, the Indians were not consulted about it at all.

In reading this text, one should not forget the impact brought by the missionaries and settlers to these Tribes in the 1830s and 1840s. There was a strong religious movement going on at the time; and no matter what happened, Indian people were blamed for the violence and strife that ensued. The Cayuse, for instance, were blamed for the 1847 Whitman incident. They thought they were doing the right thing and acted on it. The point is that the religious impact was a challenge to the Cayuse, Umatilla, and Walla Walla people. They had to prevail, even though the non-Indian religion was being so heavily imposed on them.

The Tribes' prominence does not come from any one act. It comes from steadfastness and loyalty to their own reservation and the ceded boundaries. There is a loyalty that lives in the Cayuse, Umatilla, and Walla Walla. They have had much diminishment to their reservation. They have only one treaty, and everything else has been congressionally enacted around them. After all that has been done, they still do not believe they are victims of this history. They have been oppressed and suppressed, but the leadership does not believe they are victims. There is still a Horatio Alger spirit here — one that pronounces "we can prevail."

In creating this book — a collaboration of twenty-seven different people, made up of authors, reviewers, and other informants, Indian and non-Indian — there is an effort to bring, in some way, the same set of facts to life with a different take. What advice would I give readers about what is written here? To people who have not read a lot of Indian history or do not know much about Indian history, what advice would I give them? Just read it. Find the true story for yourselves. Find it in books if you must. This will get you reading. I don't know if there is a better way. Indians are going to survive. They have the strength and the stamina and the loyalty of numbers of their own. We all have to ensure that it is going to be true.

Preface

It was not until very recently that the indigenous languages spoken by the people of the Umatilla Indian Reservation were transferred into a written form. For as many words that are in the lexicon, there are perhaps as many ways to write them down. Many language speakers choose their own phonetic structure and share that within their families. Missionaries and explorers of the past used their own preconceived sound systems of English or French to document how they heard the spoken language, often leading to confusion or miscommunication because they relied on their own understanding of the interpretations given them. Finally, tribal linguists have decided on a written system of orthography that can be universally understood by future generations. None of these practices take away from the fact that these were and are oral languages. The languages are taught to others primarily through repetition and immersion, even though curriculum and testing now have a solid footing in the learning experience.

As the culture is embedded in the language of a people, so too are the stories that give that culture its own particular context. Meanings cannot always be translated between languages, but the attempts that are made — in scholarly books and essays written by those who live outside that experience, for example — hold their own value. Like the languages of a people, the history of a people can be written in many ways. Anecdotes and oral history intertwine with seminal events in the history of native North America. And so it is with this group of tribes — the Walla Walla, Umatilla, and Cayuse. One elder, commenting on how history was recorded in the past, said that when a discrepancy occurred between people, a survey was taken among all present on how they recalled the events. Based on that, a consensus was determined, and that is how it stayed in the oral record.

The corpus and process of this project involves moving from a tradition of oral repetition to a written format, while retaining the repetition and storytelling that goes hand-in-hand with passing down the oral history. Some authors in this book felt most comfortable introducing their lineal descent as they embarked on their writing. Readers may also notice that some authors chose to interpersonally mark time through personal recollections of events, drawing directly from their own family's oral stories. As social memory and history intertwine, one story is told with many voices, creating a tapestry of information that has become this first attempt at a comprehensive history of and by the Confederated Tribes of the Umatilla Indian Reservation. As the editor of this book, I have not been the gatekeeper, but have helped usher the project along in a manner that protects the voices readers will hear from one section to the next.

Parts of this book connect with a continuum insofar as the early history lays the seeds for the later history. These become seeds of a survival story, if you will. The result is a history that is positive, not a story of victimization felt by a people. The land that was reserved in the treaty for people to live on is now part of the story of economic development.

There is no delineation between prehistory and history here. Ways of knowing the world in the time when the animals could speak are retained in the culture as ways of knowing the world as it is lived in today. The pieces of this book exemplify these ways of knowing, and readers are invited to explore and engage the history of the Walla Walla, Umatilla, and Cayuse peoples as told by them — on their own terms and in their own ways.

Thank you for taking the time to read and to listen.

Jennifer Karson
Pendleton, 2006

Acknowledgments

This book is compiled by a community of writers and a review committee made up of tribal members and scholars. There are multiple voices, none uniquely authoritative yet all with the authority of knowing their history on intimate terms. This collaborative work would not have been possible without the guidance and expertise of the following internal reviewers and contributors: Naomi Stacy, Leah Conner, Lydia Johnson, James Keyser, Clifford Trafzer, Sam Pambrun, Robert Ruby, Matthew Johnson, Christopher Burford, James Lavadour, Tom Hampson, Rich Wandschneider, Kathryn Brigham, Aaron Skirvin, and Andrew Fisher. This project would not have been possible without the efforts of the Tamástslikt staff: John Chess, Malissa Minthorn-Winks, Martha Franklin, and Dallas D. Dick. We are also grateful for the assistance and patience of Armand Minthorn, Noel Rude, Wil Phinney, Andrew Wildbill, Janene Morris, Peggy Harris, Teara Farrow, Diana LaSarge, Jacob Puzey, and Dan Haug.

Thanks also goes to the Oregon Historical Society for their early support and vision, and for the hard work and professionalism of Marianne Keddington-Lang, Joy Margheim, Eliza Jones, and Dean Shapiro. Support was provided by the Circle of Tribal Advisors to the National Council of the Lewis and Clark Bicentennial and by the Administration for Native Americans.

As Days Go By

An Introduction

Debra Croswell

For centuries, authors have documented the history of societies from around the world. Most often these histories are developed from the outside. An author — not one of the peoples being documented — studies the people, their culture, and their history and then writes a book about that society. While we have and can continue to learn much from these documented histories, they are often without the depth and point of view that can only be provided by people who are part of a particular society.

Several authors have written about the Cayuse, Umatilla, and Walla Walla tribal people, including our history and culture. We appreciate those efforts and are forever grateful to writers such as Theodore Stern, Robert Ruby, John Brown, and Alvin M. Josephy, Jr. These individuals have done much to help our Tribes preserve vital pieces of our history, and they continue to be important scholars that we consult and honor. In fact, Ruby and Josephy played key roles in making this tribal history book happen. They encouraged us to tell our own story and assisted with this project.

But our time has come — time for our people to write about our history, our cul-

ture, our way of life, and our future. As we begin the twenty-first century, we are a small group of people (nearly twenty-five hundred enrolled members) with a big story to tell, and now we have the resources to tell that story ourselves.

We are now our own authors, and we exercise the right of telling our own history. We need not rely solely on professional authors like those who have written about us previously, although they will certainly continue to be a valuable part of this and future projects. In a day when tribes, including the Confederated Tribes of the Umatilla Indian Reservation, or CTUIR, are working convincingly under the philosophy of self-determination and self-governance, documenting our history is no different. We must fulfill that responsibility. We know our story best. We must talk with our elders and document important information so that it is not lost. We must put that information into media that will benefit us and our children for the long run.

Historically and traditionally, our ancestors belonged to an oral society. They passed on traditions and values, not by writing them down but by telling them, teaching them, and living them every day. While we retain oral traditions in our tribal community today, we must acknowledge that we live in an age of technology and that the world is very different from what our ancestors knew. Our children are exposed to things our ancestors probably never imagined.

Because of our relationship with mainstream society, we no longer live the way our ancestors did. We learn traditions, values, and language in a different context than our ancestors did. Many of our children do not have access to elders who teach them customs and language every day; and since the mid-twentieth century, many of us were not fortunate enough to have close relationships with elders who, every day, taught us traditions, values, and language.

As this book will reveal, our ancestors endured heavy burdens as the non-Indian society came to dominate their land and their lives. They were punished for speaking their native tongue and for practicing their native traditions. They lived under many types of discrimination and oppression. They were forced into situations that damaged their health and well-being. Today, as we strive to recover from all this and as we strive to preserve our native language, traditions, and values, we must use whatever resources we have available, including modern technology and the written word. And we must exercise our desire and ability to tell our own story.

This history project is intended to document, from our own perspective, the past, present, and future of the Cayuse, Umatilla, and Walla Walla people and our government — the Confederated Tribes of the Umatilla Indian Reservation. We want to record our history as well as share a bit about who we are now — a living culture and people that remain in our homeland after thousands of years.

We are not attempting to record our history in a typical encyclopedic way, which simply lists facts and figures. We are documenting our history by sharing true stories, and we are telling those stories with our own voices. It is always a good feeling when we can calibrate the oral history that people pass down the generations with the written records of other observers. This book will record and share vital information that will provide our future generations with a wealth of firsthand knowledge that will educate and empower them.

Much of this book was written in 2005, 150 years after the Treaty of 1855 was signed between the United States government and the Cayuse, Umatilla, and Walla Walla people. While there are many opinions about the Treaty and what it has done for or to the Cayuse, Umatilla, and Walla Walla people, it should be acknowledged on its 150th anniversary. The ancestors who negotiated that Treaty must be honored.

As this book describes, one of the most important provisions of the 1855 Treaty was the establishment of the Umatilla Indian Reservation — a permanent homeland for the Cayuse, Umatilla, and Walla Walla people. We are among the fortunate Native American tribes in the United States who still live in the place where our ancestors have lived for thousands of years. If the Umatilla Reservation had not been preserved, at the demand of our ancestors, our tribes would have been dispersed to other reservations, not located within the heart of our homeland.

If the Treaty of 1855 had not been negotiated, the customs and traditions that are central to our culture might have been lost — fishing, hunting, and the ability to gather traditional foods and medicines. When the ancestors reserved these rights, they were certainly thinking of provisions that would help them and their children preserve elements of their way of life.

Many of our customs, traditions, and stories will be told in this book, but they are not being told to exploit our culture or our people for the sake of money. Many of our customs, traditions, and stories will not be told in this book, including parts of our religious and spiritual life — ways that could be exploited by others.

While we must constantly be aware of the danger of exploitation, we must also share enough information with the outside world so that they better understand us. By fostering an understanding of the Cayuse, Umatilla, and Walla Walla people, we are working to gain the trust of our neighbors. When we inform, educate, and gain their trust in us as a people, we will earn their commitment to help take care of the land, the water, and each other.

Understanding. Trust. Commitment. When practiced regularly, these philosophies will do much to protect the way of life that our ancestors envisioned for us, including protection of our treaty rights and resources. This history project is a key ingredient in understanding — not only understanding by our neighbors but also understanding by our own people.

Working to educate our neighbors and ourselves is something the CTUIR has done for decades, which leads to some discussion about the intended audience of this history book. Two main groups will benefit by reading this book: our local, regional, national, and international neighbors; and our own community, especially our own youth.

Our neighbors will gain a better understanding of us through this book. We all live here now, and at times our communities' needs and actions are at odds. Having a wider knowledge base about one another will help prevent and resolve conflicts between our societies. Promoting understanding and knowledge has been advocated by our tribal government, and it has been a vital piece in many of our recent successes. For example, we discussed and negotiated for years with our neighbors in the Hermiston/Stanfield area about how to return salmon to the Umatilla River and still maintain water for their needs. By getting to know one another and understand one another, we were successful in achieving that miracle. Today, as a result of fostering understanding, trust, and commitment, we now have viable salmon populations back in the Umatilla River after a seventy-year absence, and the farmers and irrigation districts continue to have adequate water for their crops.

Our tribal leaders have acknowledged, through actions and policy, that public relations and public education are essential if the Tribes are to succeed in our long-term goals.

Educating the American public about the Cayuse, Umatilla, and Walla Walla people, through projects such as this book, also does much to broaden the understanding about tribes in general. There are nearly six hundred federally recognized tribes in the United States; and unfortunately, Americans, as a whole, have a poor and often incorrect knowledge of them. Much of America continues to think of us as cultural relics or in terms of old — and sometimes new — stereotypes. We hope this book will assist in breaking down those stereotypes for the public and developing a more accurate picture of us as people and of our tribal society. And we want them to know who we were, who we are, and who we will be.

The other key audience for this unique book is our own people and our future generations. As this book is being written, the Confederated Tribes of the Umatilla Indian Reservation has just opened our first school on the reservation — the Nixyáawii Community High School. The school provides a crucial tool in the endeavor of quality education for our people — a tool that is designed to meet the unique needs of a community recovering from vast change, assimilation, and oppression. Nixyáawii is a public charter school that primarily serves our own tribal children. In addition to providing instruction in the required courses of the public school system (math, reading, science), it also provides a much-needed foundation in tribal language, history, and culture.

It is safe to say that many would like to see this book serve as a significant textbook in the Nixyáawii classrooms. From this book our children will learn about their tribal history and traditions from their own people. This book and the new school can form a unique and powerful partnership that will make a positive difference in the education of our children.

It is my hope that we can promote the use of this tribal history book in other public classrooms around the region. Students will certainly have a more valuable and meaningful learning experience if they learn about a tribe from their region rather than about tribes from elsewhere.

Tribes in the Northwest have recently made progress in having local tribal histories and culture taught in public classrooms. In 2005, the Washington legislature passed House Bill 1495 urging schools to work with tribes in their regions to teach culture and history. In Oregon, the nine federally recognized tribes have worked with the Oregon public school system on revising and updating curriculum dealing with tribal history and culture and have participated in the revision of *The First Oregonians* (published by the Oregon Council for the Humanities), a book often used as a sourcebook in schools. Progress has certainly been made in educating the public about tribes, but the job will never be done.

Although the foundation for the content of this book is history, the reader can certainly expect to gain a better understanding of our language, traditions, customs, and culture. The content of this book was developed with this concept in mind. Early sections lay the groundwork by discussing central parts of our culture, followed by historical accounts of our first contact with non-Indian societies and their effects on the people. The majority of the chapters are devoted to information about our history in the twentieth century, including establishment of the Umatilla Reservation, the formation of our modern governance structure, our quest for self-determination and self-governance in the last half of the century, and our continued pursuit of cultural preservation and enhancement. The last portion of the book will look at the future of the Cayuse, Umatilla, and Walla Walla people. As always, we look to our past while envisioning and working toward the future.

The authors of this book were chosen for their experience and interest in the Confederated Tribes of the Umatilla Indian Reservation. Some of the authors are our own people who have intimate knowledge of our traditions, customs, and language. Some of the authors are tribal members who have lived the stories they share. Some of the authors are scholars and attorneys who have become part of our tribal family over the years. Each has close ties to the CTUIR, and each brings a unique perspective and background to this project.

Readers of this book will finish with a fundamental knowledge of the Cayuse, Umatilla, and Walla Walla people — our history, our culture, our community, our government, our responsibilities, our hopes, and our aspirations. We hope this will be the first volume of this distinct and ongoing story. We hope that future generations of the Cayuse, Umatilla, and Walla Walla people will take it upon themselves to continue documenting our history as we move through time. And we hope that these volumes will help foster understanding, trust and commitment — for these are all essential if we are to successfully continue our quest for cultural preservation, environmental protection, and self-determination.

wiyáx̣ayx̣t ✳ as days go by ✳ wiyáakaaʔawn

A basic human and intellectual right is the ability to have one's own historical identity. However, this is a right that has been denied to indigenous people because they exist largely in a cultural and historical limbo overlaid by nation-states that dominate them. These nation-states often have historical inventions that rationalize the existence of the dominant society, and this history often marginalizes the history, culture, language, and thought of indigenous people.

—Donald Grinde, Jr.

From "Historical Narratives of Nationhood and the Semiotic Construction of Social Identity: A Native American Perspective," in *Issues in Native American Cultural Identity*, edited by Michael K. Green, 1995.

Tamánwit

Tamánwit *is what we refer to as "our Indian law." This native view of traditional law is more than what we think of as "law" today. In the modern world, we view "law" as a set number of statutes which guide the legal system and regulate the lives of the governed. In this view, we tend to separate the value of laws into classes of jurisdictional applicability. The classes we assign to laws may be as varied as criminal, civil, business, international, or any other class that society deems necessary. This view of law is different from that of our native past. We tend to set our modern laws first and discount the validity of* tamánwit *in our present-day lives. The* tamánwit *of the past included the concept of divine ordination and creation. In the stories of our people,* tamánwit *is an ideology by which all things of the earth were placed by the Creator for a purpose. The works of the Creator were given behaviors that were unchangeable, and until time's end, these laws are to be kept. This understanding of* tamánwit *allows for the explanation of how things are placed on the earth, according to elders, whose teachings are explained as the time before that which is spoken of in the mythological travels of coyote and his pantheon of "super-hero" animal spirits.*

— Thomas Morning Owl

Oral Traditions of the Natítaytma

Phillip E. Cash Cash

The emergence of the ancient Natítaytma, the first peoples of this land, are documented in our indigenous oral traditions known as *wálsakt* (NES) or *titwatityáaya* (NP) 'the myth' and *shúkwat* 'knowledge' (CRS). It is from these first peoples that we, the modern-day cultures of the southern Columbia Plateau, trace our emergence. Today, we are variously known as Imatalamthláma (Umatilla), Nuumíipuu (Nez Perce), Pelúutspuu (Palouse), Walúulapam (Walla Walla), Wánapam (River People), Weyíiletpuu (Cayuse), or simply 'Ichishkíin (Columbia River Sahaptin) speaking peoples. We are culturally, historically, and linguistically diverse. Our ancestral lands are distributed across the interior regions of the southern Columbia Plateau, extending along the middle Columbia and Snake Rivers and their tributaries in what is now Oregon, Washington, and Idaho.

In the ongoing study of human cultures in the Pacific Northwest, scholars have developed an intense interest regarding the ancient origins of southern Columbia Plateau peoples. A convergence of evidence from oral tradition, archaeology, linguistics, and ethnography is beginning to confirm the identity of the ancient Natítaytma (NES) or Tanánma (CRS) 'people' as belonging to the Proto-

Our Languages

Language groupings are identified by their abbreviation or by their full name, such as Sahaptin (S), Columbia River Sahaptin (CRS), Northeastern Sahaptin (NES), Northwestern Sahaptin (NWS), Nez Perce (NP), Lower River Nez Perce (LNP), Upper River Nez Perce (UNP), and Cayuse (CA).

Sahaptian linguistic family, the earliest known speech community identified in this region. The basis for such a link is one of deep cultural continuity. The descendants of the Natítaytma or Tanánma report no migration tradition that places them outside their current ancestral homelands.

Our oral traditions contain imagery of mammoths, ice-age phenomena, and ancient volcanic activity. Further, as the ancient Proto-Sahaptian speech community developed across millennia, the Nuumíipuu and 'Ichishkíin daughter languages emerged in place, along with their associated dialects. The Weyíiletpuu or Líksiyu (CA) language is considered a language isolate whose ancient origins are unknown, but in the early nineteenth century its speakers adopted Nuumiipuutímt (the Nez Perce language) as their first language. Finally, the archaeological record in the southern Columbia Plateau shows a well-established cultural adaptation of our people to riverine environments. The Columbia Plateau rock-art tradition also supports a long, unbroken cultural continuity in this region.[1] Thus, while many Plateau scholars have noted that the archaeological evidence for cultural continuity is much greater than is permitted for the linguistic record, tantalizing clues support an ongoing, deep link to both an ancient Proto-Sahaptian speech commu-

	'Ichishkíin (S)	**Nuumíipuu** (LNP, UNP)
myth	*wat'ít'ash* (NWS) *walsákas* (CRS) *wálsakt* (NES)	*titwatityáaya*
historical narratives	*tχánat* 'happenings' (NWS)	*'ikúuyn titwáatit* 'true stories' *wiyekúutpeme tamtáyn* 'news of doings'
life histories	*timnanáχt* 'remembrance' (CRS) *timnanáχt* 'story' (NES)	*'ipnatitwáatit* 'story of one's self'
informing, reporting	*talwáskt* (NES) *támapayškša* (CRS)	*tamáapaykt*
knowledge	*šúkwat* (NWS)	*cúukwen'in*
songs	*walptáaykt* 'song' (CRS) *wánpt* 'spirit song' (CRS)	*we'nipt* 'song' *wéeyekwe'nipt* 'spirit song'

nity and to the resource-rich environment of the southern Columbia Plateau.[2]

It was always looked forward to by the children to hear the words, "Ewats silay imyánashma." The meaning of the words was, "It was so, my children, in the story time long ago."

— Thomas Morning Owl

Over millennia, our oral traditions have given us an understanding of the natural world, the capacity of life, and the fundamental human relationships that are bound by it. Our oral traditions are organized bodies of discourse whose primary purpose is to provide a set of generalized statements on the meaning of reality. These deep meanings are empirically and creatively structured across different forms of talk. Today, these forms of talk are recognized by our speakers as distinct storytellings.

Sadly, our speech communities are experiencing a decline in the passing down of our ancestral languages. As the adoption of the English language increases, the vitality and continued use of the ancestral languages become endangered, including many of its culturally enriched ways of speaking. Fortunately, a record of our languages has developed over time as anthropologists, linguists, and community tribal members set out to document and transcribe our oral traditions for the benefit of future generations. This repository of information is a vital resource for understanding the role and place of our oral

The Oral Record

Charlie Whirlwind was a big doctor. He was a big warrior. He commanded a lot of respect. People didn't dare walk behind him or anything, like he wasn't supposed to be. He had a son, Charlie Shaplish Whirlwind. And he was threatening. He picked up a rattlesnake and that rattlesnake bit him. You know Indians, they could talk to them. A lot of people won't believe that stuff. I used to listen to them stories all day and they're really interesting. They [storytellers] know more about your life than you do or anybody else's. If not for them, then really nobody would ever know, but they can tell you all them things that happened.

— *átway* Glenn "Denny" Williams

This place called Elephant Rock . . .

Before people, these mountains were fighting among one another. They were throwing rocks and fireballs. Coyote came and told the people, "Leave. Go west. Keep going that way." They started going. They were going downriver, down a river canyon. This young elephant was going along with his mother. He caught up alongside his mother. "What are they doing back there?" Mother says, "Don't worry. We're told to go this way. Keep going." "What will happen if we look back?" "He says we're not supposed to look back — We're not supposed to look back." "Coyote's not around. Can I look?" Curiosity got the best of him. He looked back to where the mountains were fighting. He turned to stone. Coyote came by and saw him and said, "This is what you get for not minding. You don't have to know the reason why you're told things, because you're told for a reason, for your own welfare, for your own better."

— Fermore Craig, Sr.

Medicine doctor Charlie Shaplish Whirlwind, Sr.,
photographed by Lee Moorhouse at Elephant Rock.

tradition in the ongoing lifeways and culture of the Nuumíipuu (NP) and 'Ichishkíin (CRS) communities.

In western North America, scholarship on indigenous oral traditions has discerned a broad range of genres, including myth, tales, sacred texts, historical narratives, speeches, poetry, songs, and life histories.[3] Most of these traditions can be readily applied to Nuumíipuu and 'Ichishkíin speech practices.[4]

In a much more detailed analysis, some scholars have analyzed the internal structure and content of our native speech (or "discourse genre") in a variety of contexts.[5] Most have made generalized statements on the world-creating properties of spoken discourse, whether it be for linguistic, literary, sociological, or folkloristic purposes. As culturally enriched "ways of speaking," these genre naturally lend themselves to understanding the problems and possibilities of human experience through their narrative form and function.

Thus, in the world of human speech and expert language use, the resources of our languages impose a certain order on our experience. The semantics, syntax, and grammar of our languages give our speakers the necessary tools to create meaning in the world and ground our view of the universe in ever-important ways. Each genre type has contributed to a deeply enriched oral tradition.

The linguistic textual record shows that *wálsakt* (NES) or *titwatityáaya* (NP) 'the myth' are among the best docu-

mented and publicly known oral traditions. This is understandable given that our peoples, the Nuumíipuu and 'Ichishkíin, are primarily an oral culture, and "the myth" provided a kind of public domain of knowledge that helped shape the learning experiences of children and adults alike. For all members of our society, the myth constituted a framework for apprehending the world and its creative potential as well as serving as a guide for future adult life.[6] In using the term "myth," I in no way intend for it to mean (as it does in popular definition) that the oral stories labeled as such are untrue or made up; in fact, they represent a connection to the past that is imminently real for native people in every sense.

Myths often describe the origin of the world. For many indigenous cultures, mythic origins ground the generalized experience of ancient peoples across space and time. When we carefully examine the content of each myth, for example, we are able to discern a core cosmology that is largely shaped from events that center on the mythic emergence of the Netíitelwit (NP) 'human beings, people'.[7] In the myth, the structure of the universe is represented as a single cosmological system, one that was brought into being not so much by its creation as by its physical transformation. Its structure consists of a present world populated by modern humans and a former ancient world inhabited by supernatural entities. These two worlds are separated by a deep and ancient time dimension whereby the mythic past remotely precedes the human present.

Other discourse types (or tradition), such as *šúkwat* (NWS) 'knowledge' and ritual speech, speak more directly of a creation specific to human origins. A tribal elder connects the term for knowledge to prophecy, foretelling of future times and events:

A sukwat *is a person who knows what's going to happen. These people were blessed with certain abilities to forecast. Some of them would have visions or dreams. This is where their faith in what they believed came to focus and helped them. We had a grandmother, Grandma Ut'an'may. She was one of them who could see a long ways off. She was blind and she had a good strong mind. She used to say, "There will come a time when people around us will be living like ants. Just like when we see ants travel, they will be in lines, like when you see them crossing on a little twig. They are all in a line."*
— *átway* Lawrence Patrick*

A prominent feature in many *titwatityáaya* (NP) or *wálsakt* (NES) 'myth' is its geographically distributed myth locales, an action space characterized by the topographic embodiment of superhuman agents and superhuman events. These topographic embodiments are often the result of a mythic transformation, and their physical presence in the landscape bears witness to the changing moral character of the world — that is, a world emerging from chaos order and human form. For example, *'iceyéeye* (NP) or *spilyáy* (S) 'Coyote' often transformed lesser mythic beings into stone or the like, proclaiming: "Now human beings are coming soon, and you cannot go on being killers." Such mythic actions set the stage for the eventual arrival of the Netíitelwit and our emergence into the human era.

Myth locales and other physical environments referenced through our oral traditions provide a unique kind of map or mazeway across the cultural landscape. They take on an important role in defining "place" in a broader cultural system of knowledge and interethnic territoriality. Myth locales are considered sacred and potentially dangerous, because the deep time separation that exists between the former myth world and the present are collapsed at these sites (Figure 1).

Historical narratives are temporally distinct and make reference only to the post-mythic human era. Unlike their myth counterparts, the fundamental perspective adopted in historical narratives is an emphasis on known, reportable events. Such narratives contribute to a broad range of cultural and ecological knowledge. The manner in which a historical narrative is represented also contributes to a distinct kind of awareness, centering on human interactions and collective experiences. In this sense, discourse proceeds from one state of affairs to another, but it does so in a realistic narrative mode — that is, dramatized speech — which

---

*The expression *átway* is an honorific form used by some when speaking the name of the deceased.

directly portrays the speech of its story characters. Such portrayals can become full-fledged performances when told by an expert storyteller. This narrative strategy "evokes reality by staging it."[8]

Consider the opening sequence of a historical narrative told by *átway* Mrs. Ada Patrick. The narrative relates a historical event involving two sisters that occurred in the vicinity of *'isqúulktpe 'iyíwewiy*, a waterway on the Confederated Tribes of the Umatilla Indian Reservation in Oregon. It is told in the Lower River dialect of Nuumiipuutímt 'the Nez Perce language'.

> *Kíi híiwes 'ikúuyn titwáatit.*
> *Ne'élem hináastitwatiya.*
> *Kakáa qo'c míil'ec sooyáapoo*
> *hipáaycana kíne wéetespe.*

Kaa lepú hiwsíiine 'acíipiin.
Kaa píine, 'ácip hihíne,
"Wáaqo' kíye pe'mínenu'."

This is a true story.
My father's mother told us this story.
It happened when few whitemen had yet arrived in this place.

And there were two sisters.
And they told each other, she told her younger sister,
"Now, we will go digging [for roots]."[9]

In this brief opening, we can discern several narrative strategies. First, Nuumíipuu and 'Ichishkíin storytellers tend to make few evaluative statements on

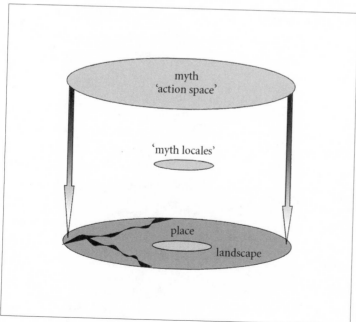

Figure 1. Myth locales

the status of the ensuing discourse. When such statements are made, they typically occur in an opening passage, as depicted here or in the closing passage. The narrator is expressing not so much the tellability of a narrative as she is identifying the story's cultural significance in reference to a wider domain of lived human experience. Second, our expert storytellers use a variety of narrative devices and performance strategies to ensure that the events are accurately reported and organized. It is in this attention to detail that the experiences and consciousness of a narrative's story characters become enacted.

The historical narrative can be further exemplified through a translation of the words that name this form of speech. In Sahaptin, historical narratives are generally referred to as *tχánat* (NWS) 'happenings, customs', the prefix *tχá-* indicating that the action is "uncaused, of its own volition."[10] In Nez Perce, this genre was referred to in the past as *wiyekúutpeme tamtáyn* (UNP) 'a narrative regarding a succession of actions' or 'history'.[11] This term is composed from the verb morphemes *wiyée-* 'as one goes' and *-kúut-* 'doings, action' to indicate the succession of events. Late twentieth-century Nez Perce speakers are recorded as using the terms *'ikúuyn titwáatit* (LNP) 'true story' and *wiyéwc'etpeme* (UNP) 'history', among other references.[12]

Historical narratives share a commonality with *timnanáχt* (CRS) 'remembrance'; *'ipnatitwáatit* (NP) 'story of one's self'; and *talwáskt* (NES), *támapayškša* (CRS), and *tamáapaykt* (NP) 'informing, reporting'. Each of these traditions share an emphasis on the narrator's personal knowledge of some aspect of the story-world. They differ from historical narratives in that the narrator manifests a

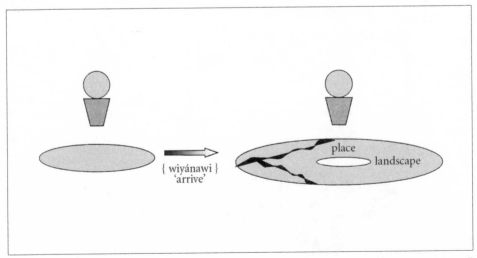

Figure 2. Event of "becoming aware."

greater degree of interpersonal involvement in the course of the narration. Typically, narrators retain the realistic narrative mode (that is, dramatized speech), coupled with the use of the first-person "I," "we," and "us."

Documented life histories are quite rare in Sahaptin and Nez Perce culture. From the few accounts that do exist, narrators typically conceive of the self in the episodic unfolding of consciousness of being in the world. Consider the opening narrative sequence of *átway* Mr. Howard Jim (Wayám), who, as a youth in the Columbia River Sahaptin village of Wayám (CRS), identifies the moment when he "first became aware."[13]

> *Míimish ináwyaw ana ku'*
> *páysh iwachá ku cháwsh*
> *páshukshamsh anwícht.*
>
> *kʷaaná kúush iwachá palaláy*
> *tanán kuna nch'inchi ttáwaxt.*
> *shks'ks kuuk kʷyáam wiyánawi*
> *kuna páysh 13 years old. . . .*
>
> Long ago, when in my youth,
> it was perhaps, although I do not
> know how many years.
>
> But at that time there were many
> people, elderly people.
> Being young, then I came into my
> true knowing there around 13 yrs
> old. . . .

Here, *átway* Mr. Howard Jim's self-awareness is metaphorically depicted as *wiyánawi* 'arriving' (Figure 2). That is, the narrated self is projected outward onto the world (the Columbia River) and "arrives" in the sense that the self is emerging aware in time and place. Thus, the world is no longer autonomously imagined; rather, it is concretely realized in the formative experience of the individual.[14]

Next, consider a brief passage from the 1950s that was given by an unidentified Nez Perce consultant to a modern-day ethnographer. This sequence depicts a highly personal and deeply spiritual experience relating to the acquisition of spirit power.

> I used to know nothing.
> One time I went down to the log
> cabin in Spalding.
> An old fellow was singing.
>
> I started shaking and crying.
> He was singing about the Stick
> Indian
> and I thought I didn't know
> nothing about it,
> but I got scared and didn't know
> nothing [e.g., was unconscious]
> for a long time.
>
> I used to always dream I was
> flying,
> especially in high mountains,
> from canyon to canyon.
> That's the way Stick Indian
> travels.[15]

In this type of narration, identified here as *tamáapaykt* (NP) 'informing, reporting', the subjectivity of the narrator

Salmon and Turtledove

Salmon and Turtledove fell in love. The Turtledove lost trust with the Salmon, so the Salmon went away. He'd leave for two years and go to the ocean without her. Every spring when the salmon comes back, the turtledove is floating up and down the river. She's singing or crying for the salmon, her lover. But salmon doesn't pay attention. He just keeps going up. This is the way Indian people always knew when the salmon was coming back, by the turtledoves' flying up and down the river looking for their long lost love affair.

— *átway* Lawrence Patrick

is highly visible. Experiential accounts such as these suggest that the function of the informing, reporting story form is to enable the acquisition of information that arises from lived experience. These accounts were not simply random personal experiences. Rather, their information value is high, and the portrayal of such life experiences often serves as a guide to others on "ways of being" and acting in the world. Given that we have emerged as a so-called ancient hunter and gatherer culture, the acquisition of information and knowledge through narrative ensures human survival and cultural continuity.

Šúkwat (CRS) 'knowledge, learning, teaching' is among the least documented genre in our oral tradition. Only a single Klikitat (NWS) text is known to exist in the literature. *Šúkwat* has been described by the linguist Melville Jacobs as "ex tempore reflections about the myths and tales, about the stages the world has gone through, about life since the advent of whites."[16] A potentially corresponding term in Nuumíipuu is *cúukwen'in* 'known empirically, known spiritually, spirited', but this term describes more a state of mind, of which knowledge is only one operative component. While little is known about *šúkwat*, it may be akin to an ancient natural philosophy that unites our knowledge about the human, spiritual, and natural worlds.

Walptáaykt (CRS) or *we'nípt* (NP) 'song' is among the most enduring and widely distributed oral tradition. In its most fundamental form, *walptáaykt* or *we'nípt* can be regarded as performance — that is, they are an "aesthetically marked and heightened mode of communication, framed in a special way and put on display for an audience."[17] Songs composed in our languages have been variously represented as church hymns, traditional war dance songs, social dance songs, serenade songs, contemporary powwow songs, nursery songs, gambling songs, Shaker religion songs, guardian spirit songs, songs from the myth, Wáashat (CRS) or longhouse songs, and songs for the arrival of the first food plants in the spring. Performing these songs is not necessarily restricted to expert storytellers or knowledgeable individuals. In our myths, for example, children are often depicted as spontaneously composing songs to communicate the deeds of their caretakers. Evidently, based on each of these wide-ranging uses, we can readily say that songs are an important but unique form of communication and that they have the potential to transcend age, gender, and religious and cultural affiliations.

Consider the following song composition by *átway* Mr. Sol Webb and *átway* Mr. John Moses, both Nuumíipuu, who said, "We just made this up, the two of us." On August 12, 1947, on the Umatilla Indian Reservation, they composed the following Chief's Song to honor Willard Rhodes, a non-native ethnomusicologist who came to document our song traditions.

A Chief's Song
Willard Rhodes híiwes
'ikúuymiyooχat.

Willard Rhodes, he's a true chief.[18]

Song composition has the unique ability to record and preserve moments in time. Songs can communicate important

Stories from the Winter Lodge

The messages of the stories were lessons for life. Stories might be cautionary on the one hand but, on the other, urging listeners to always take action and be active. *Spilyáy*, aka Coyote, as the central character of many stories, acts out his broad moral code ranging from the grossest misbehavior to the most exemplary heroism. Indian children were expected to commit these stories to memory so they would one day be able to repeat them unaltered to upcoming generations. Some of the stories are quite figurative. They encouraged children to develop vivid imaginations and envisioning powers that made the fantastical an eminently believable dimension of the real world.

— Exhibit text, Tamástslikt Cultural Institute

Fred Hill, with hand drum, and Inez Spino Reves pose in Living Culture Village,
Tamástslikt Cultural Institute.

information about our individual and collective life experiences. It should not be surprising, therefore, that song composition is so widely distributed across our culture and across so many domains of life. We can continue to expect new song compositions to emerge as our people embrace the ever-important role of revitalizing our culture, languages, and lifeways.

Signs of cultural revitalization are already emerging in a song composition by Umatilla tribal member Fred Hill. Mr. Hill (Umatilla/Yakama/Nez Perce) composed this song to encourage our emerging generation of language learners.

Our Precious Language
naamí sínwit iwá átaw
kuushkíin nash sínwisha
áykink timnákni, kunam shúkwata
chí na sápsik'wata naamí
miyánashma

Our language is precious.
That's the reason I am speaking it.
Listen with your heart and you
will understand.
This is what we will teach our
children.[19]

This brief review is not meant as a comprehensive ethnographic or narrative analysis. Rather, its primary purpose is to show the role of our oral traditions in relation to our collective experience as modern-day descendants of the ancient Natítaytma or Tanánma.

These rich and time-honored oral traditions have contributed to our overall survival as a people. In terms of the future, it is important that we begin to make room for the emergence of contemporary oral traditions that reflect our current struggles and triumphs. And, as modern-day Imatalamthláma (Umatilla), Nuumíipuu (Nez Perce), Pelúutspuu (Palouse), Walúulapam (Walla Walla), Wánapam (River People), Weyíiletpuu (Cayuse), or 'Ichishkíin (Columbia River Sahaptin) speaking peoples, we are reminded that in order to preserve our place in creation we must continue to tell our stories, speak our languages, remember the words and teachings of our ancestors, honor our *tamánwit* (CRS) or *tamálwit* (NP) 'the natural law', and name the land, the animals, and foods that are so vital to our continued survival. This will be our continuing story, our oral tradition.

Passing Down through Song

In our home, we had a grandmother, a beautiful grandmother. Every Sunday, she would take us out when the sun was coming up and we'd sing these songs. That's how we learned about the religion through her. We were taught to respect everything, everybody, all animals, everything that was alive.

— Edith McCloud

A Worship Song

Lawnxna tunx ewa
Anakush miimi iwacha
Tiichampa

Yesterday was a time
When our elders
They walked this land

They roamed this land. And they went by the law that was given them and it was a very strict law. There were laws that they lived by that were very strict. Families knew how to take care of themselves. The men knew their responsibilities. The hunters knew how to do what they were supposed to do. The women knew what they had to do in order for this family to survive. Many of our people, our ancestors, became gifted by the gift of the Creator. This Creator selected people at that time to do what they were supposed to do. He knew who would take care of children. He selected them as medicine people.

— Ethel "Tessie" Williams

Notes

1. James D. Keyser, George Poetschat, Phillip Minthorn Cash Cash, Don Hann, Helen Hiczun, Roz Malin, Carol Pederson, Cathy Poetschat, and Betty Tanberg, *Columbia Plateau Rock Art: The Butte Creek Sites: Steiwer Ranch and Rattlesnake Shelter*, Publication no. 11 (Portland: Oregon Archaeological Society, 1998). See also James Keyser, *Indian Rock Art of the Columbia Plateau* (Seattle: University of Washington Press, 1992).

2. M. Dale Kinkade et al., "Languages," in *Handbook of North American Indians*, vol. 12, *Plateau*, ed. Deward Walker, Jr. (Washington, D.C.: Smithsonian Institution Press, 1996), 49–72.

3. M. Dale Kinkade and Anthony Mattina, "Discourse," in *Handbook of North American Indians*, vol. 17, *Languages*, ed. Ives Goddard (Washington, D.C.: Smithsonian Institution Press, 1996), 244–74.

4. Haruo Aoki, *Nez Perce Texts* (Berkeley: University of California Press, 1979); Melville Jacobs, *Northwest Sahaptin Texts* (Seattle: University of Washington Press, 1929); Melville Jacobs, *Northwest Sahaptin Texts* (New York: Columbia University Press, 1934); A. Phinney, *Nez Perce Texts* (New York: Columbia University, 1934).

5. Aoki, *Nez Perce Texts*; Philip Cash Cash, *Timnakni Tiimat (writing from the heart): Sahaptin Discourse and Text in the Speaker Writing of Xluxin* (M.A. thesis, University of Arizona, 2000); Cash Cash, "*ke yóx hitamtáaycaqa ćtiqinpa* (that which is reported in talk): Reported Speech in Nez Perce," *Coyote Papers* 13 (2004): 75–85; Donald H. Hines, *Tales of the Nez Perce* (Fairfield, Wash.: Ye Galleon Press, 1984); Hines, *The Forgotten Tribes: Oral Tales of the Teninos and Adjacent Mid-Columbia River Indian Nations* (Issaquah, Wash.: Great Eagle Publishing, 1991); Virginia Hymes, "Warm Springs Sahaptin Narrative Analysis," in *Native American Discourse: Poetics and Rhetoric*, ed. Joel Sherzer and Anthony Woodbury (Cambridge: Cambridge University Press, 1987); Virginia Hymes and Hazel Suppah, "How Long Ago We Got Lost: A Warm Springs Sahaptin Narrative," *Anthropological Linguistics* 34:1–4 (1992): 73-83; Dell Hymes, "Coyote, Polymorphous but Not Always Perverse," in *Now I Know Only so Far: Essays in Ethnopoetics* (Lincoln: University of Nebraska Press, 2003); Jacobs, *Northwest Sahaptin Texts*; Karl Kroeber, ed., *Traditional Literatures of the American Indian* (Lincoln: University of Nebraska Press, 1997); Lucullus Virgil McWhorter, *Yellow Wolf: His Own Story* (Caldwell, Idaho: Caxton Press, 1940); Jarold Ramsey, *Coyote Was Going There: Indian Literature of the Oregon Country* (Seattle: University of Washington Press, 1977); Ramsey, " 'The Hunter Who Shot an Elk for a Guardian Spirit,' and the Ecological Imagination," in *Smoothing the Ground: Essays on Native American Oral Literature*, ed. Brian Swann (Berkeley: University

of California Press, 1983); Noel Rude, "Studies in Nez Perce Grammar and Discourse" (Ph.D. diss., University of Oregon, 1985); William R. Seaburg and Pamela T. Amoss, *Badger and Coyote Were Neighbors: Melville Jacobs on Northwest Indian Myths and Tales* (Corvallis: Oregon State University Press, 2000); Dell Skeels, "Style in Unwritten Literature of the Nez Perce Indians" (Ph.D. diss., University of Washington, 1949); Herbert J. Spinden, "Myths of the Nez Perce Indians," *Journal of American Folklore* 21 (1908): 13–23; Spinden, "Nez Perce Tales," *Memoirs of the American Folk-Lore Society* 11 (1917): 180–201; Anthony E. Thomas, "Piluyekin: The Life History of a Nez Perce Indian," *Anthropological Studies* (1970); Deward Walker, Jr. and Daniel N. Matthews, *Nez Perce Coyote Tales: The Myth Cycle* (Norman: University of Oklahoma Press, 1998).

6. Thomas, "Piluyekin."

7. Phillip Cash Cash, "Nez Perce (Nuumíipuu) Religious Traditions," in *Encyclopedia of Religion*, ed. Lindsay Jones, 2d ed. (Detroit: Macmillan, 2005).

8. Luc Herman and Bart Vervaeck, *Handbook of Narrative Analysis* (Lincoln: University of Nebraska Press, 2005).

9. Rude, "Studies in Nez Perce Grammar and Discourse," 256.

10. Jacobs, *Northwest Sahaptin Texts*, 150.

11. Anthony Morvillo, *A Dictionary of the Numípu or Nez Perce Language, by a Missionary of the Society of Jesus, in the Rocky Mountains. Part I. English–Nez Perce* (St. Ignasius mission print, 1895).

12. Rude, "Studies in Nez Perce Grammar and Discourse," 256.

13. Michal Conford and Michele Zaccheo, *River People: Behind the Case of David Sohappy* (New York: Filmmakers Library, 1990), documentary film.

14. Phillip Cash Cash, "To Witness Creation: A Southern Columbia Plateau Rock-Art Ethnography" (unpublished manuscript, 2004).

15. Unidentified consultant, George Coale, "Notes on the Guardian Spirit Concept among the Nez Perce," *International Archives of Ethnography* 48:2 (1958): 140.

16. Jacobs, *Northwest Sahaptin Texts* (1929), 244.

17. Richard Bauman, "Performance," in *International Encyclopedia of Communication*, ed. E. Barnow, vol. 3 (New York: Oxford University Press, 1989), 262-6.

18. Loran Olsen, *Guide to the Nez Perce Music Archive: An Annotated Listing of Songs and Musical Selections Spanning the Period 1897–1974* (Pullman: Washington State University, 1989), 12.

19. "Our Precious Language," original song lyrics by Fred Hill (Umatilla/Yakama/Nez Perce), courtesy of language program, CTUIR, Pendleton, Ore., 2003.

Indians Then and Now

Let us turn to the pages of the past. Because we so often speak of the past, we are told that we dwell too much in the past, that what has passed is past, and nothing is gained by harking back to it. Some say to us consolingly, what has happened to the Indian in this country is too bad, but it is over and done with. Deeds that I hear related have made history and are the foundations both good and bad upon which your life and the Indians have been built.

However, when "found" by the white man, they were a highly intelligent people, free from disease, adherents to rigid moral codes rigidly invoked. They were proud, courteous, and dignified. Their God, the "Great Spirit," was revered and obeyed. Though a nomadic race, they were agriculturists. Among them were orators, natural artists, dancers, and musicians. . . . They were human beings like you and me. But they were called "savages." The white man called himself "civilized." Indian laws were simple and just, and always enforced. Children very young were disciplined. The old folks were honored and reverently cared for. The highest authority on all questions and councils was composed of aged men, for they knew reckless youth lacked caution of age. There was no upper class, no middle class, and no lower class. All men were equal and all shared. Even today among Indians it is no stigma to be poor in material possessions. The unforgivable mistake and disgrace comes from being stingy, from hoarding for oneself which another needs, from withholding from another what one can give. To violate slightly this code is to suffer complete ostracism. Early Indian life was like music, it had to be composed by ear, feeling, and instinct, not by rule. Nevertheless, the young were taught the rules to avoid being misguided. The "Great Spirit" taught them that nothing but a good life here could fit them for a better one hereafter. To share with the weak, the poor, the helpless among us is universal in Indian culture. In all Indian Tribes, this is the moral code and the structure of Indian life and expected for normal social behavior.

Maudie C. Antoine, Chairwoman, Board of Trustees, Confederated Tribes of the Umatilla Indian Reservation. These remarks were made at the 1855 Treaty Centennial observance in Walla Walla, Washington, June 11, 1955.

Early Contact and Incursion, 1700–1850

Roberta Conner and William L. Lang

These co-authors are joined in history by their ancestors and their current work in public history. Roberta is a descendant of Istikus, Old Joseph, and Timothy, who participated at the 1855 Treaty Council at Walla Walla. William is a descendant of Joel Palmer, Oregon Territory superintendent of Indian affairs and treaty commissioner at the same council.

There was a time before human beings on the Columbia River Plateau. Tribal oral tradition tells of this ancient time, when all animals could communicate using a common language. The Creator spoke to *spilyáy* 'Coyote,' who forewarned the other animals of what was to come: human beings who would be like infants and who would need to be taught how to live here. An animal council was held to determine how to proceed. Salmon volunteered to be the first to offer his body and his knowledge to the Natíitayt (Walla Walla) 'the people'. Many other species followed suit from the abundant animal and verdant plant kingdom, including the roots and berries. These decisions from the animal council demonstrate *tamánwit*,

the traditional philosophy and law of the people — the foundation of a physical and spiritual way of life that would sustain Plateau peoples for thousands of years.[1] This covenant between the Creator — who made the land, the water, and all the species therein — the plants and animals who offered themselves to the people, and the people who promised to take care of all that was given them is the basis of native respect for all creation.

The Creator planted the Natíitayt on this earth, where they still live. Plateau tribal oral tradition contains no migration story, no arrival from another land to the Plateau. The origin of the Plateau peoples is in this land. How long ago is the subject of scientific theory, anthropological and archaeological investigation, and popular debate. But, for these Tribes, the answer to how long ago they came to be here has little practical consequence. Substantiation of 11,000 years over 9,000 will not restore salmon runs. Proof that it was 13,000 and not 10,000 years will not reverse the splintered factions of Plateau peoples into a whole, nor will it restore millions of acres to Plateau tribes. Evidence of life here for a greater number of millennia will not eradicate racism or abate social ills or erase historical trauma and injustice. Still, regardless of these issues or their outcomes, our community's position is constant: We have always been here.

From this land in which the people lived and its incumbent seasons came the diet, the languages, and the customs that are distinctly appropriate and associated with the homeland. The traditional diet of fishes, meats, roots, greens, and fruits defined when and where the people traveled to harvest and process foods. People who ate the same foods, lived in the same areas at various times of the year, and spoke the same languages were related — *náymuma, nay'mosha, himyúume* 'relations'. Intermarriage to neighboring, non-adversarial tribes such as the interior Salish or Crow, who spoke different languages and subsisted on similar but differing foodstuffs, created alliances that expanded the range of safe travel. Those who were not related or allied were strangers or enemies. The identity of Plateau people derived from their family, village, diet, and language and where their permanent homes were in relation to one another — upriver people, people from across the mountains, tamarack people, cottonwood grove people.

Who We Are

The tribal identities used today — Cayuse, Umatilla, Walla Walla — classify peoples with little consideration of any place-specific distinctions. These modern identifications are based on external observations and assumptions and were created for the convenience of outsiders desirous of transacting business efficiently with an unfamiliar people. These are not the names we called ourselves. While the newly arrived Euro-American interlopers would have preferred a centralized, integrated political structure with which to deal — and they tried to help create such by deeming leaders friendly to their purposes "chiefs" — that was not our system. Our vast extended families were kinship communities. These communities recognized their citizenship by relations. These communities did not share homogenous identities. Peculiarities due to village remoteness or easy accessibility, differences in obtainable foods and herbs, divergence in clothing due to climate, greater or lesser use of livestock due to available grazing, and variations in size of village all played into the dynamic identities of the ancestors whose descendants now comprise the Confederated Tribes of the Umatilla Indian Reservation.

While the development of the Sahaptian dialects and languages spoken on the

Martha Johnny (Palouse) displays an *ititámat* 'time ball'.

Plateau are an indication of the passage of vast spans of time in the homeland, these languages were not used to measure time in ways familiar to Euro-Americans. The importance of time as measured by native people was more personal than global. The most prominent and common measurement of time was indicated in the *ititámat* 'time ball' or 'to count'.[2] Usually, a young girl would begin the practice of keeping a time ball that would be maintained throughout her life, much like a diary. She would keep track of important events using a cord or string made of hair or hemp ornamented with beads and knots to provide reference to births, courtship, weddings, deaths, battles, and raids. Later in life, as an elder, she would be relied upon to remember what occurred and when. Other forms of time measurement included the number of winters passed during an expedition or in one life or references to cataclysmic events as milestones, such as floods, eruptions, and climatic changes. Today, evidence from oral histories and indigenous language vocabularies have been used in Australia and Canadian courts to demonstrate the traditional occupation and ownership by specific people of their lands, waters, and resources such as fish and game.³ The language evidence also supports conclusions of long-term occupation of homelands and the people's detailed knowledge of plant and animal species and country arising from long and intimate familiarity.

In ancient times, the animals learned of forthcoming change, and they prepared for it. Subsequently, the Cayuse, Umatilla, and Walla Walla peoples would do the same many times over. The animals did not try to escape or avoid change. Although it may have occurred to *spilyáy*

to do so, he rose to the task given him by the Creator and helped prepare for the Natíitayt by bringing order. Later, the arrival of new peoples, new modes of transportation, new diseases, and new ways of living were prophesied by tribal people who had been endowed with special gifts of seeing the future in visions. One vision said that men would come out of the ocean. Then when the first white men appeared, some had blue eyes and it was assumed that their eyes were blue (like fish) because they came from the ocean.⁴ Generations ago, one visionary tribal woman demonstrated her prophecy

Indian Trails
Gilbert E. Conner (1897–1967)
talk to the Rotary Club

The Indians of this area, the Cayuse Indians and the Waluula, or Walla Walla as they are called now, lived on the south shores of the Columbia River and the foothills of the Blue Mountains. As the seasons progressed, when their migrations took them across the Blue Mountains in the Grande Ronde area, they followed several trails. Those living near the headwaters of the McKay Creek followed the trails on over into the Grande Ronde Valley proceeding then into the Big Grande Ronde, some of them going south towards the Powder River area, to gather roots and hunt and follow the fish migrations. Some went over into the John Day area, North Fork of the John Day area and then followed eventually southeasterly towards the Huntington and Snake River area, some going on into the Boise Basin and then north towards the Payette Lakes. Others may have followed the Grande Ronde and the Catherine Creek trails around the south side of the Wallowa Mountains going then into the Snake River area, hunting in that area. Others may have followed across the Blue Mountains over the Umatilla watershed over towards the Summerville area, crossing over into Minam area, eventually going into the Wallowas.

when she used ants to travel on branches and twigs like the roads that criss-cross the country today. She also foretold of travel by air like the eagle only bigger.[5] One tribal family passed down a Coyote story that told of a different race of people who would come and ride on ribbons of light and fire that would run what they rode. The ribbons would turn out to be rails of steel, and the fire would power the train that traveled on it carrying the new-comers.[6] Change and transformation would become hallmarks of these Plateau people who lived at the crossroads for historical comings and goings of many eras.

The expansive Columbia River Plateau extends from the eastern slope of the Cascade Range to the western slope of the Rocky Mountains, and from the northern reach of the Columbia River to the Blue Mountains and Salmon River. The homeland of the people now known as Cayuse, Umatilla, and Walla Walla included islands in and areas on both sides of the mid-Columbia River; both sides of the lower Snake River; Horse Heaven Hills; the John Day, Malheur, Powder, Burnt, Umatilla, Walla Walla, Touchet, Tucannon, and Grande Ronde Rivers; and Willow, Birch, Butter, McKay, Johnson, and

The Waíiletpu or Cayuses and the Waluula Indians came across the headwaters of the Walla Walla tributaries and came over into Wenaha and over to the Grande Ronde, eventually coming down towards Looking Glass at Palmer Junction, and then meandered over towards the Elgin area, where they would camp for a period of time, catching fish, eventually following the Indian Valley area into the Minam.

Whenever these trails sometimes crossed ridges they knew just about when to follow to where the later fish migrations would necessarily take them, to the upper Wallowa region, then into the Imnaha River system, where they caught their fish later in the summer. These trails are crisscrossed in various areas either returning or going upstream to these various locations. And these are what have been the main trails now covered by most of the roads we know today.

The Umatillas who lived along the Columbia River, their migrations took them south from the Umatilla area usually across the Umatilla River towards the Heppner area, into the watersheds of the John Day. There are three tributaries of the John Day, the North, Middle, and South Forks, which area the Umatillas hunted and fished. Some Cayuses intermarried with the Umatillas also used these areas, as well as the Northern Paiutes. They usually gathered in the Ukiah

Mill Creeks, among many others. This land base provided for numerous and prosperous well-populated villages that depended on river as well as mountain and forest yields. Winter villages ranged in size from 50 persons to 700. Population estimates of Cayuse, Umatilla, and Walla Walla prior to contact ranged from 1,100 to 8,000, depending on the geographical area included and the terminology used associating the various tribes.

The Umatilla primarily occupied areas along Willow Creek, the Umatilla River, and the main stem Columbia and hunted in the Blue Mountains. East of the Umatillas, the Cayuse lived on the south side of the Columbia; in the upper reaches of the Umatilla and Walla Walla Rivers; along the Touchet, Tucannon, and Grande Ronde Rivers; and in the Blue Mountains. The Walla Walla were also at home on the lower Walla Walla River, both banks of the Columbia, the lower Snake, and the lower valley of the Yakima River. Related neighbors included the Nez Perce, Palouse, Wánapam, Yakama, Wishxam, Wayam, Tygh, Tenino, and John Day peoples. Together, these tribes used and managed the diverse topography and habitats of the region to reap great varieties of foods from the Cascade Mountains to the Bitterroot Mountains and from the Blue Mountains

area as well as the area south of John Day, just because they knew when to gather at these places, for roots in the Ukiah area, Fox area, and the John Day tributaries, and then for beaver and fish migrations they came up the Malheur River. They followed across the mountains south of Canyon City into the area, which is called Seneca or Silvies, tributary of the Malheur, then southeasterly to the headwaters of the Malheur. There was an area of two streams there where they would spend considerable time catching the fish migration that came up the Malheur River from the Snake.

There are many areas that also went west from the Blue Mountains, what I guess are known as the Ochoco Forest area, where they joined with the Warm Springs tribes, and then they eventually returned towards the Deschutes area and then back towards the Columbia River.

Some of these migrations took the tribes of this area farther along the Boise Basin into what has been known as the Green River Rendezvous in Wyoming. They followed the foothills of the Rockies and went around into the Plains area, where they got buffalo for the meat and hides and also exchanged articles of wear as well as artifacts with the Plains Indians, either acquired horses or whatever else was necessary for their economy.

to the Spokane River. Salmon, trout, suckerfish, sturgeon, freshwater mussel, lamprey, deer, bighorn sheep, antelope, moose, elk, goat, bison, bear, prairie chicken, sage hen, jackrabbit, and cottontail complemented the variety of roots, spring greens, and berries that were harvested, processed, and stored. Seasonal travel by foot and watercraft — and later by horse —followed well-established annual patterns for each village.

In 1845, Commander Charles Wilkes wrote: "The Indians of the Territory are not a wandering race, as some have asserted, but change for food only, and each successive season will generally find them in their old haunts, seeking it."[7] Major gatherings at spring and fall salmon runs and at summer camas meadows attracted hundreds or thousands of people during the height of each season, depending on the capacity of the resource. Such abundance permitted sufficient harvest to support a rich and age-old tradition of trade, gifting, and gambling. Congregating in immense numbers at places such as Celilo, Wayampam, Wishxam, Kettle Falls, the Walla Walla and Grande Ronde Valleys, and Yellowstone provided for a high degree of economic exchange and ample opportunity for cultural interaction and intertribal marriage. For Plateau

There are other tribes to the north of us, like the Yakamas, the Klickitats, Cowlitz, Chelans, and so on. These trails go northward. Either towards the Columbia or the Palouse areas, the Snake River and the tributaries of the Snake, and to the Nez Perce country were trails leaving from Walla Walla eastward across the Tucannon into Pataha Valley and Alpowa into the junction of the Snake and the Clearwater area. And then there were those that went up the Snake River to the mouth of the Grande Ronde and along the river south up towards the junction of the Salmon River.

Many places the hills were so steep and so rugged, you had to be an expert to make these crossings. . . . As I understand it, they used either canoes when they had them available or they used skin boats, rowboats, as they are known, and swam their possessions across and then drove the horses. And sometimes they ferried them with a log raft or something, to get the horses started and gather them over on the other side. There were many times when some of them were lost on these trips across these large streams like the Snake or the Salmon River, as well as the Columbia. But they usually found a shallow place to cross and that was a knowledge that not all people had, but only those who traveled to those places.

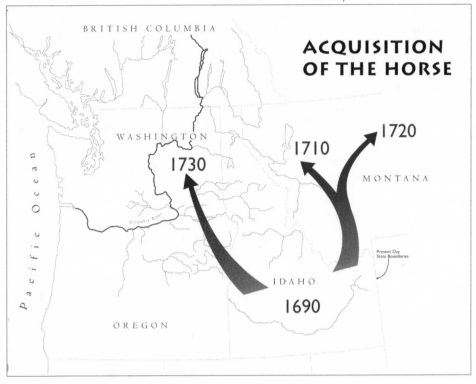

tribes, games constituted a primary method of exchange. Games were not child's play and were not just about material gain. Adult games and contests were entertaining, but they were also earnest demonstrations of personal power. Personal power included the intensely skilled observation of body language, an invocation of spiritual assistance through songs and teamwork, as well as ceremony, the ability to disorient and disturb opponents, a resolute shrewdness in estimating the skills of others, and absolute strength and stamina. The stakes for games ranged from hides, foods, and tools to captives, livestock, and, later, money. Tribal expeditions to and raids in lands of other tribes provided new goods, new gambling opponents, and news of change elsewhere, including the arrival of ships, diseases, and peoples.

Arrival of the Big Dogs

When early Spanish explorers made their landings 300 years before the first white man came to the Columbia Plateau, the most important passengers disembarking were equine. The modern horse reached the Cayuse by 1730 by way of rivers pointing northerly from New Mexico. Not every tribal person saw his or her first big dog — *kusi* (Sahaptin), *sikim* (Nez Perce) or *tuu-nap* (Cayuse) — at the same time.[8] The most renowned were the men in the joint Cayuse-Umatilla war party who rode south into enemy country, led by Ococ-tuin, and saw a man riding something the size of an elk. The men were so resolute to obtain a mare and a stallion that they backtracked to amass goods worthy of the prize and returned south.[9] The gamble paid off, as the Cayuse became one of the West's renown horse tribes. Their superiority derived from three legacies: selective breeding of the Spanish mustang into an athletic, sound, fleet equine designed foremost for stamina; feats of horsemanship that rivaled all; and herds that numbered as many as 20,000 by the mid–nineteenth century.

While visiting the Whitman Mission in 1839, Thomas J. Farnham, a reporter hired by Horace Greeley, observed Cayuse horses and their owners:

Early in the day, the Indians brought in large numbers of their horses to try their speed. These are a fine race of animals; as large, and of better form, and more activity than most of the horses in the States. Every variety of colour is found among them, from the shining coal-black to the milk-white. Some of them are pied very singularly; for instance, a roan body with bay ears, and white mane and tail. Some are spotted with white on a roan, or bay, or sorrel ground, with tail and ears tipped with black. They are better trained to the saddle than those of

civilized countries. When an Indian wishes an increase of his serving animals, he mounts a fleet horse, and, lasso in hand, rushes into his band of wild animals, throws it upon the neck of the chosen one, and chokes him down; and while in a state of insensibility, ties the hind and fore feet firmly together. When consciousness returns, the animal struggles violently, but in vain, to get loose. His fear is then attacked by throwing bear-skins, wolf-skins and blankets at his head till he becomes quiet. He is then loosened from the cord, and rears and plunges furiously at the end of a long rope, and receives another introduction to bear-skins, &c. After this, he is approached and handled; or, if still too timid, he is again beset with blankets and bear-skins, as before, until he is docile. Then come the saddling and riding. During this training, they uniformly treat him tenderly when near, and rudely when he pulls at the end of the halter. Thus they make their wild steed the most fearless and pleasant riding animals I ever mounted.

Four days later, in the course of his travel toward The Dalles, Farnham found himself again appreciating Cayuse horses:

For three hours before sunset the trail was rugged and precipitous, often overhanging the river, and so narrow that a mis-step of four inches would have plunged horse and rider hundreds of feet into the boiling flood. But as Skyuse [Cayuse] horses never make such disagreeable mistakes, we rode the steeps in safety.[10]

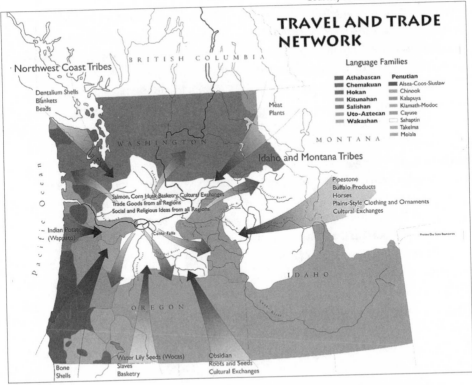

TRAVEL AND TRADE NETWORK

Language Families

Athabascan
Chemakuan
Hokan
Kitunahan
Salishan
Uto-Aztecan
Wakashan

Penutian
Alsea-Coos-Siuslaw
Chinook
Kalapuya
Klamath-Modoc
Cayuse
Sahaptin
Takelma
Molala

Northwest Coast Tribes

Dentalium Shells
Blankets
Beads

Meat
Plants

Idaho and Montana Tribes

Pipestone
Buffalo Products
Horses
Plains-Style Clothing and Ornaments
Cultural Exchanges

Salmon, Corn Husk Basketry, Cultural Exchanges
Trade Goods from all Regions
Social and Religious Ideas from all Regions

Indian Potato
(Wappato)

Celilo Falls

Water Lily Seeds (Wocas)
Slaves
Basketry

Obsidian
Roots and Seeds
Cultural Exchanges

Bone
Shells

Horses made travel to distant lands more practicable and more frequent. The presence of horses among enemies also made their incursions into the Plateau easier. Before contact, the Snakes or Northern Shoshone, Bannocks or Northern Paiute to the south, and Blackfeet northeast of the Bitterroots raided the Plateau people for their abundance of fresh and preserved foods and to take slaves. One such raid resulted in the story of the tribal heroine Ut'an'may.[11]

Ut'an'may was out digging and gathering in the Blue Mountains when Snake Indians sneaked up and captured her. In captivity, she would become a slave. Capturing rival tribal people was a way to increase productivity, and there are numerous stories of children and women captured by Bannocks and Snakes, the tribes that most commonly raided the Plateau.

Ut'an'may's hands were bound, and she was forced to ride with a Snake warrior on his horse. She managed to get her hands loose, took the man's weapon, killed him, and escaped. As a consequence, she was recognized as a warrior at large gatherings, and she became a participant in war councils and raiding parties with men. Since time immemorial, women are the makers of life and men are the takers of life as guardians of their people and lands. Ut'an'may was a notable exception.

Bannock attacks are legendary in local families. One local medicine woman and her son-in-law were killed during a Bannock raid on her camp on the Blackhawk trail along the Grande Ronde River (circa 1870s). She was a prime target, because many people showed their appreciation for her help by giving her foods. Her three children — Koots Koots Wapta, Sisaawipam, and Kipsootspaouyeen — escaped and later in life became allottees of the Umatilla Reservation. They always remembered the sounds of bullets and arrows whizzing by their heads as they raced away on horseback.[12]

In another instance, a young Cayuse boy taken captive by the Bannocks became a leader among them. He later returned to this homeland to negotiate a war alliance with the Cayuse and was killed by three Cayuse warriors to prevent further bloodshed.[13] Other oral histories recall Bannock raids on Hurricane Creek in the Wallowas and on the John Day, Deschutes, and Umatilla Rivers.

Tribal rivalry was also manifest in other practices. In years when camas yields were poor, for example, Plateau people burned the grasses on the camas prairies to prevent others from seeing the tops of the plants they had left untouched, thereby protecting the plants from immediate digging and improving the soil for the following year's yield and harvest.

Raiding rivals also yielded goods that were unavailable or limited in local trade circles. Because the marauding pursuits of the Snakes and Bannocks brought them into contact with northern and southern Plains tribes and tribes of the Southwest, successful Plateau raiders could return from counterattacks with new apparel, weaponry, and tools from distant lands.

Beads, Brass, and Other New Goods

Native peoples from lands in the colonies of the United States, from Hudson Bay to the Dakotas and from Nootka Sound to California and Mexico, had had dealings with French, British, Spanish or Russians long before white men penetrated the interior Columbia River Plateau. More than one hundred ships had visited the Pacific shore before 1800, searching for new lands and opportunities. Goods generated by these diverse explorers and would-be possessors made their way to the Pacific Northwest through other tribes.

The first European goods that Plateau Indians saw likely came up the Columbia River from the Chinook, Clatsop, Cowlitz, and other trading groups on the lower river. The trade network brought the world beyond the Columbia to Plateau Indians, with goods from northern people on Vancouver Island and up to Alaska; Plateau and Great Basin people in Idaho, Wyoming, and Utah; plus a wide range of European manufactured trade items from maritime ports on the Atlantic and Pacific oceans. The center of regional trade distribution in the Columbia Basin country was downriver at Celilo Falls, one of the great fishing places in North America. Each year, when salmon coursed up the river by the millions, thousands of people gathered at the Great Falls on the Columbia, where trading flourished. Lower Chinook people traded wapato and other foods from the lower Columbia, trade items from northern people along the Pacific Coast, and European manufactured goods acquired from maritime traders.[14] Not many maritime explorers found what they desired until the late eighteenth century, when they discovered a wealth of furs in the North Pacific that brought them riches in trade with China. A rush to capitalize on the new wealth in the maritime fur trade brought traders to the Pacific Coast and a ready source of manufactured items for trade.

Two British mariners, James Cook and George Vancouver, and American trader Robert Gray drew the first widely published charts of the northern Pacific coast. The world got its first inkling of the Great River of the West — the Columbia — from cartography based on Cook's third voyage in 1778, Gray's crossing of the bar at the mouth of the Columbia River in May 1792, and Vancouver's exploration of the river in October 1792. Vancouver dispatched Lt. William Broughton to survey and chart the river's course for 100 miles. His report became the first written description of the river and its importance to trade among native groups.

Broughton encountered Cathlamet, Cowlitz, and Multnomah Indians during his upriver paddle. Through signs, he understood that Indian groups on the lower river traded with upriver groups and that navigation up the Columbia was blocked by falls. Broughton incorrectly surmised that the Columbia was a short river, with its source likely near Mt. Hood.[15] Locally, these arrivals had no immediate impact on the tribes 200 to 300 miles distant like the Cayuse, Umatilla, and Walla Walla.

Robert Gray was the first American maritime trader to survey the North Pacific Coast and to chart the mouth of the Columbia River, but he was just one of many traders who frequented the region at the end of the eighteenth century. Most of the ships originated in Boston, and they came loaded with trade goods, which they freely traded with willing natives along the coast. They sailed in relatively small ships, which could maneuver in shallow bays and rivers. By the early nineteenth century, the "Boston men," as natives called them, had nearly taken over the maritime trading enterprise in the region. British and American traders had introduced thousands of trade articles — metal, cloth, glass, tools — into the native trade system before land explorers entered the Plateau homeland during the first decades of the nineteenth century.[16] By the mid-nineteenth century, individual tribal names would begin to reflect the Bostons by including the words *Pushton* or *Pashtun* in Indian jargon for "white man."

Not every native person saw his or her first white man at the same time. In one family's oral history, the first time anyone saw a white man was during a multi-tribal hunting expedition to the Yellowstone area for buffalo. In another family's oral history, there is a story of some Nez Perce men who were traveling on the "Nez Perce Trail." At night they saw a campfire down in the valley and went down to it. They expected to find Cayuse, but to their surprise they found two French men.[17] There is no way to date these events. Had it occurred after Lewis and Clark were in the West in 1805–1806, however, their surprise may not have been notable enough to survive for two hundred years in oral history.

Umatilla, Cayuse, and Walla Walla people had traded at Celilo for as long as people could remember, but the introduction of European trade goods subtly altered trade patterns. Trade in new materials — metal, glass, wool — became very desirable. Over time, the acquisition of goods that brought new wealth or enhanced life changed the economy among Plateau people in terms of content, quantity, quality, and price. Trade for the first European goods anticipated the visit of the first Euro-Americans to travel through Cayuse, Walla Walla, and Umatilla country — Meriwether Lewis and William Clark — in October 1805. When the American explorers traveled down the Columbia River, Clark recorded in his journal for October 21: "here we Saw two Scarlet and a blue cloth blanket, also a Salors Jacket."[18] In a way, the world of Lewis and Clark had preceded them to the interior Plateau. More important, however, the trade was a harbinger of much greater changes that would overwhelm people in the region within decades of their encounter with Lewis and Clark and their so-called Corps of Discovery.

Strangers with an Agenda

The Lewis and Clark Expedition was part of an ambitious agenda that President Thomas Jefferson had planned for years. Jefferson had instructed Lewis and Clark to pursue economic, political, diplomatic, and scientific goals on their journey west. He hoped they would find an easy passage from the Missouri River to the Columbia, but the mountains in present-day Montana and Idaho argued against it. On the Continental Divide, where Lewis looked west to see only mountaintops and deep canyons, the president's dream of a water passage to the West died.

Jefferson's ambition for a water route focused on commerce. His desire to gain knowledge about the territory west of the Continental Divide focused on science, cartographic descriptions, and the development of relations with native peoples. The explorers understood how important it was that they accurately describe the region drained by the Columbia River, a region that included Cayuse, Walla Walla, and Umatilla lands. What they learned about the land, the people, and potential resources would be extremely valuable to cartographers, scientists, politicians, and other explorers.

Lewis and Clark also entered the Columbia's sphere as natural historians. The pursuit of natural history in the eighteenth century was part of the Enlightenment, a forceful empiricist investigation of the world that was consistent with the idea of a Great Chain of Being, which categorized living creation into hierarchical orders of greater and lesser beings. Jefferson and other Enlightenment naturalists focused on the idea that order prevailed on earth in the living kingdoms of plants and animals. In the mid-eighteenth century, Carl Linnaeus' outline taxonomy of that world — the binomial naming of plants and animals — gave names to the order of being and became the scientific basis for surveying the natural world. Jefferson sent Lewis and Clark west as Linnaean discoverers, to report on an environment no Enlightenment scientist had seen and to bring back a catalog of western America. They documented their travel, as Jefferson had specified by measuring and describing the environment.[19]

When Lewis and Clark arrived at the confluence of the Snake and Columbia rivers in October 1805, two prominent Nez Perce men who were escorting them arrived in advance of the main party. They were called Twisted Hair and Tetoharsky in the journals.[20] The expedition had been among the Nez Perce for almost a month after leaving the Flathead and Lemhi peoples on the other side of the Continental Divide. Given the close relations and proximity of villages among the Cayuse, Walla Walla, Palouse, and Nez Perce on the

Snake River, word had traveled downriver ahead of the explorers, and two hundred tribal people gathered to greet them with song at the confluence. Yet other tribal people were hunting in the mountains when the Expedition passed through.

In addition to drying off goods that had been soaked and dampened in the arduous journey on the Snake, Lewis collected vocabularies and the captains engaged in their usual diplomatic overtures of speechmaking translated through signs and gifting to men they identified as "chiefs." Typically, the Expedition identified Indian men who they presumed were leaders so they could make their "friendly intentions" known and present gifts, which would serve as evidence to anyone else traveling through that Americans had been there. At that point in the journey, the gifts that Lewis and Clark used to "make chiefs" consisted mostly of shirts, handkerchiefs, small trade medals, flags, and beads.

The explorers observed a river phenomenon with which they were unfamiliar — spawned-out salmon. They could not explain the large quantities of dead or nearly dead salmon in the Columbia River and on the banks. They also observed distinctions among Plateau people: a more balanced division of labor between men and women than they had seen before — veneration for the elderly, and heads shaped in infancy by flattening boards as a mark of beauty — and they traveled upriver to see the mouth of the Taptett (Yakima) River. As they prepared to head down the Columbia, they purchased forty aboriginal dogs to supplement their diet, even as they noted the immense quantities of fish being taken and dried by Indians in village after village of tule-mat lodges.

Proceeding downriver in advance of the main party, Clark rested on a rock in the Columbia and shot a crane out of the air. The villagers witnessed this event and reacted. Clark and three men approached a Umatilla village on the north shore of the Columbia, where the Indians had fled to their lodges and closed the doors. Clark entered one of the lodges and observed the natives' level of angst. He later commented in his field notes: "I am confident that I could have tomahawked every Indian here."[21] He offered them what he had in his pockets, took their hands, smoked with them, and tried to put them at ease until the rest of the party arrived, including the Nez Perce escorts, Sacagawea, and her infant son, Jean Baptiste.

After a long, soggy winter at the mouth of the Columbia, Lewis and Clark struggled up the river against the current in the spring of 1806, eager to leave the region and speed themselves over the mountains to the Missouri River and back to St. Louis. On their return in April, they noticed a river on the south shore of the Columbia they had not recorded the previous year — the "Youmalolam riv.," or Umatilla — where they saw a sizable and well-populated encampment. Then they made their way toward the mouth of the Snake River and the camp of Yelépt, leader of the Walúulapam.[22] Lewis recorded on April 27 that Yelépt

appeared much gratifyed at seeng us return, invited us to remain at his village three or four days and assured us that we should be furnished with a plenty of such food as they had themselves; and some horses to assist us on our journey. . . . we purchased four dogs of these people on which the party suped heartily having been on short allowance for near two days. . . . the indians informed us that there was a good road which passed from the columbia opposite to this village to the entrance of the Kooskooske [Clearwater River] on the S. side of Lewis's [Snake] river; they also informed us, that there were a plenty of deer and Antelopes on the road, with good water and grass.[23]

Yelépt brought the captains "an armful of wood and a platter of 3 roasted mullets," and Lewis and Clark purchased four dogs. The next day, as Corps member John Ordway recorded in his journal, a large number of invited Indians gathered to dance in celebration of the explorers' presence. The Walla Wallas extended their hospitality to Lewis and Clark and expressed the desire, as Ordway wrote,

. . . that they Should be lonesome when we left them and they wished to hear once of our meddicine Songs and try to learn it and wished us to learn one of theirs and it would make them glad.[24]

It was clear to Lewis and Clark that Yelépt had extended himself to encourage an ongoing relationship and the promise of future trade. Eager to leave the camp

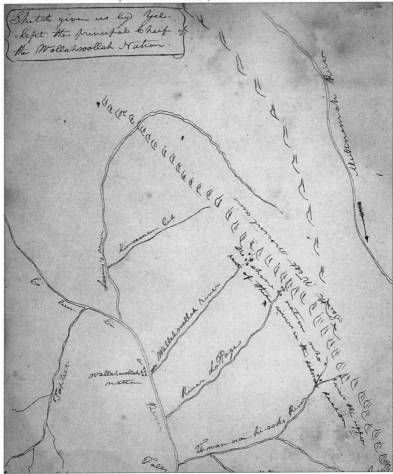

Yelépt's map of overland return route, "a good road"

and head east to the mountains, Lewis and Clark hastened to bid goodbye to Yelépt, but he entreated them to stay longer, as they had promised. He undoubtedly knew by the depth of the river that the spring runoff had not begun in earnest and that deep snow in the mountains would prevent the Expedition from getting through the Bitterroots. Lewis pointed out that there were no winds on the river that day and that it was a good day to cross. Eventually, Yelépt provided canoes for crossing the horses over the river but required the Corps to stay one more night in his camp.

On April 29, Yelépt presented Clark with "a very elegant white horse," for which he received Clark's sword. The next day, the Expedition crossed the Columbia on two canoes furnished by Yelépt, and proceeded to the Walla Walla River, where they paused overnight among twelve lodges of Walúulapams before heading overland to the Nez Perce camps.

With Sacagawea's help, through a Shoshone woman captive in the Walla Walla camp, the explorers had gained valuable information about the overland travel route. With a map in hand of the region that depicted the major tributaries of the lower Snake River — which Yelépt had sketched for Clark — the Corps of Discovery had traveled safely overland to the familiar camps of the Nez Perce on the Clearwater River in present-day Idaho.

Lewis and Clark left the Walla Walla country more knowledgeable about how the Indian population lived in their environment, but they still had questions about what they observed. Clark, for example, wondered about the health of Indians who suffered from eye maladies. He concluded that "the fine Sands of those plains and the river Contribute much to the disorder."[25]

During their time on the Columbia River Plateau, Lewis and Clark presented approximately seventeen medals to various "1st, 2nd and 3rd chiefs" in the tribal

Yelépt

"On the Umatilla Reservation," Ron Pond writes," no oral tales have survived about Yelépt, but the chiefs knew about the Jefferson Peace Medal that he received from Lewis and Clark. All that has remained is the compelling story about how he died."* Peter Skene Ogden provided the eyewitness account of that remarkable event on the lower Walla Walla River on November 14, 1825, when the tribal leader was approximately fifty years old. Dr. Theodore Stern summarized the event:

*The Eagle [Yelépt], owner of more than a hundred horses, within the space of a few months had been stricken in succession by the death, first of a younger, then of his elder son. A wife and two married daughters survived, but he had no more sons nor the hopes of any. When the funeral for the latter son was held, the chief invited Dease to be present and the other officers came along. The body having been lowered into the grave, the chief himself delivered the funeral oration, rather than employing the customary speaker who functions today. Then, unexpectedly stepping into the grave, he laid himself on the corpse of his son and ordered his relatives to fill the grave; nor could he be dissuaded.***

*Ron Pond, "The Jefferson Peace Medal: A Cultural Phenomenon Passed down from Chief to Chief in Walla Walla Culture" (Ph.D. diss., Washington State University, 2004), 287.

**Theodore Stern, *Chiefs and Chief Traders: Indian Relations at Fort Nez Percés* (Corvallis: Oregon State University Press, 1993), 76.

homeland.[26] In the Walla Walla country, after "each [chief] presented us a fine horse," Lewis and Clark gave a pistol with ammunition and two small Jefferson Peace Medals to their host chiefs.[27] From notes in Clark's handwriting, these two medals were presented to "Chief To mar lar" (Tamatapam), and one to "Arloquat" (Ollokʷot).[28] (They had presented a small medal to Yelépt on the outbound trip and promised a larger one on the return journey, but there is no evidence that he received it.) These three men were leaders of the Walúulapam (Walla Walla) and Waíiletpu (Cayuse). On the north side of the Columbia near the mouth of the Umatilla River, Lewis and Clark also had presented two small medals to "two principal chiefs" of the "Pish-quit-pah" and "War-war-wa" on April 25, 1806.[29]

Recipients of the medals did not always apply the same meaning or value to the gift as the giver. For the captains, the medals were symbols of their sovereign government, which claimed dominion over Indian nations in the vast area of the Louisiana Purchase, and of friendship and potential alliance in the Columbia River region. With tribes, gifts could gain safe passage for the Expedition. For the recipients, the coins' message and importance varied. The Cheyenne, who were suspicious of what consequence their acceptance of the medals might bring, refused them. The Nez Perce would later recall how the medals constituted their first treaty with the United States, symbolizing their agreement to peaceable relations and to not take up arms against the government. For other leaders, the medals represented mutual goodwill and promises. In all cases where medals were received, they became new objects in the native culture that represented a recognition of status bestowed on the recipients by newcomers. The Washington season medals, which were the medals most often given to Indians by the Corps, featured scenes of farming, houses, domestic livestock, and women working — providing "windows of opportunity, progress and cultural change for Indian chiefs."[30] These depictions were messages, a preview of sorts, of the "civilizing" that would follow.

There is no mention of the Cayuse people in the journals of Lewis and Clark. The explorers assumed they were yet another band of Nez Perce, and they were not called Cayuse then. While among the Nez Perce in June 1806, they recorded meeting men who they identified as Ye-E-al-po, Wil-le-let-po, and Y-e-let-pos, an attempt to write Waíiletpu.

Perhaps the most important legacy of the Lewis and Clark Expedition is the body of information found in the journals — extensive cartography, scientific descriptions of landscapes, and, most importantly, information about Indian nations. The interactions the captains had with tribal people and the names they left on the landscape were harbingers of a much larger ambition, an imperial ambition that the United States extended into the region only one generation after the Corps of Discovery returned home.

New Rules of Exchange

Lewis and Clark had promised friendship and a future trade relationship, but the Americans would not be back for more than two decades. In the meantime, another nation of intruders stepped in to pursue a quick gleaning of the wealth in the Plateau homeland. Five years after Lewis and Clark left Yelépt's camp, another explorer met the Walla Wallas at the mouth of the Snake River. Descending the Columbia River, David Thompson, a fur trader and cartographer in the employ of the Canadian-based North West Company, arrived on the morning of July 9, 1811, with seven in his party. Thompson described meeting "the Principal Chief of all the Tribes [Yelépt] . . . . a stately good looking Man of about 40 years old, well dressed." Thompson noticed that Yelépt had "an American medal of 1801 Thomas Jefferson & a small Flag of that Nation," which he likely anticipated, because he had read the account of the Lewis and Clark Expedition written by Corps member Patrick Gass and published in 1807.[31] "I found him [Yelépt] intelligent," Thompson wrote in his journal, "he was also very friendly, & we discoursed a long time and settled upon the Junction of the Shawpatin River [Snake] for a House, etcetera." Thompson smoked with Yelépt and swapped gifts, two feet of twisted tobacco to the Walla Wallas in exchange for two fat salmon.[32]

Thompson engaged Yelépt and the Walla Wallas as trading partners. Aware of the potential promises Lewis and Clark had made to the Indians in 1806, Thompson made sure that Yelépt understood the North West Company's commitment to establishing a trading house in his region. In addition, Thompson claimed the area for Great Britain, an act of imperialism and also a claim in competition with the Americans. Within one year, the United States and Great Britain would be at war, and the two nations' competing claims in the Pacific Northwest would enter a new phase, one that would last for three decades. In 1811, however, Thompson believed he had the right to make a land claim, with no apparent concern about the Walla Walla nation or any other Indians who lived on the Columbia Plateau. On a small pole that he erected near the mouth of the Snake River, Thompson attached a paper that read:

Know hereby that this Country is claimed by Great Britain as part of it's Territories and that the NW Company of Merchants from Canada, finding the Factory for this People inconvenient for them, do hereby intend to erect a Factory in this Place for the Commerce of the Country around.[33]

From his meeting with Yelépt, Thompson descended the Columbia thinking he would meet up with American partners in a larger fur enterprise that had been planned for several years by New York capitalist John Jacob Astor. Astor had created the Pacific Fur Company in 1810 to establish a string of fur-trading posts across the West and a trading port on the Pacific coast that could take advantage of the lucrative trade with Asia. Unknown to Thompson, however, the Astor deal with the North West Company partners had fallen through. When he reached the mouth of the Columbia, Astor's men greeted him and feigned agreement that they were part of a joint enterprise, even though they doubted that it was true. The Astor enterprise had included two settlement parties, one by sea from New York aboard the *Tonquin* and another overland from the Missouri, led by Wilson Price Hunt. Hunt had little experience in outfitting or leading an overland expedition, especially one that pursued a poorly planned route. After nearly six months of travel west from the Arikara Villages on the Missouri River in present-day South Dakota, Hunt and his worn-out comrades —thirty-two men, one pregnant woman and her two children, and three Shoshone Indians—struggled to get over the Blue Mountains in December. "We had only five wretched horses," Hunt wrote, "for our food during the passage of the mountains."[34]

On January 8, 1812, the hungry and dead-tired Hunt party descended the Umatilla River east of present-day Pendleton and into a large camp of Cayuse Indians. "I cannot sufficiently express my gratitude to Providence," Hunt wrote, "for having let us reach here; because we all were extremely fatigued and enfeebled." Hunt's overland group spent nearly a week with the Cayuse, resting, trading (Hunt purchased horses), and getting a general description of travel routes to the Colum-

bia. The Cayuse, "the cleanliest indians that I know of," as Hunt later described them, had revived the bedraggled party, but the Cayuse had also gotten a promise from Hunt that Astor's fur traders would return and trade with them for beaver. It was a promise that went largely unfulfilled until the establishment of Fort Nez Perces in 1818.[35]

Astor planned to make Fort Astoria, his fur post at the mouth of the Columbia, the headquarters for an extensive network of interior posts on the river and its tributary streams. Pacific Fur Company men David Stuart and Alexander Ross planned to penetrate the upper Columbia, a region David Thompson had traversed, so they joined up with Thompson on his upriver return to Canada within a week of his arrival at Astoria. Ross memorialized this trip in his *Adventures of the First Settlers on the Oregon or Columbia River, 1810–1813*, published in 1849. The entourage canoed upstream into the Columbia River Gorge near the end of July 1811 and encountered Chinook at villages near the Cascades, where Ross commented that the Indians extracted presents from the fur traders before they could pass the rapids. Thompson left the group near The Dalles, and Ross and the Astorians made their way upriver. Ross visited a village at the Long Narrows, a location he called "the great emporium or mart of the Columbia," because it was the principal location for trading on the river. Ross described the Indians negatively, calling them "troublesome," but upriver at the mouth of the

Deschutes River, he described the Indians as "very useful" in navigating their canoes upstream. At Willow Creek, upstream from the John Day River, an Indian sold Ross a salmon. On the following day, August 10, 1811, Ross camped at the mouth of the Umatilla River, where he noted many Indians "occupied in catching salmon."[36]

At the mouth of the Walla Walla River on August 12, "a large band of Indians were encamped, who expressed a wish that we should pass the day with them." As Ross recorded:

We encamped accordingly; yet for some time not an Indian came near us, and those who had invited us to pass the day with them seemed to have gone away; so that we were at a loss what construction to put upon their shyness. But in the midst of our perplexity we perceived a great body of men issuing from the camp, all armed and painted, and proceeded by three chiefs.[37]

On the plain near the camp, Ross guessed there were no "less than four thousand" horses, a display of wealth that had to impress him. The three chiefs — Tamatapam, a Walla Walla; Quill-Quills-Tuck-a-Pesten, a Nez Perce; and Ollok^wot, a Cayuse — gave orations, which Ross described as "harangues." The orations were actually speeches of welcome that quickly melded into a ceremony of friendly engagement, highlighted by women and men in fancy dress and adornment dancing and singing. Ross character-ized the dancers as "richly garnished" and wrote that they "differed widely in appearance from the piscatory tribes we had seen along the [lower] river." The point to the welcome and the orations, as Ross soon found out, was the establishment of a trading station, such as the one Thompson had promised Yelépt two months before and that Lewis and Clark had insinuated five years earlier.[38]

The location and control of a trading post in the Plateau country was a matter of great importance to fur traders and to the people who lived on the Columbia, Snake, Walla Walla, and Umatilla rivers. For Alexander Ross and the American-based Pacific Fur Company, finding Thompson's planted pole and his claim to the region for Great Britain suggested an unacceptable demarcation of the trading territory, up the Columbia for the British and up the Snake for the Americans. Ross talked it out with Tamatapam, who he described as "a middle-aged man, well featured, and of a very agreeable countenance; and what is still better, he is, to all appearance, a good man. . . ."[39]

Ross and other traders understood that the Indians wanted trade for their own reasons, but the traders focused primarily on business and the competition among themselves to lure native traders to their establishments. Ross and traders like him seemed to ignore the complexity and cultural content of Indian trading, discounting the process as fractious and characterized by theft and unpredictable exchanges. They focused instead on what they could trade with Indians to acquire furs, believing, as Ross put it, that Indians "require but little, and the more they get of our manufacture the more unhappy will they be, as the possession of one article naturally creates a desire for another, so that they are never satisfied."[40] Ross believed this was a formula for trade with the people of the Columbia and Snake rivers.

Early fur traders in the region had little desire to transform the Indians in the direction of agricultural pursuits (such as farming or gardening), English education, or conversion to Christianity. The fur traders' objective was to stockpile furs trapped and traded by Indians, an inexpensive source of production. Farming, book learning, and a change in religion would not serve their purpose. Inducements and incentives to engage favorable tribal leaders to promote business with the traders would be necessary, since the Indians had not previously been in the habit of taking animals just for their hides or taking more than was needed for their own subsistence and trade practices. Leaders who served the purposes of the Pacific Fur Company would receive gifts and honors, and those whose actions were counter to the fur traders' desires were penalized. Because these white men and their Metís, French, and Algonquin recruits did not bring women with them to the Northwest, another way to make inroads to the local culture was through intermarriage. Fur traders also induced participation by extending credit, paying for services such as delivery of wood or horses, granting storage privileges within the fort, and giving special consideration in the acquisition of guns and ammunition.

Gibraltar of the Columbia

The War of 1812, however, dashed Astor's grand scheme on the Columbia. In the aftermath of the war, Great Britain and the United States decided to avoid settling their competing claims to the Pacific Northwest. They agreed to a twenty-year joint occupation of the vast region west of the Continental Divide and north of the 42nd parallel while completely ignoring the rights of the true owners of the lands. Fort Astoria and the other posts established by Astor's Pacific Fur Company became the property of the North West Company, which aspired to Astor's dream and took the first step by gaining approval to sell furs directly to China. With Fort George — the renamed Fort Astoria — at the mouth of the Columbia, they could export furs across the Pacific. What the North West Company needed to complete the Pacific Northwest part of their scheme was an interior post that could gather furs from the lucrative Snake River district. With the establishment of Fort Nez Perces, the "Gibraltar of the Columbia," in 1818, the North West Company became a fixture among the Cayuse, Walla Walla, Umatilla, Palouse, and Nez Perce and a signal of more intrusions. The region became a field for fur-trade entrepreneurs, and it was the fur traders who soon intruded into the mid-Columbia country.[41]

A woman stands near a tule lodge in this Lee Moorhouse photograph.

The North West Company built Fort Nez Perces, on the east bank of the Columbia River just upstream from the mouth of the Walla Walla River, as a center for trade with nearby tribes. To construct the fort, the company had delegated up to one hundred men to Donald McKenzie, an experienced Canadian fur trader who had become the manager of the company's interior district in 1816. There had been friction between fur men and the Palouse, Walla Walla, and Cayuse near the mouth of the Snake River in 1813 and 1814, and the company wanted to stabilize relations with all trading Indians in the area.

The traders were apprehensive, as Alexander Ross later recorded, but they knew "plans had been formed; the country must be secured, the natives awed and reconciled, buildings made, furs collected, new territories added."[42]

The purpose was that clear, and the assembled chiefs understood it as well. The fur men needed access to trapping areas, which meant achieving agreements with the principal men of each native trading group. In 1817, McKenzie, Ross, and others carried on a long discussion, but no agreement could be reached until Walla Walla leader Tamatapam joined in the parleys.

When he arrived with a group of nearly five hundred men, fresh from a successful raid on Shoshone camps, the discussions heated up, with great contention and a steady set of orations from all sides. Ross recorded that a prime issue centered on establishing peace with the Shoshone, a necessity before trade could flourish. More than fifty Walla Walla and Cayuse men made agreements with the traders that opened the Snake River country and set the stage for building Fort Nez Perces.[43]

The fort built, McKenzie struck off in the Snake River country in September 1818, with nearly two hundred men and trapping gear. Fort Nez Perces became the launching point for brigades, well-organized expeditions that would scour the Snake and Columbia drainages for furs over the next decade. While Tamatapam and others had permitted the erection of the trading house, the leaders did not approve the construction of the post stockade. The tribes had had free access to the post previously and this new barrier, symbolizing white ownership and mistrust, angered the local tribes.

This trading structure represented the first permanent change to local tribal culture. Scotch-Irish, Metís, and Algonquin intermarriage commenced locally. Regular trade at the fort yielded wool, flannel, calico, tobacco twists, tea bricks, sugar cones, mouth harps, thimbles, beads, nails, metal cups and kettles, guns, ball and powder, dice, needles, and hats in exchange for otter and beaver pelts. This also instigated the challenge to one of the tenets of traditional law — never take more than you need.

In 1821, the North West Company merged with the more powerful Hudson's Bay Company, a trading company formed in 1670 and headquartered in London. The HBC gobbled up the old Pacific Fur Company and North West Company posts, including Fort Nez Perces. By 1824, HBC managers had decided to consolidate operations and build a new headquarters post, Fort Vancouver, on the north bank of the Columbia near the mouth of the Willamette River. HBC also recommended moving Fort Nez Perces to the north side of the Columbia to remove it from potential claim by the Americans, in case Britain and the United States divided the Oregon Country at the Columbia, as some expected. The Cayuse and Walla Walla, however, complained loudly about the proposed relocation of the fort. At least in part, the company left the fort in its location because of their concerns.[44]

Fort Nez Perces was a sturdy edifice, built of "drift logs, and surrounded by a stoccade of the same, with two bastions, and a gallery around the inside," as one observer described it in 1834.[45] HBC traders did a steady business with Cayuse, Walla Walla, Umatilla, and Nez Perce, who brought furs and especially horses for trade. One trader commented that even though some Indians were "poor in furs, they trade Horses, and a good moderate Horse, will always cost a Large Blkt. . . ."[46] The company strove to establish an atmosphere of predictable and peaceful trading, a "pax H.B.C.," as one scholar put it, but they did not hesitate to use force to gain advantage and arrange trade on their own terms. HBC controlled the landscape near each fort through armaments, sentinels, fort structures, and rules of engagement with Indian traders. They also tried to establish special arrangements with select Indians, with families that traded frequently at the fort — the so-called Home Guard, who also lived close to the fort and profited from an ongoing relationship with HBC traders.[47]

Walla Walla families dominated in this group, while Cayuse had the reputation of exerting influence on the Columbia as far downriver as Celilo Falls. Botanist David Douglas recounted an incident during his 1826 tour up the Columbia, when a Cayuse chief protected him from harassment at the hands of Chinook at the falls:

Just at this time a chief of the Kyeuuse [Cayuse] tribe and three of his young men, who are the terror of all other tribes west of the mountains and great frends of the white people, as they call them, stepped in and settled the matter in a few words without any further trouble. This very friendly Indian, who is the finest figure of a man that I have seen, standing nearly 6 feet 6 inches high, accompanied us a few miles up the river, where we camped for the night. . . .[48]

The Price of the Fur Trade

The London headquarters of HBC set early policies that prohibited sexual relations with natives and prohibited having white wives in the trading forts. Over time, however, the usefulness of taking Indian wives to solidify tribal relations and ensure smooth trading led to the company issuing reminders against the "detestable sin of whore-mongering," referring to casual exploitative relations between fort men and native women. Eventually, HBC officials would note that while all wives were a distraction to their husbands' work, Indian wives were less distracting than white wives. All of this intermarriage would lead to disputes in which HBC men left inheritances to Indian wives and "reputed" children that other family members would contest. This practice — known as a custom of the country, blanket marriages, *á la façon du pays* — led HBC Governor George Simpson, who would later be assigned to the Northwest, to write in a private letter in 1822, "White Fish seems to be favorable to procreation and had I a good pimp in my suite I might have been inclined to deposit a little of my Spawn but have become . . . vastly tenacious of my reputation." By the early 1830s in Red River, Simpson had a legitimate marriage to his cousin Frances, who "was always terrified to look about her in case of seeing something disagreeable" — including, perhaps, her husband's progeny.[49]

In late 1824, Peter Skene Ogden undertook his first Snake country expedition, one of several HBC forays bent on thoroughly trapping out beaver east of the Blue Mountains to provide a buffer that would keep American competitors at bay.

Ogden's aggressive trapping was new to the country and surely must have raised questions among tribes about the company's larger intentions. Trapping out the region contradicted any justifiable relationship with the environment, but there were other purposes than simply accumulation of wealth. George Simpson, the head of HBC operations in North America, hoped to create a "fur desert" in the Snake River country that would stave off American settlers by halting the advance of American fur trappers. Ironically, the Snake country brigade trail that Ogden and other HBC traders used in pursuing Simpson's policy became integral to the Oregon Trail, which would serve American emigrants some twenty years later.[50]

By the early 1830s, it was clear that HBC's trapping policy had blunted the efforts of American fur traders. In 1831, John Work, a company trader who would later become a chief factor for the HBC, took over trapping the Snake region. The following year, he reported to John McLoughlin at Fort Vancouver that there were too few fur animals in the Snake country to justify further expeditions.[51] Nonetheless, the Walla Walla knew that American traders generally offered better exchanges for furs, and several had traded with Americans at rendezvous meetings east of their homeland. Establishing loyalty among Indian traders became one of the principal strategies at Fort Nez Perces, but the intrusion of American competitors could break connections between HBC traders and Indians. That happened

graphically in 1836, when Fort Nez Perces trader Pierre Pambrun found himself bound by upset Cayuse who demanded that he pay them prices equivalent to what the Americans paid.[52]

Local Pambrun family history and other sources indicate that Pambrun was beaten twice by local tribal leaders. In 1832, Pierre was beaten by Old Looking Glass over the extension of credit while Tawatoy looked on. In 1836, Tawatoy bound and beat Pambrun over the British rate of return compared to the American price paid by Bonneville while Looking Glass observed. The HBC policy had generally succeeded in holding off American traders such as Nathaniel Wyeth, who tried to compete at Fort Hall on the banks of the Snake River in present-day Idaho, but Americans came anyway.

Cultivating Souls

Wyeth, a New England entrepreneur who hoped to establish a trading business on the Columbia, traveled west through the Cayuse and Walla Walla homeland in 1834. His entourage included Jason Lee, a Methodist missionary, and John Kirk Townsend, a physician and ornithologist who later wrote a memoir of his experiences. In late July, Townsend arrived at a large village near the mouth of the Umatilla River.

At noon, to-day, we arrived at the Utalla, or Emmitilly river, where we found a large village of Kayouse Indians, engaged in preparing kamas. Large quantities of this root were strewed about on mats and buffalo robes;

some in a crude state, and a vast quantity pounded, to be made into cakes for winter store. There are of the Indians, about twelve or fifteen lodges. A very large one, about sixty feet long by fifteen broad, is occupied by the chief, and his immediate family. This man I saw when I arrived at Walla-Walla [Fort Nez Perces], and I have accepted an invitation to make my home in his lodge while I remain here. The house is really a very comfortable one; the rays of the sun are completely excluded, and the ground is covered with buffalo robes. There are in the chief's lodge about twenty women, all busy as usual; some pounding kamas, others making leathern dresses, moccasins, &c. Several of the younger of these are very good looking,— I might almost say handsome.[53]

Lee had a much different purpose when he encountered Walla Walla and Cayuse men who frequented the HBC fort. He had heeded the "Macedonian cry" in 1830 from Northwest Indians who had traveled to St. Louis and requested Christian missionaries to minister to their people. A Methodist from New York, Lee was the first of a mid–1830s group of Protestant evangelicals who established mission outposts in the Clearwater, Snake, Spokane, and Willamette River valleys. He recorded in his diary that Tamatapam wanted him to establish a mission near the fort and that he should "preach to them now." Lee had received gifts from Tamatapam and a Cayuse chief, and he may well have wanted to establish a post near the Snake or Walla Walla rivers; but he left with HBC traders

and traveled downriver to Fort Vancouver, where John McLoughlin advised him to site his mission in the Willamette Valley.[54] Lee's departure, however, did not dampen interest in Christian missionaries at the fort. When Samuel Parker, a Protestant evangelical missionary from the American Board of Commissioners of Foreign Missions, arrived in 1835, Cayuse headmen welcomed him and his purpose. Parker toured the area that would become Marcus Whitman's mission at Waíiletpu, where he told assembled chiefs:

I come to select a place for a mission, but I do not intend to take your lands for nothing. After the doctor [Whitman] is come there will come every year a big ship loaded with goods to be divided among the Indians. Those goods will not be sold but given to you. The missionaries will bring you ploughs and hoes to learn you how to cultivate the land, and they will not sell but will give them to you.[55]

Parker's promise to bring goods but not offer them for sale underscores one of the principal bases of discord that would develop between missionaries and natives, as more and more whites invaded the homeland. By the late 1830s, Marcus and Narcissa Whitman had established a mission at Waíiletpu, Henry and Eliza Spalding had done the same on the Clearwater River among the Nez Perce (1836), and Jason Lee and Henry Perkins had established the Wascopam Mission at The Dalles (1838). Indians on the Columbia

Plateau now engaged with two distinct groups of whites: HBC and American fur traders and their entrepreneurial operatives and missionizing Protestants, who themselves divided up as Presbyterians and Methodists.

Whitman and Spalding were not immediately convinced that they had successfully converted Indians to full-time, year-round Christianity. Spalding performed his first baptisms — on Timothy, Old Joseph, and James Conner — in 1839, after the missionaries had been here three years. The first Roman Catholic missionaries in the Oregon Country did not hesitate to baptize natives. Fathers Francois Norbet Blanchet and Modeste Demers came west with the 1838 Hudson's Bay Express, and after baptizing nineteen at Fort Colville, were welcomed to Fort Nez Perces by Pierre Pambrun, a Catholic. There, on November 18, 1838, the priests conducted three baptisms before moving on to Fort Vancouver.[56]

In his 1839 journal, Thomas Farnham wrote of "Crickie," a Cayuse man who guided him from the Blue Mountains to the Whitmans. En route, Farnham observed:

A fire burned brightly in front. Water was brought, and the evening ablutions having been performed, the wife presented a dish of meat to her husband, and one to myself. There was a pause. The woman seated herself between her children. The Indian then bowed his head and prayed to God! A wandering savage in Oregon calling upon Jehovah in the name of Jesus Christ! After the prayer, he gave meat to his children, and passed the dish to his wife.

While eating, the frequent repetition of the words Jehovah and Jesus Christ, in the most reverential manner, led me to suppose they were conversing on religious topics; and thus they passed an hour. . . . a strain of music awoke me. . . . The Indian family was engaged in its evening devotions. They were singing a hymn in the Nez Percés language. Having finished it, they all knelt and bowed their faces upon the buffalo robes, and Crickie prayed long and fervently. Afterwards they sang another hymn and retired. This was the first breathing of religious feelings that I had seen since leaving the States.[57]

Clearly, Farnham was more impressed than Commander Wilkes, who wrote regarding the missionaries generally:

Little has yet been effected by them in christianizing the natives. They are principally engaged in the cultivation of the mission farms, and in the care of their own stock, in order to obtain flocks and herds for themselves, most of them having selected lands. As far as my personal observations went, in the part of the country where the missionaries reside, there are very few Indians to engage their attention; and they seemed more occupied with the settlement of the country and in agricultural pursuits than missionary labours.[58]

Farnham might have agreed after the following experience at Whitman Mission:

. . . in the presence of Dr. Whitman. He was speaking Skyuse at the top of his voice to some lazy Indians who were driving their cattle from his garden, and giving orders to others to yoke their oxen, get the axes, and go into the forest for the lower sleepers of the new mission house.[59]

In explaining the competing religions, a few metaphors have been employed in tribal households where the rivalries were manifested. In one dinner table discussion, where a schoolboy told his family how the Catholic priest referred to the local Protestants as "heathens," the recently converted Presbyterian father said his son should not return to the Catholic school. His wife observed that it did not matter whether you rode a horse or took a wagon; you could get to the same place.[60] In another family, the poles of the tepee served to illustrate that all of the poles go from their separate placement in the ground to one direction — up — like the prayers of the people.[61]

In the old ways, when you died, there was not a bad place to go to. Sexual intercourse; birth; bodily elimination of saliva, urine, feces, and gas; nudity; taking the life of another living being — all were natural. Killing was a natural part of life, too, and tribal individuals paid with their lives many times to maintain safety of the whole.

From a Trickle to a Flood

Marcus Whitman brought Christian missionizing into the Cayuse homeland, but he also brought an imperial outlook. In fundamental ways, he became an agent of empire in the early 1840s through his active promotion of overland immigration from the United States. In part, Whitman's enthusiasm for immigration masked his mixed record as a missionary among the Cayuse, Walla Walla, and Umatilla people. He failed to convert many Cayuse and seemed to pay more attention to the increasing immigrant traffic than to Indians at Waíiletpu. The immigration, which began in 1841, received an important boost from Whitman's successful wagon journey over the Blue Mountains in 1843, bringing more than two hundred wagons through the heart of the homeland. The Oregon Trail cut across prime hunting territory and created a months-long disturbance that was more disruptive to daily life than anything the fur traders had created.[62]

When the immigration of whites to the West began with the explorers, it was a trickle passing through the homeland. By the 1830s, with migrations from the Red River in Canada and Americans leaving by way of Missouri, it became a stream of people. All the early contacts were hospitable, and many tribal oral histories demonstrate how curious the immigrants were to local people. One day on the upper Umatilla River, some white children walked into a tribal camp, holding out their hands and saying a word that sounded like *piish* (rawhide) to the woman who was there. She handed them strips of rawhide. When the children began to chew on it, she realized they were hungry and wanted food. She ended up hosting the mother and children while the father went on to the Whitman Mission for supplies. She noticed the pitifulness of the children's feet and made them moccasins while they stayed with her. Another family remembers how the immigrants would yell out from their wagons, "How far Willamette?" — eager for any reply that might mean they were close to their destination.[63] Usually, the Blue Mountain crossing was the most difficult part of the journey for the travelers, and weary and weak livestock were frequently left behind. From 1843 to 1846, the stream of immigrants became a river, with thousands of immigrants and livestock each year. By 1847, it was a flood. Thomas Jefferson once wrote that American Indians were

Endowed with the faculties and the rights of men, breathing an ardent love of liberty and independence, and occupying a country which left them no desire but to be undisturbed, the stream of overflowing population from other regions directed itself on these shores; without power to divert, or habits to contend against, they have been overwhelmed by the current, or driven before it. . . .[64]

In 1842, a Bureau of Indian Affairs sub-agency was established in the Willamette Valley, and Dr. Elijah White was assigned as Indian sub-agent for the Oregon Territory. In the three years that he held the post, he instituted what became known as White's Law of the Nez Perce, which would govern daily relations between Indians and whites. Penalties for infractions were accepted and agreed upon in December by the Nez Perce. Penalties ranged from variously prescribed numbers of strikes to hanging.

All of the changes affected young tribal people, too. In 1811, John Clarke of the Pacific Fur Company hanged a young Palouse boy for allegedly stealing a silver goblet. In the 1830s, three tribal boys were sent to the Anglican School at Red River (present-day Winnipeg, Manitoba) to be educated. PeoPeoMoxMox's son, Elijah Heading, was shot at Fort Sutter, California, in 1843 because his party was in possession of a mule that had been previously stolen. These dramatic events pale in comparison to the childhood diseases brought by young immigrants. Chicken pox, scarlet fever, whooping cough, dysentery, typhus, measles, and smallpox would take more young lives.

Those who came on the Oregon Trail were not all innocents. In 1845, Charles Wilkes reported: "The white American population, as far as I have been able to judge of them, are orderly, and generally industrious; although they are, with the exception of the missionaries, men who have led, for the most part, dissolute lives."[65] Some immigrants were accustomed to the bottom rung, to poverty, to rough life. The seasoned, wizened, and jaded had less to learn and brought with them their knowledge of injustice, persecution, or depravity. But none of them knew what lay ahead when they left Missouri to travel west. At best, they were ignorant of the variety and number of tribes in the West, and many of them came equipped with a healthy bias against Indians. Yet, they would be aided by and would trade with tribes in the Blue Mountains and on the tributaries and main stem of the Columbia. Most were ill prepared and arrived in the homeland of the Cayuse, Walla Walla, and Umatilla somewhat destitute, usually as winter approached.

A consequence of the invasion of the homeland by traders and immigrants was the spread of deadly pathogens. Disease had accompanied European exploration and settlement of North and South America from the earliest contact with native people, and waves of pestilence had swept both continents from the sixteenth century to the twentieth. Smallpox was the most devastating disease to invade the Columbia Plateau. Most evidence suggests that it came from the Plains, striking in the early 1820s. A decade later, malaria sickened people in the homeland, most likely brought here from the lower Columbia, where the epidemic devastated Chinook populations below the Cascades and up the Willamette and Cowlitz rivers.[66]

Change Brings New Challenges

Our people had lived according to the order, discipline, and cycles of our culture, in which communal values, family expectations, and individual autonomy could vary greatly while still remaining congruent with the covenant between the Creator,

all other creations, and the Natítayt. This covenanted community experienced many changes between 1700 and 1850.

When the horse came to the homeland, the Tribes adopted this new being and adapted their lives around it — to greater and lesser degrees. When the French, Scottish, British, Métis, Algonquins, and Americans came, each provided opportunities for the Tribes to infuse change into their lives. In each case, the Tribes chose what they liked from these other cultures and adopted and adapted it. Whether it was the fleur-de-lis pattern, the abstract floral beadwork designs, the brass ornaments, or intermarriage, each person and family elected the amount of exposure to the new people and things he or she would have — that is, until the time when tribal people would no longer be at liberty to choose for themselves. From the arrival of the horse to the arrival of the immigrants, our communities selectively incorporated a range of new elements: technology, religious ideas, non-Indian marriage partners, and allies. But by 1850, new patterns of power, disease, and morality would threaten our covenant with the Creator and the strength of our culture.

From explorers to missionaries, the Tribes hosted and traded with all comers. Why would we do so? There are many answers. First, the Tribes had been welcoming travelers to their lands for a very long time. The land given to them by the Creator provided for them well, and they were usually well-off enough to provide for others because they stored preserved food in caches. Second, tribal people had honed their trading skills for thousands of years and were eager to trade, especially for new and uncommon goods, including weaponry. Third, they were typically unafraid of strangers. They were at home and seriously outnumbered all early arrivals, and usually the travelers were escorted by someone known to the locals. Fourth, the people coming between 1805 and 1836 espoused their intent to be good for the Indians. From all outward appearances, they did not intend any harm. Early on, in the first contact stories, there were no major issues of scarcity or threats to control or ownership. Those would come later.

Competition in the homeland changed dramatically; it was no longer competition between locals and neighbors for goods or with enemies for arms. Many new layers of competition blanketed the region: for the conversion of Indian souls between Catholics and Protestants, for business and claims to the region between the Americans and British, for control between regular army and the militia, and for power between federal authorities represented regionally by the army and the recently arrived territorial governments.

"It was visitor Alexis de Tocqueville who most accurately foresaw the future," wrote historian Kent Richards.

He described how the Americans would take the Indians "by the hand and transport them to a grave far from the lands of their fathers," and he noted that it would be accomplished "with a singular felicity; tranquilly, legally, philanthropically." Tocqueville predicted they would remain undisturbed in their new homes only until the whites needed the land. He erred only in placing that need at a point in the distant future.[67]

Thomas Jefferson anticipated that it might take a thousand years to fill in the lands of the Louisiana Purchase. In less than one hundred years, Indian displacement, diaspora, and disentitlement would be complete west of the Mississippi. The changes that next came to the Cayuse, Umatilla, and Walla Walla people would challenge every aspect of the culture.

Notes

1. *Tamálwit*, in Nuumiipuutímt.

2. Northeast Sahaptian.

3. See *Wik Peoples v. State of Queensland* (1996), 141 ALR 129; *Mary Yasmirr & Ors v. Northern Territory of Australia & Ors* (1998), 771 FCA; *Lardil Peoples v. State of Queensland* (2004), FCA 298; and *Delgamuukw v. British Columbia* (1997), 3 SCR 1010.

4. Lydia Johnson, Tamástslikt Convocation of Scholars, Elders, and Students, 2000, archived at Tamástslikt Cultural Institute [hereafter Tamástslikt Convocation].

5. *Átway* Lawrence Patrick, interview at Tamástslikt Cultural Institute, with Tama Tochihara and Jennifer Karson, 2001.

6. Fermore Craig, Tamástslikt Convocation.

7. Charles Wilkes, "Report on the Territory of Oregon," *Oregon Historical Quarterly* 12 (1911): 269–99.

8. *Kusi* is horse in Sahaptin, *sikem* is horse in Nez Perce, and *tuunap* is horse in Cayuse. Aboriginal dogs predate the arrival of the horse and share the same root word in their names. *Kusi kusi* is the Sahaptin word for dog; saying the word *kusi* twice makes it diminutive. *Sikemkal* is the correlative Nez Perce term for dog.

9. Theodore Stern, *Chiefs and Chief Traders: Indian Relations at Fort Nez Percés* (Corvallis: Oregon State University Press, 1993), 41.

10. Reuben Gold Thwaites, ed., *Early Western Travels, 1748–1846*, vol. 28, *Part 1 of Farnham's Travels in the Great Western Prairies, etc., May 21–October 16, 1839* (Cleveland: Arthur H. Clark, 1906), 343–4, 351.

11. *Átway* Lawrence Patrick. Myrna Williams Tovey told a similar story of a woman who lived near the north fork of the Walla Walla River, east of Milton-Freewater, Oregon. Fermore Craig, Sr.'s grandmother told the story of a woman who was captured, escaped, and killed her captors, which is transcribed and archived at Tamástslikt Cultural Institute.

12. Leah Conner, story of the grandmother of *átway* Elsie Spokane Conner and *átway* Vera Spokane Jones, author's family oral tradition.

13. In 1878, on the brink of starvation, the Bannock and Northern Paiute broke free from the confines of their reservation and united in a desperate war of survival. After several violent encounters with the U.S. Army, they retreated north toward the Columbia River. The resistance weakened by the time they reached Umatilla territory. Promises of an alliance were shattered when three Cayuse warriors parlayed with and killed war leader Egan, thus ending the war. Chief Egan, who was Cayuse, had been abducted as a child by the Bannocks.

14. Stern, *Chiefs and Chief Traders*, 22–23.

15. *The Exploration of the Columbia River by Lieutenant W.R. Broughton, October, 1792: An extract from the Journal of Captain George Vancouver* (Longview, Wash.: Longview Daily News; Portland, Or: Davis & Holman, 1926).

16. James R. Gibson, *Otter Skins, Boston Ships, and China Goods: The Maritime Fur Trade of the Northwest Coast, 1785–1841* (Seattle: University of Washington Press, 1992), 37–39.

17. Dan Motanic, Tamástslikt Convocation.

18. William Clark, October 21, 1805, *The Journals of the Lewis and Clark Expedition*, ed. Gary E. Moulton, 13 vols. (Lincoln: University of Nebraska Press, 1990), 5:317.

19. On Lewis and Clark as Enlightenment explorers, see William L. Lang, "Describing a New Environment: Lewis and Clark and Enlightenment Science in the Columbia River Basin," *Oregon Historical Quarterly* 105 (Fall 2004): 360–89.

20. Twisted Hair was also known as Walammottinin, meaning hair or forelock bunched, tied, braided, or twisted; ancestor of Mylie, Archie, and Margaret Lawyer (also known as Tsopsokalpskin), who the explorers met at a fishing camp on the Clearwater and cared for their horses over the winter of until their return in the spring of 1806.

21. Clark, October 19, 1805, in Moulton, ed., *Journals*, 5:303.

22. Ron Pond, "The Jefferson Peace Medal: A Cultural Phenomenon Passed down from Chief to Chief in Walla Walla Culture" (Ph.D. diss., Washington State University, 2004), 240–1.

23. Clark, April 27, 1806, in Moulton, ed., *Journals*, 7:173–4. Clark records the name variously as Yelleppit, Yel-lep-pit, Yel lep-pet, and Yelleppet on the outbound and return treks. Lewis consistently spells the name Yellept or Yel-lept. In Aoki, *yelépt* means friends sworn to die together or blood brothers in Nez Perce, and *yalípt* means trading partner in Sahaptian. Chief Stwire Waters described *yalupt/yah-lipt*, or *yah-y-lipt* this way: "I come to see you. I bring blankets, furs, beads, clothing, and many things with me. These, I give to you. I do not say anything. I leave them without words, You are glad to see me. You take me in and feed me. We are Yah-lipt. I am your Yah-lipt and you are my Yah-lipt . . . Indian never says any thing about paying back. . . . The Old Indian way of friends!" Quoted in Robert Boyd, *People of The Dalles: The Indians of Wascopam Mission* (Lincoln: University of Nebraska Press, 1996), 65.

24. John Ordway, April 28, 1806, in Moulton, ed., *Journals*, 9:299.

25. Clark, April 28, 1806, in Moulton, ed., *Journals*, 7:180.

26. Including Twisted Hair and two other Nez Perce chiefs, a Wanapam principal chief and a second chief and a chief of the upper villages, a second chief who came down by canoe, To-mar-lar-pom, Yelleppet, Ar-lo-quat, Tow-wall, two inferior Walla Walla chiefs on return, Chief Cut nose, Tin-nach-e-moo tolt and Hoh-hats-ill-pitp, Yoom-park'-kar-tim and son of late great chief of Choppunish. The total inventory of eighty-eight medals taken on the Expedition included three of the 105 mm Jefferson Peace Medals, 13 of the 75 mm Jefferson Peace Medals, 16 of the 55 mm Jefferson Peace Medals, 55 of the 45 mm Washington season medals, and one perforated silver dollar. See Moulton, ed., *Journals*.

27. Lewis, April 29, 1806, in Moulton, ed., *Journals*, 7:183.

28. Clark wrote on December 31, 1805: "To-mar-lar—Grand Chief Wla lar war lar, Yel lep pet Chief made a Cheif an gave a Small medal by name of Ar-lo-quat—of the Chopunnish Nation—." In Moulton, ed., *Journals*, 6:148n1. Arloquat, also known as old Ollokʷot or Walamatkin, was the father of Old Joseph by a Nez Perce wife and the father of Five Crows, Tawatoy, Itshowlale, Talchslolo, and Petints by a Cayuse wife.

29. April 25, 1806, Moulton, ed., *Journals*, 7:166–7.

30. Pond, "Jefferson Peace Medal."

31. Barbara Belyea, ed., *David Thompson: Columbia Journals* (Montreal: McGill–Queen's University Press, 1994), 152.

32. T.C. Elliot, ed., "Journal of David Thompson," *Oregon Historical Quarterly* 15 (March 1914): 58.

33. Belyea, ed., *Thompson*, 152.

34. Wilson Hunt Price, quoted in James P. Ronda, *Astoria and Empire* (Lincoln: University of Nebraska Press, 1990), 192.

35. Hunt, quoted in Robert H. Ruby and John A. Brown, *The Cayuse Indians: Imperial Tribesmen of Old Oregon*, Commemorative edition (Norman: University of Oklahoma Press, 2005), 29.

36. Alexander Ross, *Adventures of the First Settlers on the Oregon or Columbia River, 1810–1813*, introduction by James P. Ronda (1849; reprint, Lincoln: University of Nebraska Press, 1986), 129, 133, 135.

37. Ibid., 136.

38. Ross, *Adventures of the First Settlers*, 136–8.

39. Ross, *Adventures of the First Settlers*, 139–41; Ruby and Brown, *Cayuse Indians*, 27.

40. Ross, *Adventures of the First Settlers*, 141.

41. Richard S. Mackie, *Trading Beyond the Mountains: The British Fur Trade on the Pacific, 1793–1843* (Vancouver: University of British Columbia Press, 1997), 17–18.

42. Alexander Ross, *Fur Hunters of the Far West*, 1855 reprint (Chicago: Lakeside Press, 1924), 164.

43. Ibid., 170–4; Mackie, *Trading Beyond the Mountains*, 20; Clifford E. Trafzer and Richard D. Scheuerman, *Renegade Tribe: The Palouse Indians and the Invasion of the Inland Pacific Northwest* (Pullman: Washington State University Press, 1986), 18–21.

44. Stern, *Chiefs and Chief Traders*, 154–5.

45. John Kirk Townsend, quoted in Mackie, *Trading Beyond the Mountains*, 104.

46. Simon McGillivray, quoted in James R. Gibson, *The Lifeline of the Oregon Country: The Fraser–Columbia Brigade System, 1811–47* (Vancouver: University of British Columbia Press, 1997), 173.

47. Boyd, *People of The Dalles*, 144–5; Cole Harris, *The Resettlement of British Columbia: Essays on Colonialism and Geographic Change* (Vancouver: University of British Columbia Press, 1997), 34–35.

48. John Davies, ed., *Douglas of the Forests: The North American Journals of David Douglas* (Seattle: University of Washington Press, 1980), 59–60.

49. Jennifer S.H. Brown, *Strangers in Blood: Fur Trade Company Families in Indian Country* (Vancouver: University of British Columbia Press, 1980), 130.

50. Mackie, *Trading Beyond the Mountains*, 110; John Philip Reid, *Contested Empire: Peter Skene Ogden and the Snake River Expeditions* (Norman: University of Oklahoma Press, 2002), 39–41.

51. Francis Haines, ed., *The Snake Country Expedition of 1830–1831: John Work's Field Journal* (Norman: University of Oklahoma Press, 1971), xx–xxiv; Ruby and Brown, *Cayuse Indians*, 50–51.

52. Alvin M. Josephy, Jr., *The Nez Perce Indians and the Opening of the Northwest* (New Haven: Yale University Press, 1965), 112–13; Ruby and Brown, *Cayuse Indians*, 57–58.

53. John Kirk Townsend, *Narrative of a Journey Across the Rocky Mountains to the Columbia River* (1839; reprint, Corvallis: Oregon State University Press, 1999), 181.

54. "Diary of Reverend Jason Lee," *Oregon Historical Quarterly* 17 (Spring 1916): 254–8; Stern, *Chiefs and Change in the Oregon Country: Indian Relations at fort Nez Percés, 1818–1855* (Corvallis: Oregon State University Press, 1996), 258.

55. Samuel Parker, quoted in Ruby and Brown, *Cayuse Indians*, 68.

56. See Clifford M. Drury, *Henry Harmon Spalding* (Caldwell, Idaho: Caxton Printers, 1936).

57. Thwaites, *Part 1 of Farnham's Travels*, 331–2.

58. Reuben Gold Thwaites, ed., *Early Western Travels, 1748–1846*, vol. 29, *Part 2 of Farnham's Travels in the Great Western Prairies, etc., October 21–December 4, 1839* (Cleveland: Arthur H. Clark, 1906), 101.

59. Thwaites, *Part 1 of Farnham's Travels*, 333.

60. Dan Motanic, telling his folks about an incident at St. Andrews School, personal communication with author.

61. Fermore Craig, Tamástslikt Convocation.

62. Julie Roy Jeffrey, *Converting the West: A Biography of Narcissa Whitman* (Norman: University of Oklahoma Press, 1991), 205–6; Stern, *Chiefs and Change*, 95–100.

63. Spokane Jim, Elsie and Vera Spokane's father, author's family oral tradition.

64. Thomas Jefferson, Second Inagural Address, March 4, 1805.

65. Wilkes, *Synopsis of the Cruise of the United States Exploring Expedition during the years 1838, '39, '40, '41, and '42*, printed in Reuben Gold Thwaites, ed., *Early Western Travels, 1748–1846: a series of annotated reprints . . .* vol. 29 (Cleveland, Ohio: A.H. Clark, 1904–1907), 99.

66. Robert Boyd, *The Coming of the Spirit of Pestilence: Introduced Infectious Disease and Population Decline among Northwest Coast Indians, 1774–1874* (Seattle: University of Washington Press, 1999), 92–95.

67. Kent D. Richards, *Isaac I. Stevens: Young Man in a Hurry* (Provo, Utah: Brigham Young University Press, 1979).

Indians Then and Now

These colonists, strangers to the hardships and struggles in the new world, often had to call on friendly Indians for help in the hard life of the first frontier. More than once, they were saved from certain starvation by them, who in all kindness, brought food and showed them how to fertilize the soil. But as more colonists came to claim the land, shadows began to fall across the friendships of the two races.

The white man learned quickly how rich this new country was and determined he must have it, all of it. There were vast regions of unused land, unused in the sense that the white man conceives of land use. The question was not to drive the Indian to another place after the white man gained a good hold, but to destroy him. To the Indian, there was only one place where he belonged — in his homeland made sacred by the ageless sleep of his ancestors, made fruitful by the spirit of his children yet unborn. Here and only here could the life rhythm of his race beat on in unbroken harmony. To tribes all over the land, the earth was their mother, wise and loving in her care for her children. Our love, therefore, is a kind of mystical devotion, for this wise mother has cradled our race since the beginning of time. She has been dedicated with the life-blood of our ancestors and made sacred with their graves.

Land belonged to all the people, to use and to cherish. That one man could claim a piece of the earth for himself, to hold against all others, was as unthinkable in Indian philosophy as it is to you and I — that one may keep a piece of the sky above us, the sky that in this present day conception is the one thing man must share in common. In Indian economy, man may keep a plot of ground for himself so long as he needs and uses it. The newcomers could not understand the spiritual feeling the Indian had for the land. War between the Indian who owned the land and the white man who was determined to take it was inevitable. They fought with all the skill and cunning at their command to defend their very racial existence. They answered brutality with brutality, and felt that right was on their side. "Did not the Creator make us all as well as the white man?" they cried out for understanding. "Did he not place us on the land, and give us strength to defend ourselves against any invaders? Does he not expect us all that we shall exert ourselves in preserving that which he gave to our forefathers, both for themselves and their offspring forever?" War spread in all its fury wherever the white man set foot in Indian country. The innocent of both races suffered with the guilty. Look to every nation surrounding our own today where wars have been and are being waged, and to which Americans have rallied to help to protect its own shores. They are fought with brutality and savagery unknown to the Indians when they fought for their country. Look to the natives of Africa being dispossessed the same as our ancestors were and by whom. History today repeats itself so that we might remember.

For the Indians, it was a hopeless fight. The wise leaders knew how hopeless. They knew all was being taken that they had to give. All could not die for some must live. From the more personal conflict of the old days before they were introduced to firearms, suddenly war became a grim and deadly business. They were outnumbered, and the flood of white immigrants into their country continued ever greater. The grim shadows could not blot from the Indian mind the sacred knowledge that the land and all its riches belonged to him, for the Creator had placed him here. Tribes, who through these bitter years remained friendly to the white man, were moved from their homes and robbed of their lands. They remained friendly to the last, and when they were forced from their homes they didn't resort to war. As people who were already on the land, they were dispossessed. In the names of their homes, the respective kings (explorers) took everything they could conquer. They drove their stakes on the new continent and ran up their flags of nations. The aborigines, Indians, of course, were overpowered — their lands stolen, their religions called "Pagan." Thus, the minority changed from "fewer in number" to "weaker." The subdued became the minority, the conquerors the majority. For centuries, the strong, the powerful, the privileged ruled. For them, the weak, the powerless, the underprivileged had no rights that the strong must respect. They accepted the white man from the beginning and quickly adopted his ways. They intermarried with the whites who came among them. Their sons became educated in early missions. Missionaries were welcomed with respect, and under their patient teaching, Christianity became the faith of many Tribes.

Maudie C. Antoine, Chairwoman, Board of Trustees, Confederated Tribes of the Umatilla Indian Reservation. These remarks were made at the 1855 Treaty Centennial observance in Walla Walla, Washington, June 11, 1955.

Wars, Treaties, and the Beginning of Reservation Life

Antone Minthorn

My name is Himeeqis Kaa'awn (which translates in Nuumiipuutímt or Nez Perce language to Big Dawn). That namesake was my relative, a Nez Perce of the White Bird band. Big Dawn was the camp crier at Salmon River in Idaho. He announced the beginning of the Nez Perce War of 1877. I am an enrolled member of the Confederated Tribes of the Umatilla Indian Reservation, and I am of Cayuse, Nez Perce, and Umatilla descent. The Umatilla Indian Reservation is my home place. When I would come home on military leave in the late 1950s and the Greyhound bus reached the top of Rieth Ridge Grade, I would say to myself, as I looked eastward across to the Blue Mountains, "I am home. I can walk from here!"

Our ancestors were faced with an invasion of white settlers by the thousands coming west to find a place to live in the new world. They came on the waterways of the Clearwater, Snake, and Columbia rivers on their way to the Pacific Ocean. They claimed the Oregon Territory for the American government. Our tribes were in that territory. The starting point of that invasion was the earlier 1805 Lewis and Clark Expedition. The Expedition did stop and talk with our people as they passed Wallula Gap.

The message from their Great Father was for peace and friendship. At the time, the Great Father was Thomas Jefferson, president of the United States.

It is important to know how young the country was at that time. The Revolutionary War was over and the U.S. Constitution had been adopted. Also, Europe was in the Industrial Age. Thomas Jefferson was only the third President of the United States in 1805. Jefferson's policy called for national expansion, and colonization would make its way to the Oregon Country.

The Lewis and Clark Expedition met with the Walla Walla chief, Yelépt. The Jefferson Peace Medal (1805) and Clark's saber (1806) were presented to the Indians. Furthermore, the Tribes were asked to recognize the president as the Great White Father and them as his Red Children. There was a celebration held for Lewis and Clark at the confluence of the Columbia and Snake rivers on the return trip. American expansion policy to Oregon Indian Country began in earnest from that point forward. The treaty council was held fifty years after the 1805 Lewis and Clark Expedition crossed the Oregon Country to the Pacific Ocean. The Expedition was the vanguard of the American government's policy of colonizing Oregon Indian Country, and several events followed that led up to the 1855 Treaty.

Chiefs Yellow Bird (Walla Walla) and Lawyer and Looking Glass (Nez Perce) met the Lewis and Clark Expedition and were also present at the 1855 Treaty Council in the Walla Walla Valley. After the Lewis and Clark Expedition, a fort and trading post were built at the confluence of the Walla Walla and Columbia rivers. It was called Fort Nez Perces and later became Fort Walla Walla. It was owned by the British Hudson's Bay Company. The company chief was John McLoughlin.

The fur-trading business was established in the region in 1818, and native people could now trade for manufactured goods. The Indian people have always been impressed by technology, often blending that technology with their own creative innovations. By the first half of the nineteenth century. French and English traders were now institutionalized at the confluence of the Walla Walla and Columbia rivers. All of this sets the stage for the struggles that were to come over sovereignty, protection, and recovery.

The Cayuse Meet the Whitmans

In the early 1830s, a delegation of Indians from the interior Pacific Northwest made a journey to St. Louis, Missouri, seeking the white man's law. When this became known to the Christian church people, a mission was sent to the Oregon Country. Two Christian ministers from New York heeded the call — Dr. Marcus Whitman and Henry Spalding. Marcus Whitman built the Waíiletpu Mission, and Henry Spalding went on to Lapwai to establish a mission with the Nez Perce. These missionaries brought the white man's law. The Waíiletpu Mission was in Cayuse country.

The horse was the main means of transportation at the time. That is, it was not for recreation purposes or use. The Spanish (Cayuse) Mustang is the symbol of great military and political power and mobility. The Cayuse were proud and fierce warriors. They were also expert horsemen. The Cayuse, Umatilla, and Walla Walla bands traveled to the Great Plains to hunt buffalo and to Mexico to trade for cattle. The Cayuse, Umatilla, and Walla Walla became very wealthy stock owners.

By 1836, Marcus Whitman had established his Protestant mission among the

Marcus Whitman attempts to aid the sick Cayuse.

Cayuse. The mission's purpose was to convert the Cayuse "savage" to Christianity and to "civilize" them in the ways of American society. A more important plan of Marcus Whitman's was to actively promote the colonization of the Oregon Country. He had an arrogant attitude toward the Cayuse, which created resentment and hostility toward him.

Dr. Whitman later founded a wagon trail over the Blue Mountains and across the valley of the Umatilla River. This was the Oregon Trail, and it connected to the Willamette Valley, which lay west through the Cascade Mountains. The trail opened the Cayuse land to white settlement and deadly disease. The Cayuse asked Marcus Whitman to close his mission and trading business, but he refused. In November 1847, the Cayuse attacked the Whitman Mission and killed Marcus Whitman and twelve others and took prisoners. The Cayuse had retaliated because of a measles epidemic, the taking of more land for the mission, and the bringing of more settlers to their country. This started the Cayuse War of 1848. Of note is that in 1843, the American Bureau of Commissioners for Foreign Missions (ABCFM) in New York had decided to close the Waíiletpu Mission for lack of converts to Christianity. Marcus Whitman did not agree and returned east to persuade the ABCFM to keep the mission open. He was successful, but he returned leading a covered wagon train of immigrants over the Blue Mountains and through Cayuse territory on their way to the Willamette Valley.

The 1848 Cayuse War with the U.S. Army had its roots in the Whitman incident. I choose not to call it a "massacre," as it has been labeled in popular historical literature. The use of "massacre" prejudges and freezes the event in time, ignoring the context from both sides of the account, including the hundreds of people who died in the epidemic that Whitman could not cure. The incident must also be understood from the standpoint of *tewatat* 'medicine doctor tradition', which calls for the life of the healer to be taken if he fails to cure the sick. When Marcus Whitman returned east to protest the proposal to close Waíiletpu Mission and, on the return trip, when he brought more people to settle the Oregon Country, the Cayuse leaders warned him that what he was doing was not the understanding they had with him. His expressed purpose for being with the Cayuse was to teach them about the Christian religion. But he brought more people, developed more land, and brought sickness that killed many Cayuse. Whitman refused to listen to the warnings, and the Cayuse killed him and the others living at the mission.

This act of killing was quickly seen as an act of war by the non-Indians in the territory. For the next three years, the Cayuse were harassed by American militia hunting for those who killed the people at Waíiletpu Mission. The objections that started the war — the taking of more land to expand the mission grounds, bringing more emigrants to Cayuse Territory, bringing disease and death to the Cayuse, and haughty treatment of the Cayuse — were never a direct opposition to being missionized. Interestingly, there were no baptized Cayuse converts to Christianity by Marcus Whitman.

It is now 1850. The war lasts for three years with continual harassment of the Cayuse and other Indian bands. Five Cayuse headmen surrender to military authority at a military outpost in what is today The Dalles, Oregon, and are taken to Oregon City for trial. The Cayuse Five (as they are now called) are found guilty for the Whitman incident and hanged. They were Clokomas, Kiamasumkin, Isiaasheluckas, Tomahas, and Tiloukaikt. (Tomahas was the grandfather of Red Moccasin Tops, who was one of the three Red Coat Warriors who was killed at the Big Hole battle during the Nez Perce War of 1877. The mother of Red Moccasin Tops was a Cayuse married to Yellow Bull, a Nez Perce war chief.) Those five Cayuse remain buried at Oregon City. Their purpose and sacrifice for surrendering themselves were to protect the Cayuse homeland and people from further harm. Tiloukaikt's own words provide a clue: "Did not your missionaries teach us that Christ died to save his people? So die we to save our people."* It was a noble cause. This war ended when the five Cayuse men

---

The Works of Hubert Howe Bancroft, vol. 30, *History of Oregon, Vol. II, 1848–1888* (San Francisco: History Company, 1888), 95.

surrendered to the U.S. Army at Fort Dalles.

There were Cayuse tribal members present at Oregon City when the Cayuse Five went on trial for the killing of Marcus Whitman. After they were judged guilty and sentenced to hang, the Cayuse who were present left Oregon City and went home. There must have been discussion of what happened and why the bodies of the Cayuse Five were not returned to the Cayuse Tribe. The reason for the hanging was not only revenge but also to prevent other areas from uniting for an all-out war. They were hanged for political reasons.

The Whitman incident took place on November 29, 1847, and was the opening salvo of the Cayuse war. History books distinguish the "massacre" as a separate episode from the skirmishes that followed, which is not the case. They were utterly connected in that the killings marked the beginning of the Cayuse War and the first Pacific Northwest Indian war. Skirmishes followed in January 1848 against volunteer troops who were organized to come to Cayuse country to confront the Cayuse.

The 1850 executions were a political act by the territorial provisional government. There was no proof that those particular five Cayuses were the ones who killed Marcus Whitman and his people. This raises both jurisdictional and procedural questions. The Cayuse Five were insurgents acting on behalf of their sovereign people and the war initiated by the Whitman killings. Should these five men have been tried as individuals or detained as prisoners of war? The American settlers were now colonizing the Oregon Indian Country of the Cayuse, Umatilla, and Walla Walla Tribes. Those settlers urged the federal government to hold treaty negotiations and to extinguish title to all tribal lands.

Treaty Making

Five years after the hanging of the five Cayuse, a treaty council with the Cayuse, Umatilla, Walla Walla, Nez Perce, and Yakama and the United States government was convened in the Walla Walla Valley.

Treaty-making had become the hallmark of American Indian policy as early as the 1780s, when the new nation was just emerging from the American Revolution, and this type of treaty council had convened many times in the eastern part of the United States before 1855. For thousands of years, Indian people had made oral agreements with each other, sealing their compacts with wampum belts, prayers sanctified by tobacco, and gift-giving. Europeans brought new traditions to the Americas, including written documents to detail their agreements with Indian people. Unfortunately, most Native Americans could not speak or read English, which put them at a distinct disadvantage that was exploited by non-Indians.

The Cayuse, Umatilla, and Walla Walla people had an idea of what was going on in the East. By the time of the Treaty of 1855, some of the Indians at the Treaty Council already knew how to read and write English. One of Gustav Sohon's

Walla Walla Treaty Council: A Synopsis

May 29, 1855 — The Walla Walla Treaty Council opened near Fort Walla Walla.* Isaac I. Stevens, governor and superintendent of Indian affairs for the Washington Territory, and Joel Palmer, superintendent of Indian affairs for the Oregon Territory, were the negotiators for the United States at the Council. Tribal chiefs and headmen from the Cayuse, Nez Perce, Umatilla, Walla Walla, and Yakama tribes and bands were also represented. The objective of the United States was to negotiate treaties with the tribes to establish reservations for their homeland, and large tracts of tribal aboriginal territory would be ceded to the United States to accommodate the increasing immigration of non-Indian settlers.

In the opening days of the Council, Governor Stevens stated that the United States wanted the tribes "to agree to live on tracts of land which shall be your own and your children's."

May 30, 1855 — By way of example, Governor Stevens referenced another treaty council in which the United States provided a tribe "a tract of land into which no white man could go without their consent, they sent them an agent, they had schools, they had mills, they had shops, and they had teachers, they had farmers, they had doctors. I repeat again no white man could go there unless the red man consented to it."

May 31, 1855 — Both Governor Stevens and General Palmer also promised that the tribes would have the authority to hunt, gather roots and berries, graze their cattle, and fish on lands outside of the reservations.

June 2, 1855 — Considerable pressure was being placed on the tribal chiefs and headmen to agree to the treaties and the reservations. Both Governor Stevens and General Palmer discussed the threat posed by "bad white men" and warned that white settlers were going to be arriving in ever larger numbers. Palmer suggested that the wave of non-Indian settlement was unavoidable. "Can you stop the waters of the Columbia River from flowing on its course? Can you prevent the wind from blowing? Can you prevent the rain from falling? Can you pre-

*Unless otherwise noted, all quotes are from Darrell Scott, ed., *A True Copy of the Record of the Official Proceedings at the Council in the Walla Walla Valley [held jointly by Isaac I. Stevens Governor and Superintendent W.T. and Joel Palmer, Superintendent of Indian Affairs, on the part of the United States with the Tribes of Indians named in the treaties made at that Council June 9 and 11, 1855]* (Fairfield, Wash.: Ye Galleon Press, 1985), May 31, 1855.

vent the whites from coming? You are answered no! Like the grasshoppers on the plains, some years there will be more coming than others, [but] you cannot stop them, our chief cannot stop them. . . ."

In response to this unstoppable influx of settlers, Governor Stevens and General Palmer recommended a treaty establishing a reservation for the tribes. Claiming that time was of the essence, General Palmer stated that "if we enter into a treaty now we can select a good country for you, but if we wait till the country is filled up with whites, where will we find such a place?" Most importantly, the United States negotiators promised that the treaty promises of the United States would be honored and that the tribes could count on the terms of the treaties being enforced. General Palmer stated that "if we [the United States] make a treaty with you and our Great Chief and his council approves it, you can rely on all its provisions being carried out strictly, my heart is that it is wise for you to do so."

June 7, 1855 — The United States came to the Walla Walla Council to negotiate two treaties, one with the Yakama and one with the Nez Perce. The United States planned to place the Cayuse, Umatilla, and Walla Walla Tribes on the Nez Perce Reservation.* This proposal was unacceptable to the tribal representatives.

June 8, 1855 — The United States negotiators made it clear that they wanted the ceded territory to be made available to non-Indian settlers. General Palmer, speaking to tribal representatives, stated that the United States wanted the tribes "to allow the white people to come and settle in the country anywhere outside of the reservation."

June 9, 1855 — As a result of the concerns of the Cayuse, Umatilla, and Walla Walla chiefs, General Palmer proposed to establish a Umatilla Indian Reservation for the Tribes. General Palmer described the boundaries of the Reservation as currently set forth in Article I of the Treaty of 1855, as well as the off-Reservation grazing, gathering, hunting, and fishing rights set forth in the same Article I. General Palmer also set forth promises to develop schools, mills,

*Governor Stevens made the proposal on June 4, 1855, in part in response to the statement made by the Walla Walla Chief Pio-pio-mox-mox earlier that day that Governor Stevens had "spoken for lands generally" but had not "spoken of any particular ones [lands]."

drawings recording the events shows an Indian writing on a tablet. They were also familiar with other kinds of technology, such as guns and pots and pans. The Plateau tribes went to the plains to hunt buffalo and to raid. They came back with new ways, new dress regalia, new ceremonies, new dances, and new music.

At the 1855 Council

The treaty commenced on May 29, 1855, and adjourned on June 12, 1855. The Cayuse understood that the purpose of the 1855 Treaty was to remove them from their land. Their first choice was to not sign any treaty at all. If that meant killing the treaty negotiators, then so be it. The second choice was for the Cayuse to move and live on the Yakama or Nez Perce reservation, which meant giving up their homelands. This was not acceptable, and the proposal was rejected. If that meant war, then it was going to be war. The third choice was the establishment of an additional reservation in Oregon Territory.

This proposal was accepted, and the Umatilla Indian Reservation was thereby created and established in Cayuse territory. The Umatilla and Walla Walla moved to the Umatilla Reservation. All of their land had been ceded to the United States government, but some land — the tradi-

farms, and blacksmith shops and to make payments for lands ceded by the Tribes to the United States.

June 11, 1855 — Even after they received the promise from General Palmer of their own Umatilla Indian Reservation, there still was some lingering opposition to executing the Treaty and giving up the remainder of their aboriginal lands. It took some last-minute pressure by the United States negotiators to persuade the chiefs of the Cayuse, Umatilla, and Walla Walla Tribes, as well as the Nez Perce and Yakama, to execute their treaties. There is evidence that the United States representatives added threats to their other arguments to persuade tribal chiefs to execute the treaties. Terence O'Donnell cited the writings of two settlers present at the meetings on the night of June 8, 1855, that "[Governor] Stevens told the interpreters to tell the chiefs that 'if they don't sign this treaty they will walk in blood knee deep.' Threats, the promise of increased annuities to the chiefs, and probably a great weariness finally combined to force the chiefs' submission."*

*Terence O'Donnell, *An Arrow in the Earth: General Joel Palmer and the Indians of Oregon* (Portland: Oregon Historical Society Press, 1991), 207. According to O'Donnell, fifty-six chiefs signed the three treaties (the first for the Cayuse, Umatilla, and Walla Walla; the second for the Nez Perce; and the third for the Yakama Tribes) that ceded some 60,000 square miles to the U.S.

Treaty Council, by *átway* Philip Guyer. The scene portrays the Walla Walla negotiations, with interpreters translating words from "Boston" into Chinook jargon and from Chinook jargon to the Sahaptian dialects.

tional home of the Cayuse — had been saved, and the Umatilla and Walla Walla were welcome to live together there with the Cayuse. The reservation held the name of Umatilla for the river that intersects it.

Some thirty-six chiefs and headmen of the Cayuse, Umatilla, and Walla Walla Tribes put their "X" mark on the Treaty of 1855.* The principal chiefs signing for the Tribes were Pio-pio-mox-mox, Chief of the Walla Walla; Weyatenatemany (also known as Young Chief), Chief of the Cayuse; and Wenap-snoot, Chief of the Umatilla. Governor Isaac Stevens and General Joel Palmer executed the Treaty on behalf of the United States. By message dated July

29, 1856, President Franklin Pierce presented the Treaty to the United States Senate for ratification, as required by Article 2, Section 2 of the United States Constitution. The Treaty of 1855 was ratified by the Senate on March 8, 1859, one month after Oregon became the thirty-third state admitted into the United States. Statehood

---

*They were: Pio-pio-mox-mox, Meani-teat or Pierre, Weyatenatemany, Wenap-snoot, Kamaspello, Steachus, Howlish-wampo, Five Crows, Stocheania, Mu-howlish, Lin-tin-met-cheaunia, Petamyo-mox-mox, Watash-te-waty, She-yam-na-kon, Qua-chim, Te-walca-temany, Keantoan, U-wait-quiack, Tilch-a-waix, La-ta-chin, Kacho-rolich, Kanocey, Som-na-howlish, Ta-we-way, Ha-hats-me-cheat-pus, Pe-na-cheanit, Ha-yo-ma-kin, Ya-ca-lox, Na-kas, Stop-cha-yeou, He-yeau-she-keaut, Sha-wa-way, Tam-cha-key, Te-na-we-na-cha, Johnson, and Whe-la-chey. Spellings of names are as they are recorded on the Treaty.

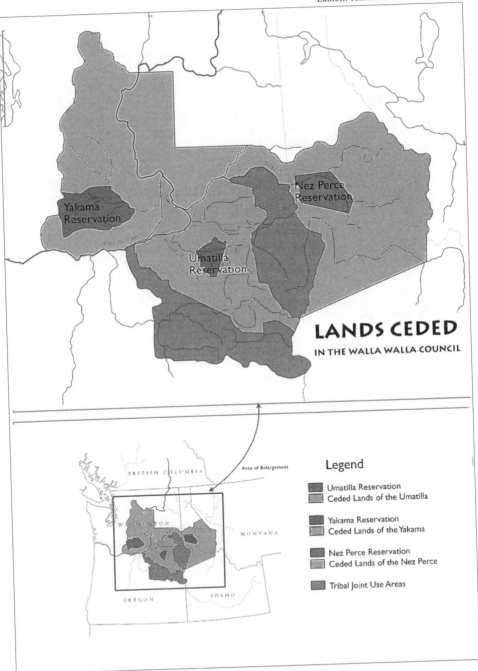

LANDS CEDED
IN THE WALLA WALLA COUNCIL

Legend

Umatilla Reservation
Ceded Lands of the Umatilla

Yakama Reservation
Ceded Lands of the Yakama

Nez Perce Reservation
Ceded Lands of the Nez Perce

Tribal Joint Use Areas

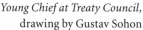

Young Chief at Treaty Council,
drawing by Gustav Sohon

PeoPeoMoxMox at Treaty Council,
drawing by Gustav Sohon

was approved prior to legal dispossession of the lands from the Tribes.

In 1855, Governor Isaac Stevens and General Joel Palmer acted on behalf of and for the benefit of their own country, not the Indian nations of the Northwest. Their methods and actions in dealing with the Cayuse, Umatilla, Walla Walla, and other tribes followed the well-worn path of the United States to negotiate treaties, open up millions of acres to white settlement, and confine Indians to reservations where the Office of Indian Affairs could control them.

Nearly five thousand people representing the various tribal bands of the Plateau were present at the Treaty grounds in the Walla Walla Valley. This was to be a momentous event for all the tribes present. In the Treaty minutes, the ancestors talk about how important the land is and how the children are the consideration because they will need a place to live. This was the vision expressed by our ancestral leaders at the Treaty of 1855, and for this they are to be commended. The Umatilla Indian Reservation became the anchor for

Prophecy and the Dreamer Religion

A powerful and unifying force that came into being in the early 1800s was the Dreamer religion, also known as Seven Drums or Wáashat (literally, 'the dance'). Smohalla was one of several influential prophets who led the movement that revived religious tenets that were being forgotten and blended them with new callings for Indian people. Born around 1815 at Wallula, near the mouth of the Walla Walla River, Smohalla later lived as a holy man among the Wánapam band in the Snake and Columbia River region. His teaching was for Columbia River tribes to remember and keep practicing their Indian ways, and his vision was that all Indians would again arise and take back the land. This teaching was in response to the flood of white immigration into Oregon Country.

The Smohalla religious doctrine and those of the other prophets in the region at the time of the Treaty gave hope to the Tribes that they would regain the power to enjoy life free of oppression. The vision and practice of this religion are an important aspect of the story and history of tribal involvement with Lewis and Clark and the 1855 Treaty. The prophets' teachings were a strategy in response to the powerful belief of Manifest Destiny. Settlers believed they had the God-given right to exploit, or subdue, the Mother Earth for the purpose of making a living. The land was not just for the Indians but for the white people as well. If the white people have to take the land by force to remove the Indians, then force will be used. That was the clear message given to the Indians at the 1855 Treaty Council.

The Tribes of the Umatilla Indian Reservation are historically followers of the Dreamer religion. They are believers in the idea that the earth is the mother of life, that Indian culture and children are to be valued and protected, and that the Indians will triumph to retake their place in the world. This was a message of hope at a time when the Indian way of life was undergoing shattering change. It was the vision of promise and strength that we would survive as a people and once again find happiness. The Dreamer religion has guided and sustained the Plateau tribes during extremely difficult times in our continual fight for freedom and justice. In that respect, the longhouse at Mission represents the security and heart of our cultural and religious interests. The teachings of Smohalla and the other influential prophets are still with us in the longhouses of the Plateau tribes.

Even though the longhouse is reestablished on the reservation today, many people remain strict followers of the Catholic Church, which maintains a mission, or are members of the Presbyterian Church, which is now led by native families. Many people have also embraced the longhouse ceremonies and taken Indian religion back into their lives — if they had not always kept it alive all along over the generations, however quietly. While it now remains a choice for all tribal members on how they will worship, the underlying philosophy of *tamánwit*, which dictates the indigenous view of the relationship to the land, still rings true and has not faded.

the survival of the Cayuse, Umatilla, and Walla Walla nation, the stronghold that protects our culture and sovereignty as unique people.

The thousands of Indians who met in the Walla Walla Valley vastly outnumbered the few non-Indians, or *suyápo*, representing the government of the United States. For a variety of reasons, other Indians did not attend the Council, but the leaders of our tribes attended to listen and learn what the white men had to propose.

The Cayuse, Umatilla, and Walla Walla cultures and peoples are distinguished from other Native Americans by certain important historical events that have shaped our lives and tribal communities. One of these events is the Treaty of 1855 with the United States Government, held in the Walla Walla Valley in Washington Territory. Only fifty years after Lewis and Clark presented the Jefferson Peace Medal in order to promote peace and friendship, the United States government obtained most of the lands of the Cayuse, Umatilla, and Walla Walla peoples through a treaty. The original pro-posal of the federal negotiators was for the Cayuse, Umatilla, and Walla Walla to go to either the Yakama or Nez Perce reservations. That offer was rejected. A dramatic treaty negotiation led by the Cayuse designated the third reservation.

The Cayuse Stronghold

All the tribes attending the Treaty Council understood that the U.S. government was forcing the Indians to choose a place for a reservation to prevent war and to stay out of the way of the settlers rushing in to make claims of their land. The Cayuse, already experienced with the white man's war, made the decision that they would not leave their ancestral homelands. This was the Cayuse rebellion.

So far as the Cayuse were concerned, they already had a place to live. The people needed enough land, water, and food to keep them alive. There had to be enough land to graze their stocks of cattle and horses. The Cayuse would not sign the Treaty. They were ready to fight, but they knew they had to win. They pressed other tribes at the Treaty Council for an alliance to kill the federal negotiators or to leave the Treaty grounds. The other tribes were unwilling. The one last hope was Chief Looking Glass.

It was learned at the Treaty grounds at Walla Walla that Chief Looking Glass was coming from a Montana buffalo hunt. The Cayuse would wait for Looking Glass before they would sign the Treaty. When Looking Glass got to the Treaty grounds, he challenged the leadership of Nez Perce Chief Lawyer regarding the future status of the Nez Perce homelands. Chief Lawyer retained the tribal leadership. Looking Glass signed the Treaty. The Cayuse, under duress and understanding the futility of further resistance, signed the Treaty as well.

(It is interesting to note that Nez Perce Chiefs Lawyer and Looking Glass and Walla Walla Chief PeoPeoMoxMox were present in 1805 when Meriwether Lewis and William Clark visited with the Nez Perce in the Clearwater River region and the Walla Walla and were reminded of this fact at the Treaty Council.)

The Cayuse had been to war with the white people, and when they came to the Treaty grounds they were hostile. The Indians attending the Treaty negotiations understood they were going to lose their land. The Cayuse bands camped away from the main Treaty grounds and accepted no gifts of rations. They feared losing all of their land and a place for their children to live. Because some Cayuse had been to war after the 1847 Whitman incident and had fought with white people over land, they did not want to agree to treaty terms that would take their land.

In the Cayuse camp, they discussed what they should do. They did not want to sign any treaty, but they knew they would have to fight and they were not strong enough to win an all-out war. They knew that Chief Lawyer was siding with the American negotiators. The other tribal chiefs were not stepping up with other strategies, such as "let us do it later." The Walla Walla and Yakama eventually did go to war but in separate battles, and all lost.

(Interestingly, when Looking Glass arrived at the treaty grounds and joined the negotiations, he stated that the Cayuse should have a larger reservation, because of their huge herds of cattle and horses [20,000]. The federal negotiators did not agree with Looking Glass, and the Umatilla Reservation remained undersized at 512,000 acres.)

The Cayuse went head-to-head with American doctrine of Manifest Destiny. This unyielding determination forced the federal government to propose a third reservation to be in Cayuse land — the Umatilla Indian Reservation. It was a major victory. The head Cayuse Chief Weyatenatemany, called Young Chief, was responsible for winning the establishment of the Umatilla Indian Reservation on Cayuse land in Oregon Territory. It was a victory that saved the Cayuse Nation and made it possible for our children to have a home today. This reservation homeland includes the Umatilla and Walla Walla Tribes, and we are now united as the Confederated Tribes of the Umatilla Indian Reservation. Young Chief will be with us so long as there is a Umatilla Indian Reservation.

The Dreamers

The Cayuse feelings were hostile because of the recent Cayuse War, which had ended with the hanging of five Cayuse men in Oregon City. The Cayuse were followers of the Dreamer religion. The Dreamers believed that the land, people, and culture and the children were valuable and were to be protected at all costs. It was Young Chief's duty to protect the Cayuse Nation.

At the time of the Treaty Council at Walla Walla, there was a powerful spiritual and religious force present in the Plateau Indian country. It was the Dreamer belief of the Prophet Smohalla. This doctrine was strongly stated by Young Chief on Thursday, June 7, 1855, at the Treaty Council. In part, the doctrine teaches: ". . . I wonder if this ground has anything to say . . . though I hear what this earth says . . . God on placing them (people) on the earth, desired them to take good care of the earth and do each other no harm. . . ." Young Chief further explained that he did not understand the U.S. government offer and did not know if he could take it. But on the same day, General Palmer, in response to Young Chief, suggested that the Umatilla Valley afforded some good land.

On Friday, June 8, Young Chief proposed the Grande Ronde Valley, south of the Treaty grounds, as the best place for them to reside. General Palmer, in turn and again, proposed the Umatilla River Valley as a reservation for the Cayuse, Umatilla, and Walla Walla. Young Chief had earlier explained to Governor Stevens why he did not understand what was being proposed:

You embraced all my country, where was I to go, was I to be a wanderer like a wolf. Without a home without a house I would be compelled to steal, consequently I would die. I will show you lands that I will give you, we will then take good care of each other. . . . I think the land where my forefathers are buried should be mine; that is the place that I am speaking for. We will talk about it, we shall then know, my brothers, that is what I have to show you, that is what I love the place we get our roots to live upon (meaning the Grande Ronde). The salmon comes up the stream — that is all.

They were being told what country to go to and live without their having a voice in the matter. Further, they had many horses and cattle and needed good land on which to graze them.

Of the three treaties, two were signed on June 9, 1855. The Nez Perce did not sign until June 11, 1855, because Chief Looking Glass was intent on changing the boundaries agreed upon previously with Chief Lawyer. As I try to understand the Cayuse position, they seemed to hope that Looking Glass would somehow prevail and stop the treaty negotiations or get a larger Nez Perce and Cayuse reservation. Young Chief was

Two men pose on horseback for photographer Lee Moorhouse.

holding out for a better deal than what was being proposed by Stevens and Palmer. There were several places considered for a Cayuse reservation, such as the country around the Tucannon, Touchet, and Grande Ronde rivers. In the Treaty minutes, Young Chief supported Chief Looking Glass right up to the end, until he gave up and agreed to sign the Treaty. Then the Cayuse knew it was over, but they had protected their nation. It is important to get the dates and times of the Treaty signing right and the attitude of the Cayuse about the signing. There were important life-and-death decisions being made that need to be understood, respected, and honored. When Old Chief Joseph (also known as Tuekakas and Walamuitkin, or Hair Knotted in Front) later went to the 1863 Nez Perce Treaty Council at Lapwai, Young Chief was with him. That is the time when General O.O. Howard threw Nez Perce Chief Tooholholzote into jail for taking such a strong stand against giving up more land. He and other Dreamers believed that the land was the mother and that the U.S. government had no right to sell it.

The Dreamer religion was a powerful spiritual force present at the 1855 Treaty Council at Walla Walla. It inspired the resistance to the Manifest Destiny doctrine of American expansionism, which was the interest of the federal negotiators Isaac Stevens and Joel Palmer. It was the force of this teaching that was behind Young Chief's refusal to bargain away the land of the Cayuse Nation.

The Presence of *Tamánwit* at the Treaty Council

[EDITOR'S NOTE: *This section was contributed by historian Clifford Trafzer.*]

For the Indian people attending the Walla Walla Council, the meeting provided an opportunity to articulate their view of the white settlement and the proposals put before them. Naturally, they emphasized the native view of *tamánwit* (Columbia River Sahaptin) or *tamálwit* (Nez Perce), which is literally defined as "throw down," but which means Indian law, natural law, or divine law handed down by the Creator at the beginning of time. *Tamánwit* is essentially the "rules to live by" that come out of the Indian religion and that are espoused in song and ritual. *Tamánwit* emerged when life first began on earth. This was the time when Natíitayt, 'the people', received the spirit and the law. Through their translators, the Indian leadership at the Walla Walla Council tried to convey to Stevens and Palmer their deep and profound belief in *tamánwit*, so that these non-Indians might understand that the Indian leaders could not sell their land and resources. To do so would violate *tamánwit,* or Indian law. To sell the land, the leaders would have to break the spirit and the law, handed down to them for generations from the time of creation to 1855. The idea of selling their land was abhorrent to the Indian leaders, so in their presenta-tions at the Council, they emphasized the sacredness of the earth and all its bounty. This became the underlying theme of the native leadership at the Council as recorded in the speeches given by Indian leaders, a theme common to Indian people in their dealings with whites.

Throughout the proceedings of the Walla Walla Council, the Indian leadership explained again and again that they had a singular relationship with the prairies, mountains, valleys, rivers, lakes, trees, roots, berries, fish, and animals. The relationship had emerged at the beginning of creation, before mankind, when the plants, animals, and places made ready for the arrival of human beings. The Creator and all the creative powers had prepared the earth and its bounty so that humans could exist. Every Indian leader that attended the Walla Walla Council understood this precept, and every leader tried — in his own way — to protect the special relationship of their people to the earth. In their attempt to explain *tamánwit*, the Plateau Indian leaders at the Walla Walla Council followed in the path of Native American leaders in American history.

Many times in the past, American Indian leaders living east of the Mississippi River had used similar words to explain their close relationship with the earth, plants, places, and animals. They had told non-Indians many times that their lands had been blessed by the blood and bones of their people, buried in the heart of Native America. Tribal leaders had presented their position to deaf ears, to people of European and American stock who viewed the earth and its bounty in economic terms, not spiritual terms. The United States proposed to liquidate American Indian title — their native or natural title — to nearly all native land, containing billions of dollars worth of water, gold, silver, oil, timber, farmland, rangeland, medicine, and other resources. For the Cayuse, Umatilla, Walla Walla, and other Indians of the Great Columbia Plateau, the earth was sacred ground hallowed by past events of the Natíitayt, village sites, gathering areas, fishing places, cemeteries, and so forth. The first nations of the Columbia River framed their religious philosophy in terms of *tamánwit*, expressing beliefs through values, oratory, stories, songs, rituals, and ceremonies. Like so many other Indians, the people of the Columbia Plateau lived their religion and strongly expressed their spiritual beliefs throughout the Walla Walla Council.

Cayuse Chief She-Ca-Yah or Five Crows, half-brother to the Nez Perce leader Old Joseph, spoke first, explaining: "We have but one Father in Heaven . . . who had made all the earth." Five Crows explained that the Creator had "made us of the earth on this earth" and "gave us this earth." Cayuse Chief Stikus suggested that he would be more generous if he "owned" two rivers — saying to Governor Stevens and General Palmer that if he had "two rivers I would be content to leave the one and live on the other" — but he did not "own" any rivers that he could sell. He asked the American negotiators to think of the lands of the Columbia Plateau as if it were their mother. Then Stikus asked: "If your mothers were here in this country who gave you birth, suckled you and while you were sucking some person came and took your mother and left you alone and sold your mother, how would you feel then?" Referring to his belief in *tamánwit*, Stikus concluded by saying: "This is our mother, as if we drew our living from her."

Cayuse Chief Weyatenatemany or Young Chief provided one of the most moving speeches of the Walla Walla Council when he asked "if this ground has anything to say: I wonder if the ground is listening to what is said. I wonder if the ground would come to life and what is on it." He understood that in his world, the earth was a living, breathing being. It was alive in the largest sense of the word. The earth and all its elements lived, including inanimate objects like mountains, rocks, valleys, rivers, oceans, and lakes. Young Chief was not saying that life simply lived on the earth or in the seas. Of course it did. But Young Chief asserted that the earth itself and all its components were alive. He and other leaders believed the earth to be alive, because Plateau Indians felt this to be a central tenet of *tamánwit*.

Young Chief explained that the Creator had instructed the earth to provide plants and animals so that life could sustain itself in a balanced manner of life and death. Plants and animals gave their lives so that humans could live; but in return, humans had to follow ritual in their treatment of plants and animals. Indians had to offer praise and thanks through ceremonies. Salmon, deer, bear, and other animals understood their relationship to humans. Camas, *kouse*, huckleberries, and other plants also had life, being, and spirit. They understood their relationship to humans. Young Chief knew this through ancient teachings, songs, ceremonies, and other experiences. Every Indian person at the Walla Walla Council understood all this and much more, because these beliefs formed the basis of their being as Umatillas, Cayuses, and Walla Wallas.

Just as other tribes understood their relationship with the earth, so did the tribes of the Columbia Plateau. In this, the Confederated Tribes of the Umatilla Reservation shared with other Indian tribes far and wide. We also shared a cultural gap with the Americans who knew little of this philosophy and cared less about it. For white Americans, land and resources — the economic value of property — reigned supreme. As a result, Governor Stevens and Superintendent Palmer did not understand the meaning of Young Chief's words: "God has given our names and we are told those names; neither the Indians or the Whites have a right to change those names."

When the earth was in its infancy, the Creator had instructed Coyote to plant various roots and to give them names. The Creator had given the plants names, just as the Creator had given the animals, mountains, valleys, rivers, and lakes their names. The Creator had looked one way

and then the other, but the Creator had named certain lands for the Umatillas, Cayuses, and Walla Wallas. The Creator intended for these names to last forever, and Stevens intended to change the names and steal the land from Indian people. This was the greatest violation that could befall our people, and they knew that to surrender their birthright — a gift of the Creator — could mean illness, calamity, and death. Of course, the people were correct. This is exactly what happened to us after the signing of the Treaty, but we survived and continued our fundamental beliefs in *tamánwit*.

Throughout the Council, Walla Walla Chief PeoPeoMoxMox or Yellow Bird had asked to end the meeting so the leaders could inform the people of the American proposals to limit Indian land, create reservations, and open their homelands to white settlement. His request matched that of many Indian leaders throughout the territories and states who wanted to confer with their own people in a democratic manner before making decisions. Like other American negotiators, however, Stevens and Palmer pushed the people to make a bargain and sign a treaty as quickly as possible so the leaders could not drift away from the Council, where they would reflect, consider, and discuss the implications of the treaties. PeoPeoMoxMox realized the ploy, saying, "from what you have said, I think you intend to win my country." He told Stevens and Palmer that they had "Spoken in a manner partly-tending to Evil."

This excerpt from the Nez Perce Sketchbook shows an Indian charge. The Sketchbook came from the Long Hair and Black Elk ledger given to Hilda Halfmoon and later presented to Dr. Theodore Stern.

The Americans proved impatient, and PeoPeoMoxMox became irritated. He asked Stevens and Palmer to adjourn the meeting so there would be "no bad minds among the Indians," but the Americans pushed hard to get the treaties signed. "Let us part and appoint another day," PeoPeo-MoxMox said. But Palmer responded that before the people could meet again, "we might have a great deal of trouble." Palmer threatened the people, reminding them of the California Gold Rush and the killing of so many Indian people. Miners, Palmer proclaimed, would come to the Northwest "by the hundreds" and among the immigrants would be "some bad people" who would "steal your horses and cattle." Palmer warned the people, saying that white settlers would overrun the Indians without the protection afforded them by signing the treaties. PeoPeoMoxMox called the negotiations "crooked," stating that he had been "blown away like a feather."

In the Midst of War

There were thirty years of war between the Plateau tribes and the federal government, from the 1847 Cayuse War to the 1878 Bannock War. The Cayuse were involved in all of the wars, fighting the federal government's military forces. For the American people, the conquest and taking of Indian land was ordained by God. The Indians were thought of as savages to be subdued by any means necessary. This was the doctrine and force behind Manifest Destiny. The Cayuse, Umatilla, and Walla Walla, however, believed in the doctrine that the land could not be sold because they did not own it. The land was to be respected as the mother who provided for her children. Wealth was not understood in terms of resource exploitation for personal gain, such as in the mining of gold.

The last war for the Cayuse, Umatilla, and Walla Walla Tribes was with the Shoshone–Bannock Tribe on the Umatilla Indian Reservation. The battle was fought on the eastern side of Mission Creek, near the confluence with the Umatilla River, and continued up Mission Creek into the Blue Mountains. It ended somewhere near Emigrant Springs, where the surrender of the Bannocks took place in 1878.

Stories passed down within families underscore the personal side of war. My father told me that the Cayuse had to identify themselves with a marker as "friendly" during the Cayuse War. My mother told me a story about the silverware that was taken during the Whitman slayings. It was taken not as a theft but as a statement. Cornelius Towatoy was a prisoner of war in World War II. When he returned home, he went to Umapine, to his ancestral land on the reservation. But Towatoy's land was on mission land. The Catholic mission of St. Anne's closed due to the Cayuse War, and treaty-era people are still buried there today.

Many battles were fought over the thirty-year period. We should recognize those we know who fell in those battles. Additionally, the Cayuse Five should be elevated to a status of national hero for the Cayuse Nation. They were the first to stand in harm's way. Let us not allow them to die in vain. We also recognize as warriors Chief Joseph, Ollokʷot, Red Moccasin Tops, Earth Blanket, Egan, and others and especially the treaty negotiators who had to see that the "children" would have a place to live. We should reestablish the military traditions of our nations, such as the farewell ceremony, the war dance with the whipman, and the pipe ceremony in their honor.

The actual whip carried by the whipman is a horsewhip decorated with guardian spirit inspiration known as *wéyekin*. It is carried by a designated warrior-commander and is the symbol of discipline on the battlefield, of tribal military power and of authority. It is to be carried with honor and respect. The whip was brought to Thornhollow after the Ban-

Thirty Years of War

Cayuse War, 1848

As a response to the slaying of the Whitman party in November 1847, the Oregon Volunteer militia fought the Cayuse Tribe on multiple fronts in pursuit of those responsible for the incident. Some 300 militia troops fought the less numerous Cayuse warriors (who were joined by members of Tenino and Wascopam bands) in the largest battle on February 24 at Sand Hollow. The war ended in 1850 with the hanging of five Cayuse men. Whether or not they were responsible for the Whitman party deaths is uncertain to this day. These men of the Cayuse Nation will be recognized and honored for the sacrifice of their lives, which has not been in vain.

Yakama War, 1855–1856

A major cause of the Yakama War, which erupted in October 1855, was the influx of white settlers across the inland empire before ratification of the treaties and establishment of the inland reservations. The low-intensity conflict swept through the Columbia Gorge and over the mountains to the Pacific Coast as other tribes allied with the Yakama, including the three inland Tribes. Congress reacted to the war by delaying ratification of many Oregon treaties until 1859.

Coeur d'Alene War, 1858

The Coeur d'Alene War of 1858 in Washington and Idaho territories was the second phase of the Yakama War. The conflict spread to more tribes, including the Coeur d'Alene, Spokane, Palouse, Northern Paiute, Walla Walla, and Cayuse. Chief Kamiakin of the Yakama had been calling for a general alliance among the tribes on both sides of the Columbia River, citing the growth of the mining frontier in the Colville region and the pattern of forced treaties and land cessions. Federal troops under Major Edward Steptoe marched out of Fort Walla Walla and across the Snake River into Indian country. A combined force of about one thousand attacked and routed Steptoe's forces. The allied tribes met the enemy on an open field, the Spokane Plain. In that battle, the Indians suffered high casualties, whereupon they scattered to their villages. The army column continued its trek through Indian lands, rounding up dissidents.

Walla Walla War, 1855–1858

After the treaty of 1855 was signed, unfounded rumors circulated that the Indians were organizing to kill all of the whites in the area. After the nock War of 1878. The Bannock surrendered to the Cayuse in the Blue Mountains after Chief Egan had been killed. The whip was brought and presented by the Bannock to the Cayuse. The whip has become a symbol of peace between the Cayuse and the Bannock. It is not known what happened to the whip presented and used in the ceremonies celebrating the existence of a State of Peace, not war, between the Bannock and Cayuse Nations.

Looking Back for a Better Understanding: Lewis and Clark Pave the Way

Returning briefly to the 1805 Lewis and Clark Expedition and the 1855 Treaty in the Walla Walla Valley with the Cayuse, Umatilla, and Walla Walla to note how they are connected. How do historical events describe tribal culture? Meriwether Lewis and William Clark and the members of the Expedition were not strangers. Indians knew about them. After the Corps passed,

Hudson's Bay post of Fort Walla Walla was looted and burned, Colonel James Kelly blamed and targeted the Walla Walla Chief PeoPeoMoxMox as the prime instigator. PeoPeoMoxMox and other companions approached a camp of Oregon Volunteers under a white flag of truce to offer peace and to protect the women and children in their village. On December 7, 1855, they were taken hostage and in the ensuing battle of Walla Walla in the vicinity of the old Whitman Mission and Frenchtown, PeoPeoMoxMox was killed. He was scalped by the Volunteers and parts of his mutilated body were later distributed throughout Oregon Territory. The war raged intermittently for three years and ended with the military slaying of about 1,000 Indian horses at the Battle of Spokane Plains in August 1858. The U.S. Army conducted hangings of war chiefs and tribal leaders for many months across the inland northwest.

Nez Perce War, 1877

When Old Joseph died in 1871, Young Joseph inherited his birthright and vowed forever that he would not sell the land of his forefathers. In 1873, Indian agents tried to force the Joseph Band off of their homeland and onto the Nez Perce reservation. Chief Joseph refused to go, still claiming that the Treaty of 1863 did not represent all Nez Perce. In 1877, the long fight began. This war pitted the non-treaty Nez Perce bands against a force of 2,000 U.S. Army soldiers. Under the orders of General O.O. Howard, Joseph's band was being forced from his birthplace in the Wallowa Valley to the Clearwater River. Many were able to flee what did the people here think of them? What did this visit mean? What did the Corps of Discovery mean?

There were ceremonies accorded to the strange visitors by the Tribes, particularly, at a place across from the confluence of the Columbia and Snake rivers the night before Captain Clark received a white horse from Yelépt.

Lewis and Clark were putting their stamp down here on our homeland. Our Plateau region in the Far West became known as the Oregon Country and would be claimed by the United States government. The Cayuse, Umatilla, and Walla Walla were witnesses and subject to this expansionist doctrine of the United States. That is the view on a macro level, but there is a micro level also playing out. The trouble started with Lewis and Clark.

The hard fight to preserve Plateau Indian culture and resources had started. Marcus Whitman arrived in 1836, and disease and measles followed. The Cayuse told Dr. Whitman to leave, and they attempted to force him out, but he would not go. When more immigrants came, Dr. Whitman went to the Blue Mountains to cut timber and to make lumber. He established the first mill in the region. There is

into Canada to avoid capture. After six major battles were fought with heavy losses on both sides and weary of his people's suffering, Joseph negotiated an end to the fighting. His people were removed to Kansas and Oklahoma, then later to the Colville Reservation, with many descendants of Joseph's band settling on the Umatilla Reservation. The outbreak of the Nez Perce difficulties in the Wallowa country east of the Umatilla Indian Reservation caused the Umatilla Indian agent to move about 220 Walla Walla and Umatilla people onto the reservation.

Bannock War, 1878
On the brink of starvation, the Bannock and Northern Paiute broke free from the confines of their reservation and united in a desperate war of survival. After several violent encounters with the U.S. Army, they retreated north toward the Columbia River. In July, they made a hostile raid on the Umatilla Reservation and herded off a large number of horses and cattle, burned houses and barns, and destroyed some crops. The resistance weakened soon after they reached Umatilla territory. Promises of an alliance were shattered when three Cayuse warriors parlayed with and killed war leader Egan, thus ending the war. Ironically, Egan was of Cayuse descent and had been abducted as a child and raised by the Bannock, only to die later at the hands of a Cayuse, Umapine.

Bannock War scene on the Umatilla Reservation,
painted by tribal member *átway* Philip Guyer

the influence of the Hudson's Bay Company on Whitman in the existence of nearby Frenchtown. Fort Vancouver was already established to the west.

The Lewis and Clark Expedition and the missionaries were followed by hordes of immigrants who brought traumatic political and cultural change to the Tribes. When the Expedition came to the Plateau country, the Cayuse, Umatilla, and Walla Walla had horse technology. They had adopted much of the Plains culture in ways of living, dress, and ceremony. The Cayuse, Umatilla, and Walla

Walla traveled great distances on horseback to the Great Plains and into California and Mexico. The Tribes became expert horse people. For the Cayuse, Umatilla, and Walla Walla, the survival of the people was always of deepest concern. Survival was tied to the land, and a total loss would be catastrophic. There was some relief of that fear when the Umatilla Indian Reservation was created in 1855, giving promise of safety and survival for the people. The Cayuse, Umatilla, and Walla Walla would not have to relocate to another place far away from their homeland. That may be the very basis of their cultural survival. That incident is, therefore, a victory. The Cayuse called it *hiwah* 'relief'. The Tribes were able to protect their sovereignty.

The CTUIR lost a tremendous amount of resources and culture from the time of Lewis and Clark in 1805 and the 1855 Treaty signing, but we can never go backward to make things right. That is done. It is over. The only way we are going to recover what we have lost of our original reservation promise is to move forward using the sovereign powers we have retained. We have to learn how to use our sovereign powers to rebuild our nation and take our place in this world. The CTUIR has made significant gains since the devastation of the cultures of the Cayuse, Umatilla, and Walla Walla Tribes caused by the signing of the 1855 Treaty.

The strategy that has made it possible for us to restore and protect our homeland was the federal legislation that returned the power of sovereignty. With it, we could make and implement our own plans to shape our own destiny without the interference of the BIA and other outside influences. We know the difference between oppression and freedom.

The turnaround for our people came with the adoption of the 1949 Constitution and By-Laws. This was probably the first tribal legislative action taken to break the hold the BIA had over the Cayuse, Umatilla, and Walla Walla Tribes. The people were free to elect their leaders and, it is of interest, Indian women were elected to tribal office. In fact, one of our first Board of Trustees (BOT) officers and chair was a woman. So far as I know, CTUIR is the only tribe that had that distinction in the very early days of modern government. Maudie C. Antoine was the 1955 BOT chair at the time of the Treaty centennial in 1955. Her words serve as a transition between the parts of this book. It is also interesting to note that the 1855 Treaty centennial year of 1955 was the time of the 1953 termination policy of the federal government. Although there were invitations sent out to the vice president, senators, congressmen, the secretary of the Interior, and governors, not one of them accepted an invitation to attend the centennial events.

The Vision and Power for Change

The 150-year anniversary of the Treaty is a victory celebration of survival for the Cayuse, Umatilla, and Walla Walla Tribes in this Plateau country, in this place where the Indians watched Lewis and Clark as they passed through. This is the place of the Hudson's Bay trading post, the Waíiletpu Mission, and the Treaty grounds.

The 150th anniversary of the Walla Walla Treaty Council of 1855 commenced with a horse procession. The pageantry of the 2005 horse parade was the first of its kind to honor our ancestors since their spectacular grand entry into the Treaty grounds in 1855 to meet and greet the federal negotiators Isaac Stevens and Joel Palmer. At that time, there were two thou-

Douglas Minthorn (far left), Fred Hill, Marvin Burke, and Antone Minthorn ride at the Treaty sesquicentennial commemoration in Walla Walla.

sand Nez Perce and five hundred Cayuse riders demonstrating on horseback. There were no more than fifty Indian riders mounted on horses for the 2005 commemoration. Even so, tradition remained. Our horse pageant was led by the *wéeptes téhey* carrier 'eagle feather flag', *tewyelenewéet* 'crier or announcer', and the *mimimiyóoxat tu'ynú'suusiin* 'men with warbonnets'. Others followed and mixed in, such as veterans and military colors. It was a proud moment and wonderful to see Indians with the warbonnet headdresses on horseback singing and *hayaytám* 'war whooping'. There is a belief among our Tribes that says: We have known battle from antiquity, and if any will threaten us, we will fight them, because that is our honor.

Our history is our strength. Our traditional cultures define us. Although we are all Indians, we are unique among ourselves and tribal bands. The best way to protect our culture is to learn and practice the teachings of the Indian ways. So far, we are succeeding in both worlds. The powerful spiritual force present during the 1855 Treaty encampment and negotiations was the force that was behind the resistance of all the tribes present. This force was not

Edward James (left) and Fermore Craig, Sr., are shown here at the
Veterans' Memorial during the July Fourth celebration.

Christianity. It was the Dreamer religion
with the tenets of *tamánwit*, which taught
that the earth was sacred and the mother
of life, and she was to be respected at all
times. Old Chief Joseph of the Wallowa
Nez Perce believed that he and the earth
were of one mind. To lose your place on
earth meant that you would be a traveler
without a home, with no place to stop and
rest.

One other important Dreamer doctrine is the vision of a resurgence of
Indian tribes. It was a vision that gives
Indians hope for the future. All of the
Indians will come together, both living
and dead, to take back the land. At the
Treaty of 1855, Young Chief was stating
these principles of *tamánwit*. That is why
he had such great trouble of mind in giving up Cayuse land. It is very important

for all people to understand that the
Indian religion is very much alive and
practiced by the Plateau tribes in the
Columbia River Basin. It is the guiding
light by which we make important decisions for our people.

The Treaty sesquicentennial is a victory celebration of survival for the Cayuse,
Umatilla, and Walla Walla Tribes. We
should go back to the 1855 Treaty grounds
in the Walla Walla Valley and talk and
pray with our ancestors from time to time.
We need them just like they need us, to
help each other.

The interior Oregon Country is Plateau tribal land. It is now an integral part
of the formation of the United States of
America, the most powerful nation in the
world. The legacy of the 1805 and 1855 commemorative events are the reestablishment

of tribal history and ceremonies that recall for our people the immense responsibility our ancestral leaders had in making the right decisions to ensure the survival of the Tribes and the children. They succeeded in achieving that goal by creating the Umatilla Indian Reservation. In this respect, our circle of life goes on.

Indians Then and Now

For centuries, our ancestors yielded ground to the advancing white man, and at his hands, suffered the most grievous loss of life and property. Government soldiers erected stockades and herded Indians of all ages and sometimes whole bands into them. There, they were to suffer and die slow deaths from diseases caused by malnutrition. Whole bands died from want of a will to live. Many preferred death to such imprisonment and fled. They were mercilessly slaughtered and massacred by military soldiers under government orders.

Reservations were established to protect the Indian from complete annihilation, but more truly to keep him under surveillance and to protect the white man from the Indians, that they could seize more land unmolested. Indians couldn't thrive under reservation life. How could a freedom-loving people so often transplanted from lands they loved to lands barren of game for food, streams for fishing, to lands and all other necessities provided by nature on lands taken from them, be expected to survive? Here, he lost the right to govern his own affairs, his economic independence and self-reliance. Self-confidence was destroyed, creating something like racial shock, which stopped, for a time, all impulse toward progress for the whole of our people, holding them imprisoned in misery and despair. Whole generations gave themselves up to grief and hopelessness. Bitterness too had its place in their hearts. Disappointment, deep sadness, ending in

inexpressible grief. Such grief and sadness is evident today in countries where wars have ended, leaving many of this generation despoiled, homeless, hungry, and without hope. So history lives again.

After the horrible finale of these so-called Indian wars, our people began their slow and painful struggle back to freedom. That struggle is not yet ended. Deeds of such magnitude cannot be done and over with, as many of you believe. They cannot stand alone in a period of time. Their tentacles reach out to oncoming generations and touch the lives of our people. We live centuries after the deeds themselves seem only echoes in history. I am an Indian living in the present now, but I, like all my people, carry the burden of those distant years. So do you, whether Indian or white. We cannot be understood separated from the past, for what has happened to our ancestors over the past centuries has had its large share in molding the character that is ours today. The past shadows every act and thought for my people today; it circumscribes our dreams and, to a large degree, has limited our future. Thus today for us, past history is living history. These truths have been handed down to us over the generations, not to create hatred but understanding and the ability to enable us to meet with faith and courage our responsibilities in a time and age when we face confusing accusations of being the offspring of generations of savages. Only one who understands the forces compelling the Indian and white relationships during those years can comprehend the dilemma of the living Indian today.

The Indian Bureau was established in 1834 and kept under military control until 1849, when it was transferred to the Department of Interior. Many campaigns were instigated as a direct result of military policy of total annihilation of the Indian. Pressure of white settlers for more land demanded that reservations be reduced in size, they argued. Indians were a dying race and didn't need all the land set-aside for them. The result was loss of the best lands, the richest soil, and the richest forests.

Treaty after treaties were negotiated, forcing alienation upon Indians from their lands and homes. Treaties dealt with land purchase from Indians for paltry pennies and exchange of rations to some. Treaties provided for education and learning the white man's way of farming, farming on lands, that today's farmer with the most modern scientific knowledge and equipment is hard-pressed to make a living on. The obligations and responsibilities of the government to the Indian today are the result of these treaties. The white man and the Indian together pledged themselves in the keeping of these treaties for "so long as the creeks and the rivers shall flow, and the sun and the moon and stars endure."

Maudie C. Antoine, Chairwoman, Board of Trustees, Confederated Tribes of the Umatilla Indian Reservation. These remarks were made at the 1855 Treaty Centennial observance in Walla Walla, Washington, June 11, 1955.

Through Change and Transition:
Treaty Commitments Made and Broken

Ronald J. Pond and Daniel W. Hester

Of the three treaties signed at the Walla Walla Council, the Cayuse, Umatilla, and Walla Walla Treaty was the one that the United States never intended to enter. The difficult birth of the Treaty of 1855, as it turns out, would be a good indicator of the difficult life it would lead. The story of the Treaty — its origin and implementation, the ongoing assault on the homeland it established, the resources it reserved, and the sovereignty it reflects — encompasses the conflict between Indian and European cultures and the pendulum-like swings in federal Indian policy. It is a testament to a tribal leadership determined to preserve their land and culture in times of rapid change caused by an unprecedented wave of non-Indian settlers moving west. It is also a story of the failure of the United States to honor its treaty promises. The Oregon Trail, which crosses the Umatilla Indian Reservation, funneled settlers to the rich river valleys of the Columbia Plateau, creating competition for the land, water, fish, and wildlife that the Tribes thought they had reserved in their Treaty.

Time after time, to accommodate the growing demands of settlers, the Treaty commitments made by the United States were violated. Congressional legislation and federal agency action took land, water, or other resources that tribal leaders thought they had reserved in their Treaty. For decades after the Treaty was ratified, non-Indian settlers agitated to have the reservation withdrawn, the Tribes moved, and its lands opened for settlement, and tribal leaders were constantly under pressure to consent to such proposals. Despite their strong resistance, the Tribes suffered serious losses of their reservation land base, water resources, and the highly valued salmon fishery, which Article 1 of the Treaty had reserved for their exclusive use on the reservation and at usual and accustomed stations off-reservation.

When tribal leaders celebrated the centennial anniversary of the Treaty in 1955, the damage to the Treaty was clear to see. The Umatilla Indian Reservation was a fraction of the size described to tribal leaders a century earlier. Salmon, once abundant in the Umatilla River, had been wiped out for over thirty years due to dams and irrigation diversions; and the federal government had spent millions on a project to store and deliver water derived largely from snowpack on the Blue Mountains to farmers downstream of the reservation. Congress had just passed Public Law 280 giving the state criminal and civil jurisdiction over the Umatilla Indian Reservation.[1] Indian law scholar, Charles Wilkinson has described the middle of the twentieth century as "the all-time low for Tribal existence on this continent."[2] But, at least the Treaty and the reservation survived. That was not the case for many Oregon tribes. Just the year before, in 1954, Congress had terminated the Klamath Tribes and several Oregon coastal tribes. Of all the treaty tribes in Oregon, only two — the Umatilla and the Warm Springs — have had their treaties and reservations survive without termination.

Cultural Change and Transition

The efforts of the headmen of the Cayuse, Umatilla, and Walla Walla people to secure our own treaty and reservation set the stage for the long-standing struggle that our leaders would need to engage in to preserve their reservation and the resources and rights reserved in the Treaty. The treaty period in the United States actually extended from 1778 to 1871. With the passage of the Monroe Doctrine of 1823, the United States became recognized as a world power and established the legal parameters of Manifest Destiny. The young nation developed a policy to separate itself, politically, from its overseas European counterparts and, by that, extended its sovereign powers over indigenous nations.[3] In 1853, Isaac Ingalls Stevens, with the approval of Congress, made plans to survey an overland railroad route across and through Plateau country to Puget Sound and, at the same time, reconnoiter the traditional homelands of the mid-Columbia River and Northwest Coast Indians for treaty-making purposes. The railroad surveys of 1853–1854 gave Stevens cartographic and demographic information on coastal Indians, which set the stage for the Treaty Council that took place in the Walla Walla Valley in 1855. In 1859, when the Treaty provisions were ratified, the Umatilla, Walla Walla, and Cayuse had no recourse but to relocate to a federal reserve in northeastern Oregon. With their traditional freedom suppressed, they fell under the paternalistic control of the United States government.

As for the three principal related tribes, the acculturative mechanisms that were put in place through Indian policy would erode their traditional value system based on their age-old Seven Drum religion. The Anglo-American mind-set

Charlie Bellman, photographed by
Lee Moorhouse.

placed native peoples in an inferior role, which justified their taking of the land. After all, the government's main goal was to save the Indians from their pagan ways and bless them with Christianity. This provided a unique challenge for the dominant society, because it had to develop a policy to separate Indian children from their elders and oral teachings. The children were placed in a new and alien environment, sent in the early years to mission and government schools and later to public schools. In large part, such policy measures were intended to "whitewash" the minds of the children and absorb them into mainstream society.

After the treaty process drew to a close in 1871, native people lost 95 percent of their aboriginal land base and were driven onto Indian reserves in droves. A few years later, the U.S. government was persistent in opening up more Indian land for white settlement. As one Indian commissioner recommended: "The remnant groups of Indians should be relocated to five territorial reserves in (1) the Great Lakes region, (2) the Central Great Plains, (3) the Northern Rocky Mountains, (4) the Great Basin–Southwest, and (5) to the Pacific Northwest."[4] This exemplified the predatory nature of the United States in shaping policy, with genocidal tendencies, to remove the First Americans from the ancient lands of their ancestors. "The policy of assimilation — which has continued to the present under the names of 'allotment,' 'termination,' or 'abrogation' was a way to get around the political reality that the new United States . . .was setting out to destroy Indian nations for the sake of real estate."[5]

In 1859, when the Treaty was ratified, the Cayuse were militarily escorted to the Umatilla Reservation and, with the Umatilla and Walla Walla bands, ordered to migrate and settle there by the late nineteenth century. These two groups were forced to surrender their ancestral homelands along the Columbia River near the confluences of the Umatilla and Walla Walla rivers. The three principal bands had relatives that also moved onto the

Umatilla Reservation with them, including scattered bands of Palouse Indians who inhabited the lower parts of the Snake and Palouse river systems. Many of them were refugees of the Nez Perce War of 1877, who had escaped into Canada and returned to settle among their relatives. At least one-third of the descendants of the Nez Perce War now live on the Umatilla Indian Reservation.[6] It was the ancestors of these related bands who first greeted Meriwether Lewis and William Clark in 1805–1806 and performed their ancient religious songs and dances for the explorers. And it was the modern-day descendants of the "old river people" who revived the ancient Seven Drum religion on the Umatilla Reservation after it had almost disappeared.

In the early years of Indian-white contact, a familiar pattern developed that involved native depopulation and land reduction. Based on one estimate, about five million people inhabited North America in the contact period; by 1890, their numbers had fallen to 250,000.[7] Because the natives had no immunity to the hidden vectors that carried pathogens from abroad, disease epidemics such as typhus, smallpox, and measles wiped out whole villages. Many tribal groups became extinct. This, in effect, created a new wilderness vacuum that was void of native peoples and, with that, fit into the whites' stereotyped image of "a vanishing Indian." In 1807, after Lewis and Clark returned to St. Louis, they reported that the mid-Columbia River Indians had lost about one-half to one-third of their numbers to imported diseases. This depopulation held true for the Walla Wallas, too. During the Lewis and Clark Expedition, they reportedly numbered 2,600 strong; by the time of the Treaty of 1855, there were 800 tribal members in Oregon and Washington. By 1910, their numbers were drastically reduced to a mere 397 tribal members. Before the Treaty, the three related bands' traditional homelands consisted of 6.4 million acres. That territorial domain was ceded to the United States government in exchange for a small Indian reservation in northeast Oregon that comprised 245,699 acres.[8]

This reservation land base would be further reduced as a result of the General Land Allotment Act, or Dawes Act, of 1887. As for the Indian tribes west of the Rocky Mountains, the treaty process — and the whites who negotiated or struck them — became more corrupt. Reminiscent of the removal policies of the 1830s, for instance, Oregon's Donation Land Claim Act of 1850 foreclosed on 2.5 million acres of land in western Oregon without recognizing Indian title.[9] The idea of isolating and encircling Indian nations on reservations became an important part of the federal government's illegal land acquisition policy measures.

When the Indians agreed to the reservations, a certain kind of life was proposed by the treaty stipulations. The very structure of Indian lifestyle was to be changed forever. No longer would the Indian be able to move freely about the country gathering his needs for living without trespassing on the private property of the new owner — the Whiteman. The treaty further legislated that the reservation was to be a farming community — a replica of the civilized, White community.[10]

Therein was the crux of Indian policy development. The Umatilla, Walla Walla, and Cayuse would be forced to live on a

small parcel of land and would become so amalgamated that the government — especially through its public education initiatives — fully expected to wipe out their cultural heritage and zero out what was left of their aboriginal land base. As the Umatilla, Walla Walla, Cayuse, and Palouse peoples were thrust into such an adverse environment, it was a struggle for them to preserve and maintain elements of their inherent sovereign power — based

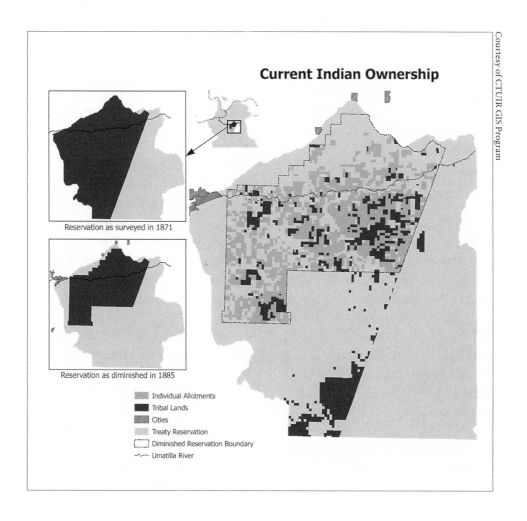

Current Indian Ownership

Reservation as surveyed in 1871

Reservation as diminished in 1885

Individual Allotments
Tribal Lands
Cities
Treaty Reservation
Diminished Reservation Boundary
Umatilla River

on deeply held religious beliefs — to govern themselves. The longer story of the Treaty, therefore, is one of commitments made and broken, and of the commitment of the Confederated Tribes to restore its promise.

Treaty Implementation

Once the Treaty was ratified, it needed to be implemented. The U.S. had many promises to keep, and implementation problems occurred immediately. The U.S. Supreme Court declared in 1920 that treaties are "the supreme law of the land," but treaties are only as effective as their implementation and enforcement.[11] In addition federal courts held in 1903 that Congress has "plenary power of Indian affairs," which means that Congress can amend or revise treaties.[12]

An interesting window into implementation of the Treaty can be found in the annual reports prepared and filed by the Indian agent stationed on the Umatilla Indian Reservation. The reports document the influx of settlers brought by the "immigrant road" — that is, the Oregon Trail — the unending pressure to open the reservation to settlement because of the fertility of reservation lands, and the frustrations in securing the resources to construct the mills, schools, and agency buildings needed to carry out the government's obligations under the Treaty. The reports also document the circumstances that led to the congressional statutes that decimated the reservation land base reserved in the Treaty.

The early agent reports spoke glowingly of the reservation. In 1860, the agent reported that the size of the reservation, citing an estimate by General Joel Palmer, was 800 square miles. He described timbered forests, fertile farmlands watered by mountain springs, and a "natural pasture [that] can scarcely be excelled for beauty and productiveness."[13] In 1862, the agent characterized the reservation as "admirably located" in "the very best location that could have been made," containing "a very large area of fine arable land" that could "be made not only self-sustaining, but a source of revenue to the [Interior] department."[14]

The agent also had high praise for the Tribes. The 1860 report referred to the Tribes as "once proud and powerful," expected to make "rapid advances in civilization," and led by "intelligent" chiefs.[15] The agent went so far as to describe the Tribes as "justly considered the most advanced of all the tribes in Oregon."[16]

The agent expressed early frustration at the United States for not providing funding to construct the mills, schools, and other facilities required by the Treaty. In Article 3, the United States agreed to expend $50,000 for the "erection of buildings on the reservation, fencing and opening farms, for the purchase of teams, farming implements." In Article 4, the government agreed to erect a sawmill, a flouring mill, a hospital, two schoolhouses, a blacksmith shop, a building to make wagons and ploughs, and homes for the agent, teachers, physicians, millers, blacksmith,

Lucien Williams, Richard Burke, Poker Jim (Richard and Clarence Burke's father), Clarence Burke, and Charlie Johnson, as photographed by Lee Moorhouse.

and so forth. Under Article 5, the United States committed to constructing homes and farms for the "head chiefs of the Walla Walla, Cayuse and Umatilla Bands. . . ."

The United States, according to their own agents, was slow or incompetent in carrying out their treaty obligations. In 1862, the agent commented extensively on these failures. Based on the agent's review of progress on the mills and the report by his predecessor, he reported that he was "thoroughly convinced that the original plan, if completed, will never operate suc-

cessfully. . . ." The relationship with the Tribes was at stake, the agent concluded, and he admonished the government: "If we expect to maintain friendly relations with these Indians, the [Interior] department must make some reasonable show towards complying with the stipulations of their Treaty."[17]

The Pressure to Open the Reservation for Settlement

An ongoing concern, fueled by rumors of settlers' designs on reservation lands and

These women and children in front of a teepee were photographed by Lee Moorhouse.

resources, that the reservation would be eliminated and opened for settlement and the Tribes moved. In the first agency report after ratification of the Treaty, in 1860, the agent reported that "a special vigilance will be required to guard the Indians from the corrupting influence of unprincipled white men."[18] In 1866, the agent reported that the "only cause of discontent [among the Indians] is the constant fear that the reservation will be taken from them and thrown open to settlement by the whites."[19]

As time marched on and the number of settlers increased, the pressure to open the reservation for settlement and for its resources intensified. In 1869, the Oregon superintendent for Indian affairs reported on a trip he took to the Umatilla Agency about the activities of white settlers to take reservation lands. All of the commissioner's discussion about the Umatilla Agency and the reservation focused on this subject. He wrote:

The Indians, who are superior to most tribes in intellect and energy, are very much attached to their home, and very reluctant to abandon it. Some thoughtless whites have talked quite freely about driving the Indians off and taking possession by force. During a visit last spring to that agency and vicinity I heard threats of that sort repeated many times. Public meetings of citizens have been held to devise means to have the tract opened to settlement, and petitions for the same object to Congress and to the State legislature have been circulated and numerously signed. The Indians are hence very uneasy and very much alarmed.[20]

The commissioner's visit led him to conclude that the Tribes were attached to their reservation, would not leave it, and would not be responsible for any hostilities that might arise between settlers and Indians. But the commissioner also respected the military prowess and allies of the Tribes and feared the cost associated with such an outbreak.

The Indians are peaceable and quiet and wish to remain so, and if any outbreak should occur, the fault will be with the whites originally, and as these tribes are among the most warlike, intelligent, and best provided with horses and arms, a war with them will be no trifling matter. As they are connected by intermarriage and otherwise with the powerful Nes Perces and Spokane tribes of Washington and Idaho, these tribes would probably join them, and the magnitude of the expenditure of life and money necessary to close the contest would be enormous.[21]

In 1860, the agent reported that the road could be "easily diverted" and that the appropriated funds would "be ample for its survey and construction." Even relocated, the immigrant road still delivered settlers in growing numbers. In 1869, the Oregon superintendent of Indian affairs reported that "the amount of travel and freight transportation [on the immigrant road] is immense." Another contributing factor, according to Indian agent reports, was the discovery of gold in the region, an issue that arose during negotiation of the Treaty of 1855.[22] According to historian Terence O'Donnell, the Treaty Council at Walla Walla was disrupted by the uncertainties associated with news that gold had been discovered north of the Walla Walla country in the Colville region. This meant that "miners would soon be passing through the Indians' lands," making it "more urgent than ever to settle the land question."[23] While the relationship between settlers and Indians varied, the relationship between Indians and miners was always bad. O'Donnell describes the experience when gold was discovered in the Klamath River in 1851:

Miners in Indian country almost always meant trouble. Settlers had a stake in peace. For one thing, they had their womenfolk and children to protect. They had barns and crops that could be burned and oxen that could be killed. Also, Indians were often employed by settlers. There were many accounts of good relations between settlers and Indians. Miners, on the other hand, often were young, single, and rambunctious. This led, among other things, to the giving of their attentions to Indian women, an attention not always appreciated. The men were transient, and their personal possessions were few. In short, they had little stake in peace and, in fact, often relished a fight.[24]

Perhaps most significant was the growth of the small settlement that became the Umatilla county seat — the town of Pendleton.

Pendleton

Pendleton had its beginning in the early 1860s.[25] Umatilla County officials selected Pendleton for the Umatilla County seat in 1868, but the town did not officially incorporate until October 25, 1880, when it had 730 residents. While small, Pendleton would grow, and it would need both land and water. The town looked east, to the Umatilla Indian Reservation, to provide both.

Pendleton was first surveyed in 1867. The surveys apparently did a very questionable job, according to local historian Mildred Searcey:

In December, 1867, E.A. Wilson, a county surveyor, was sent to lay out a town. The first stakes were set "near a thorn bush," a description somewhat indefinite as thorn brush was thicker at that time than inhabitants are today. It is said that the ambitious proprietor of the town, anxious to encroach as much as possible upon the reservation line on the south and fully understanding the surveyor's propensity for a stimulant on a cold day, placed a jug of ardent near a tree to the south, with the injunction that if the line reached that point the jug would be emptied, otherwise creek water was good enough. It is hardly fair to presume that the jug attracted the needle of the compass, but it is a fact that the line at that time reached the point designated. The line was changed later by the government survey.[26]

On March 29, 1870, several Pendleton residents petitioned the Umatilla Agency for the right to construct an irrigation ditch from the Umatilla River across reservation lands to Pendleton for agricultural and related purposes. The petition claimed that the withdrawal could be "without any injury or detriment to the Indians residing on said reservation."[27] By letter dated April 23, 1870, the Oregon superintendent of Indian affairs, A.B. Meacham, sent a letter to the commissioner of Indian affairs in Washington, D.C., recommending that the Pendleton residents request be granted.

The Office of Indian Affairs in the Interior Department authorized the Umatilla Agency to

. . . grant the privilege asked for in said [Pendleton] petition if it can be done without injury or detriment to the Indians . . . upon the express conditions that no permanent rights shall attach or become vested . . . and that any ditch or canal . . . and the use of the same shall be subject to the control of and to be discontinued at the pleasure of the Department [of Interior].[28]

The petition must have seemed harmless when it was originally filed, but soon the water needs in Pendleton expanded. In a few short years, the 1870 license was sold to W.S. Byers. He used the license to record a water-rights claim in Umatilla County, claiming "the right to take all the water out of the Umatilla River . . . for the purpose of running the Byers grist mill."[29] The Byers license was the beginning of non-Indian diversions downstream of the reservation, which damaged, and later destroyed, the salmon fishery in the Umatilla River and its tributaries.

The growing population in Pendleton and other settlements surrounding the Umatilla Indian Reservation in the 1870s led to increasing turmoil and local and federal actions to open the reservation to settlement. In its 1870 annual report, the acting agent at the Umatilla Agency reported:

The subject of the removal of these Indians has been often presented and thoroughly discussed in former reports. The last Congress "authorized the President to negotiate with these people for their lands." I would respectfully suggest that immediate action be taken in this matter. . . .[30]

By joint resolution on July 1, 1870, Congress authorized the president of the United States to appoint commissioners to negotiate with the Cayuse, Umatilla, and Walla Walla on the terms under which the Tribes would vacate their reservation or take lands in severalty — that is, allotments. The commission was appointed and met at the Umatilla Agency on August 7, 1871. According to the agent, "after the

matter had been fully discussed, the Indians declared that they would not part with their present reservation, and none of them expressed a wish to take their lands in severalty."[31]

Hostilities persisted. The 1880 report by the Umatilla agent contained detailed planning for the allotment of the reservation and for opening up a portion of the reservation to non-Indian settlement. In the 1881 annual report, the commissioner of Indian affairs, Hiram Price, again addressed the City of Pendleton's need for additional land to accommodate its growing population and the availability of reservation lands to meet that need. According to the commissioner, "land is much needed to meet the growing necessities of the town, and it appears that there is none to be held elsewhere than upon the reservation." He also referenced a petition signed by citizens of Pendleton setting forth their interest in purchasing reservation lands for these purposes. Commissioner Price acknowledged that Congress would need to enact legislation to authorize the sale. In 1882, that is exactly what happened. Congress enacted legislation authorizing the sale of 640 acres of land on the western boundary of the reservation to the City of Pendleton.

The 1882 Act authorized the secretary of the Interior to survey, dispose of, and sell lands within the Umatilla Indian Reservation that were contiguous to or in the vicinity of Pendleton, so long as those lands were not in excess of 640 acres.[32] The funds generated by the sale of reservation

The Umatilla Allotment Act, 1885

The essential elements of the Umatilla Allotment Act are as follows:

1. Allotments of tribal lands were made to tribal members in varying amounts of acreage depending on their status: 160 acres to each head of household, 80 acres to single persons over 18 and orphans under 18, and 40 acres for all other persons under 18.

2. "Reasonable" amounts of pasture and timberlands were to be reserved within the reservation for the use by tribal members.

3. 640 acres of agricultural lands were to be set aside for a tribal industrial farm and school.

4. A commission of three disinterested persons were to be appointed by the president to go on the reservation to do the following:

   a. determine the number of tribal members entitled to allotments and the acreage needed to satisfy the allotments;

   b. determine the location and quantity of "sufficient pasture and timber lands for their [tribal member's] use";

   c. determine the location of an industrial farm and school on 640 acres of agricultural land;

   d. keep all allotments, pasture lands, timberlands, and school lands on a reservation not to exceed 120,000 acres, which "shall be in as compact a form as possible"; and

   e. report to the secretary of the Interior the number and classes of persons entitled to allotments and their location, the location of pasture and timberlands, the location of the tract of the industrial farm and school, and "if the same shall be approved by the Secretary of the Interior the said tract shall thereafter constitute the reservation for said Indians and within which the allotments herein provided shall be made."

Source: Section 1, Land Allotment Act imposed on the Umatilla, Cayuse, and Walla Walla, ratified on March 3, 1885.

lands were to be deposited in the U.S. Treasury to the credit of the Tribes and was to be used to support an industrial school for tribal members. The survey was made to separate the purchased lands from the "lands of said reservation," which "shall from the date of the approval of said survey by the Secretary of Interior, be and constitute the line of said reservation between the same and the Town of Pendleton."[33] As a result of this legislation, 640 acres at the western edge of the reservation was severed from reservation status to provide room for Pendleton's expansion.

The Umatilla Allotment Act

The 1882 Act accommodated the immediate needs of the City of Pendleton, but it did little to quench the desire to open the reservation to white settlement. Congress was working on legislation to open up the Umatilla Reservation as the 1882 Act was being implemented. While Congress did not agree to extinguish the reservation, it did enact legislation on March 3, 1885, to provide individual allotments to tribal members, to provide certain lands for tribal use, and to open the remainder of the Reservation to white settlement.[34]

The bill was supported by Senator Henry L. Dawes of Massachusetts, who sat on the Senate Indian Affairs Committee. In 1887, Senator Dawes would sponsor the General Allotment Act, which opened for settlement reservations throughout the United States and resulted in the loss of 90 million acres held by Indian tribes.[35] But in 1885, Senator Dawes and Senator James H. Slater from Oregon were focused on the Umatilla Indian Reservation in Oregon. The impetus for action on the reservation had everything to do with its location relative to the Oregon Trail, with its influx of settlers, and the availability of federal soil for agricultural purposes at the base of the Blue Mountains within the Treaty reservation boundary. The Senate report accompanying Senate Bill 66, which would allot and open the Umatilla Indian Reservation, justified the legislation by claiming that it had been requested by the Tribes and that the revenue generated by the sale of reservation lands would provide needed goods and services to the Tribes. According to the Senate report:

These Indians for some years have in various ways manifested their desire to take lands in severalty, and secure titles to homes for themselves and children. In April, 1879, several of the chiefs and headmen visited Washington to confer with the Indian Office in respect to making a permanent settlement on their reservation, or, in lieu of such settlement, to remove to some other locality. The matter was to be left to the Indians upon their return to their reservation, which was determined by them the following November in favor of remaining upon their present reservation and taking lands in severalty. . . .[36]

The disposition of lands outside the reduced Reservation were to be disposed of under provisions in the remaining sections of the Umatilla Allotment Act. Sec-

Legislative Acts

This timeline lists the major legislative acts passed and events that took place to precipitate the social and cultural changes on the Umatilla Indian Reservation in the first half of the twentieth century:

1907 — Commissioner of Indian Affairs calls Indian boarding schools "educational almshouses," which perpetuate dependence, and calls for a system of day schools on the reservations.

1910 — The power of the Bureau of Indian Affairs is evident. The Bureau has the power to deny individuals the power of attorney and the power of representation, and it can keep individuals from speaking to Indian groups on reservations. Congress authorizes the BIA to create competency commissions to determine which Indians are capable of managing their own affairs. "Competent" Indians are to be given title to their land (which means they can then sell it) and be declared citizens.

1917 — The commissioner of Indian Affairs releases the declaration of policy to speed up the assimilation of Indians and to terminate government support to tribes. The new policies take "blood quantum" into account in determining competency.

1919 — The Citizenship for Veterans Congressional Act passes, providing citizenship for all Indians who served in the military or in naval establishments during World War I.

1921 — The BIA issues a lengthy "List of Indian Offenses" for which corrective penalties are provided. One concern is the reckless giving away of property; another is Indian dances, which the Bureau describes as a "ribald system of debauchery."

1922 — Charles Burke, through the commissioner of Indian Affairs, recommends that people be educated against Indian dances and that government employees work closely with the missionaries in matters that affect the "moral welfare of the Indians."

1924 — The Indian Citizenship Act states that "the citizenship decree was the political form of the assimilation program that had begun with the unsuccessful allotment policy of the Dawes Act." Historian Lawrence Kelly notes, "The

tion 2 provided that the "residue" of the reservation — that is, those lands outside the "new boundaries of said reservation" — were to be surveyed, classified as timbered and untimbered lands, and sold accordingly. In Section 3, Congress provided that the funds generated by the sale of reservation lands were to be placed in the U.S. Treasury "to the credit of said Indians." Finally, before the act was executed, the Tribes' consent must be obtained "in writing and signed by a majority of male adults upon the reservation and by a majority of their chiefs."[37]

A three-person commission was appointed by the president on August 13, 1887.[38] The commission determined that 120,000 acres was insufficient acreage to provide for the allotments, pasture lands, timberlands, and school lands promised to the Tribes in the Umatilla Allotment Act. The commission requested, and Congress provided, additional acres to satisfy the requirements of the act in legislation enacted in 1888.[39]

The 1888 amendment to the Umatilla Allotment Act makes it clear that Congress intended to diminish the Umatilla

passage of the Indian Citizenship Act in 1924 brought with it an expectation that Indians would be brought in line with other Americans in the areas of civil and criminal law."

1934 — The Indian Reorganization Act (also known as Wheeler–Howard Act) passes. It does not affect tribes that are not designated as an IRA tribe or that do not have a tribal constitution. The commissioner of Indians Affairs lifts the ban on Indians practicing their traditional religions.

1940 — The Golden Eagles Protection Act is passed, which means eagles are protected for Indians' ceremonial practices.

1946 — The Indian Claims Commission is established, of which the Umatilla Tribes are a part.

1948 — Congress passes legislation allowing Indians to consume alcohol only for mechanical, scientific, or medicinal purposes.

From the 1960s until 1978, the Claims Commission was inundated with Indian claims against the U.S. government. The same era saw the BIA reorganization and the creation of the Portland-area office.

Sources: E.B. Eiselein, Lawrence C. Kelly, *Indians of the Pacific States: A Winter Count of the Indian Nations of Washington, Oregon, and California* (Browning, Mont.: Western Textbook, 1998); Lawrence C. Kelly in *The Commissioner of Indian Affairs, 1824-1977*, ed. Robert M. Kcvasnicka and Herman J. Viola (Lincoln: University of Nebraska Press, 1978), 256-61.

Indian Reservation. Whereas the Umatilla Allotment Act refers to the "new boundaries of said reservation" and to the sale of "the residue of said reservation," it avoids the word diminishment. When Congress amended the act in 1888, there is frequent mention of the diminishment of the Umatilla Indian Reservation. For example:

That the [Umatilla Allotment] Act is hereby, amended by repealing so much thereof as limits the total quantity of the diminished reservation proposed to 120,000 acres, and the Secretary of the Interior shall set apart such further quantity of land of the existing Umatilla reservation . . . required by said Act to be selected, designated, and reserved for the uses and purposes of said Indians, and the said Secretary is authorized by order to establish such diminished reservation accordingly. . . .

Thus, while the 1885 Act clearly indicates that the Umatilla Reservation was to be diminished, the 1888 Amendment expresses Congress's intent to diminish the reservation.

Shortly after the enactment of the 1888 amendment, the secretary of the Interior issued an order defining the new boundaries of the reservation. The purpose of the order — dated December 4, 1888, and issued by William F. Vilas, secretary of the Interior — was to satisfy the Umatilla Allotment Act requirement that the secretary approve the proposal for the

new boundaries and the allotment of land to tribal members, lands set apart for agricultural, pasture, and timber purposes as well as 640 acres for an industrial farm and school. It is clear in the secretary's order that the Umatilla Indian Reservation was being diminished.[40]

In 1890, the commissioner of Indian affairs described the actions of the commissioners to implement the 1885 statute. He focused on the opening of the reservation for settlement by whites.

I am unable to say just how much land will be subject to sale as above, as the plats of the survey have been sent out for the use of the appraisers, but I should think it would not fall far short of 125,000 acres.[41]

In April 1891, the "residue" of the reservation was open for sale to white settlers. The Umatilla Agency agent reported that 25,000 acres were sold for a total of $210,000, leaving about 70,000 acres of former reservation land unsold. The agent also reported concern among the Tribes about the unsold lands and the Tribes' request that if the land was not sold then "the unsold portion adjacent to the diminished reserve be restored to them."[42] Years later, in 1902, Congress enacted legislation to permit the sale of lands outside the diminished boundaries of the Umatilla Indian Reservation to be sold at private sale. The purpose of this legislation was to facilitate the sale of reservation lands not purchased at the public auction in 1891.

Indian Land Terms

Checkerboarding. Since the General Allotment Act allowed for a significant amount of land to pass out of tribal or individual Indian hands, lands within reservation boundaries may be in a variety of types of ownership — tribal, individual Indian, non-Indian, as well as a mix of trust and fee lands. Thus, the pattern of mixed ownership resembles a checkerboard. Checkerboarding seriously impairs the ability of tribes or individual Indians to use land to their own advantage for farming, ranching, as a home site or for development. It also hampers access to lands that the tribe does own and uses in traditional ways.

Fee Simple. In this, the most basic form of ownership, the owner holds title and control of the property. The owner may make decisions about the most common land use or sale without government oversight.

In Indian country, however, whether the owner of fee simple land is Indian or non-Indian is a factor in deciding who has jurisdiction over the land. Because of the checkerboarding of Indian reservations, different governing authorities — such as county, state, federal, and tribal governments — may claim the authority to regulate, tax, or perform various activities within reservation borders based on whether a piece of land is owned by an Indian or non-Indian. . . .

Patents-in-Fee. The word "patent" means the title deed by which the federal government conveys or transfers land to people. "In fee" refers to the fee simple ownership in land. The term "patent-in-fee" describes the title document issued by the U.S. federal government to terminate the trust created by the trust patent issued to the allottee. The patent-in-fee operates to vest fee-simple ownership in an allottee or their heirs.

Trust Patents. Individual Indian allottees were issued documents called "trust patents" to verify that their land was held in trust by the government.

Trust-to-Fee Conversion. The conversion of lands held in trust by the U.S. Government to fee simple status. . . . [I]n 1906, Indian lands held in trust were converted to fee status if the Secretary of the Interior determined that the Indian landowner was competent.

Reprinted from Indian Land Tenure Foundation, Glossary, www.indianlandtenure.org/ILTFallotment/glossary/terms.htm (accessed July 8, 2006).

Congressional Restoration of a Portion of the Treaty Reservation

All lands open for settlement on the former Umatilla Indian Reservation were not purchased at either the public auction or private sale, particularly in the mountainous area in the southern tip of the Treaty reservation. These lands were eventually restored to the reservation, due in large part to a change in federal Indian policy away from the policies of the Umatilla and General allotment acts and in favor of a policy more respectful of tribal sovereignty, as reflected in passage of the Indian Reorganization Act in 1934. Preceding the passage of that act, Congress enacted statutes that stopped the granting of patents on former reservation lands that had been opened up to settlement.

In 1928, Congress enacted a statute specific to the Umatilla Reservation that withheld from sale or disposition any lands within the Treaty reservation boundary that had not been sold.[43] In 1939, Congress restored to tribal ownership and to reservation status some 14,000 acres that had never been sold pursuant to the Umatilla Allotment Act.[44] This tract of land includes Lake Hume-Ti-Pin, frequently referred to as the Johnson Creek Restoration Area. It was restored to reservation status by secretarial order dated March 20, 1940.[45]

Tribal Water Rights

In 1908, in *Winters v. United States* (which is also known as the Winters Doctrine), the Supreme Court held that when the federal government sets aside lands for an Indian reservation, it reserves sufficient water to the extent that it is needed to fulfill the purposes of that reservation. The Treaty of 1855 clearly states the purposes for which the reservation was established and for which, under the Winters decision, the Tribes possess federally reserved water rights. The Treaty guaranteed exclusive use of all reservation lands to the Tribes as a homeland, "which tract for the purposes contemplated shall be held and regarded as an Indian reservation."[46]

The Treaty also provided that the Tribes have an exclusive on-reservation fishing right as well as the right to fish at usual and accustomed fishing stations located outside reservation boundaries. It contained numerous provisions regarding the development of an agricultural and cattle-grazing economy within the reservation.[47]

That the Treaty of 1855 necessitated a reservation of water to fulfill its purposes is supported by a long line of Supreme Court cases. Following the Winters decision, it was determined that tribes have federally reserved water rights for agriculture, to protect treaty-reserved fishing rights, for livestock watering, and for municipal, domestic, and commercial purposes.[48] Just as in the case of the Treaty land base, the United States also failed to protect the water rights implicitly reserved in the Treaty of 1855.

The Social and Cultural Cause and Effect of Legislation

In 1988, Jeffrey C. Reichwein wrote:

Acculturation will be broadly defined as a continuous, though perhaps irregular, process of culture change which results from either directed or non-directed contact between two or more distinctly different cultures. . . . It is my position, however, that assimilation is a process that goes beyond acculturation since it requires complete acceptance of, and thereby submission to, the alien sociocultural system.[49]

The first half of the twentieth century on the Umatilla Indian Reservation can only be described as decades of historical transition, almost entirely externally imposed as a result of rapid legislative action in the post-treaty period. Based on the treaty-making process, Congress had "plenary powers" to legislate laws to reduce Indian landholdings and break down tribal traditions. These were the hallmarks of the Jeffersonian Indian policy. Later, policies were designed to enclose the Indians on federal reserves and force them into religious and educational institutions (such as schools operated by churches and the government) and absorb them into mainstream society.

In some ways, these policy measures were very successful, because our sociopolitical, religious, and cultural values began to disintegrate. In writing our own history of what took place during the period of transition, we present a story of rapid cultural change that our people underwent in the face of adversity.

The United States' east-to-west treaty-signing era spanned from 1778 to 1871, a time when over four hundred treaties were signed. Once the period passed, tribes were no longer recognized as sovereign powers. Even though the minutes from the Walla Walla Treaty Council recorded the statement, "You shall be known from this point on as the Umatilla Nation," insinuating full independence, Indian tribes were no longer recognized as sovereign nations after 1871.

Tensions were evident early on when many families resisted the move to the reservation. The Cayuse moved first, escorted by the military because the non-Indians wanted them out of the settled areas. By 1870, Chief Homli, who succeeded Chief PeoPeoMoxMox, was removed to the reservation time after time because he kept returning to the Columbia River.

Congress ordered the Bureau of Indian Affairs to find ways to outlaw traditions and make the natives conform. The Umatilla Tribes were considered successful in the eyes of the BIA because of the decline in language use and ways of life. The Tribes were a good model of Indians conforming quickly. Those picked for termination were shown to be the most progressive toward the white man's way, but the threat of termination was not met without resistance on the Tribes' part. Our

Some of the Last Chiefs

According to Walla Walla elder Joseph Johnson's written account, he identified the following Walla Walla chiefs: "Peo-peo moxmox (Original); Chief Homelye, Chief Noshirt, Chief Kanine, Charley Johnson and Clarence Burke." This list alluded to a Jefferson Peace Medal that was passed down from chief to chief before and after reservation settlement. Chief Willie Wocatsie, who was the adopted son of Chief No-Shirt, did not appear on the list. As the story went, he was offered the peace medal but turned it down.*

Based on a recent study, Chief No-Shirt was born in 1845 and passed away in 1917; Chief Kanine was born in 1872 and passed away in 1952; Chief Charley Johnson was born in 1885 and passed away in 1954; and Chief Wocatsie was born in 1879 and passed away in 1950.** Some of the last chiefs were:

Jim Kanine, last Walla Walla Chief, died April 25, 1951 (*Oregonian*, December 7, 1952)

Clarence Burke (Chief Sunset), Walla Walla, July 29, 1889 – July 2, 1987 (1936 Round-Up Chief)

George Spino, Umatilla/Warm Springs, tribal leader, died March 15, 1962

Captain Sumpkin, Peace Chief of the Umatillas, died during Round-Up of 1928 (*Oregon Motorist*, July 30, 1928)

Jim Badroads, shared honors of Chief with two other Jims, Jim Kanine and Poker Jim (*East Oregonian*, June 2, 1933)

Amos Pond, Umatilla Chief, succeeded Chief Peo; succeeded by Allen Patawa; Captain Sumpkin, Last Chief

of the Cayuse; Jim Kanine, Walla Walla Chief (*East Oregonian*, July 30, 1934)

George Red Hawk, named Cayuse Chief, supported by Mrs. Young Chief — widow of former chief — died July 20, 1942 (*East Oregonian*, July 20, 1942)

Willie Wo-cat-se (Wocatsie), cousin of Clarence Burke, co-Round-Up Chief, died October 22, 1950

Poker Jim (Sap-at-kloni — "White Swan"), Walla Walla (*Oregon Journal*, January 23, 1952; *Oregonian Magazine*, September 7, 1952)

Jim Billy, last Umatilla Chief (*East Oregonian*, December 20, 1952)

Luke Cowapoo, Cayuse, Round-Up Chief (*East Oregonian*, July 6, 1954)

Raymond "Popcorn" Burke, Umatilla, died June 27, 2006

*Joseph Johnson, "Articles Of Agreement," adopted by the Umatilla Tribes' Board of Trustees, 1973.
**From Ronald James Pond, "The Jefferson Peace Medal: A Cultural Phenomenon Passed down from Chief to Chief in Walla Walla Culture, circa 1805-1986" (Ph.D. diss., Washington State University, 2004), 323, 334, 341.

elders donated money for tribal leaders to travel to Washington, D.C., to testify against some of the termination acts. The chiefs went to Washington to speak against the Dawes Act even before our Tribes adopted the Constitution and By-Laws that transferred chieftanships to modern governance. Our tribal elders also traveled down the Columbia River with survey teams and identified cultural use areas of the three Tribes.

Attempt to Terminate the Umatilla Indian Reservation

In 1874, the Oregon legislature weighed in with its request that the Umatilla Indian Reservation be terminated and the Tribes moved. On October 1, the Oregon Senate passed "an act to extinguish the title to the Umatilla Indian Reservation." The Oregon House passed the act the next day. The legislature's action was based on its view that too much good land was being given to the Tribes whose members were few and who made little use of the reservation lands. According to the act:

... *the legislative assembly of the State of Oregon, represent that the reservation occupied by the Umatilla Indians contains about five hundred thousand acres, and is held by only five hundred Indians; that the grass is eaten out, the game destroyed, and is destitute of fisheries, so that the Indians go off to hunt, fish, and graze, while they give little or no attention to the cultivation of the soil, although a large proportion of the tract is admirably adapted to agricultural pursuits,*

being of the very best lands along the slope of the Blue Mountains.[50]

The legislature even offered a proposal for the relocation of the Cayuse, Umatilla, and Walla Walla Tribes, suggesting they be moved to the Nez Perce Reservation because of the intermarriage between tribal members, the similarity of cultures, and the availability of fish and game.

While the request of the Oregon legislature was cast in the diplomatic terms of intergovernmental correspondence, local sentiment in the community surrounding the Reservation was not so restrained. The *East Oregonian*, Pendleton's newspaper, editorialized in 1877: "We favor their removal as it is a burning shame to keep this fine body of land for a few worthless Indians."[51]

Later in the 1870s, the Umatilla agent reported the Tribes' feeling of unease and anxiety about "what the policy of the government will be toward them upon the expiration of their treaty next year. They are aware that the press and the people of this section of the country are clamorous for their removal. . . ."[52] In 1878, the commissioner of Indian affairs made special comments on the Umatilla Reservation in his annual report, noting settlers' increasing interest in having the Umatilla Reservation opened for settlement. The commissioner wrote that several bills to open the reservation had been introduced in Congress and that the settlers' desire to open the Reservation "gains strength yearly, is well known to

The delegation to Washington, D.C., were (front, from left): Chief Peo II (Umatilla), Chief Homli (Walla Walla), Young Chief (Cayuse); (back, from left) John McBean (interpreter), Chief Showaway (Cayuse), Chief Wolf (Palouse), and Lee Moorhouse (agent).

the Indians, and begets a feeling of restlessness and uncertainty. . . ." The commissioner went on to recommend that the Tribes be removed from the reservation, that the reservation lands be sold, and that the proceeds of the sale be used to pay the costs associated with removal, for reimbursement of reservation improvements, and for a new tribal reservation and associated facilities.[53] The clamor to eliminate or, at a minimum, open the reservation for non-Indian settlement would eventually lead to congressional legislation that did just that.

Acculturation, Termination, and the Role of the BIA

When the Umatilla, Walla Walla, Cayuse, and Palouse moved onto the Umatilla Reservation, they held onto their age-old religious beliefs. For instance, "Luls" was a well-known Umatilla prophet, and the Prophet Smohalla was well-known among the Walla Walla, Cayuse, and Palouse people. As for the Umatillas, Chief Peo assumed leadership until his passing; he was later succeeded by Chief Amos Pond. The practice of installing lineal chiefs (or headmen) led into the reservation era. On chieftainship, and according to early BIA observances, it was said of the Umatilla Tribes:

Culturally speaking, a minority made up of mostly full bloods still cling to vestiges of racial culture. This group, because non-English speaking, have depended for the most part on the reputedly lineal Chiefs for emotional, cultural, and religious satisfactions as handed down to the Chiefs of former generations. Scientific knowledge as such has had no impact on the minds of this group resulting in a general static state of attitude toward all change of progress. This group is fearful of innovation, dwells forebodingly upon the inroads made by the white civilization and without reason or rhyme, disapproves any program looking to any intensive activity of an economic sort on their part. It is but natural that this group should fear what it does not know.[54]

Bureau officials, in further summing up the situation, mentioned that this group of people was growing weary of the growing number of mixed-blood members on the Umatilla Reservation, because they advocated cultural change. The more traditional group did not trust the BIA in any way and resisted change because they had already lost most of their aboriginal land base as a result of the 1887 Allotment Act. After all, according to their religious belief, it was the land, as Earth-Mother, who had sustained them since time immemorial. BIA officials also reported that this traditional group, along with their chiefs, held General Council meetings, which according to the officials' biased view, accomplished very little on behalf of the people.

Fifty years after the Umatillas were moved to the reservation, population figures were at an all-time low: "the number enumerated in 1910 was 272, of which 152 were in Oregon and 35 in Washington."[44] As for the Walla Wallas, their numbers were 579 in 1907, 490 in 1908, and 397 in 1910, with 390 living in Oregon. The Walla Walla count may have included the Cayuse numbers as well.[55]

By 1909, the three principal bands, along with many Palouses, were settled on the Umatilla Reservation. As a result of the Bureau of Indian Affairs' acculturative measures, the principal bands were reduced to a subordinate role, where they were subjected to the BIA's blood-quantum enrollment requirements. They were labeled as "full blooded Indians," even though those of mixed Umatilla descent (such as Umatilla and Walla Walla) became full-blooded Umatillas and those of mixed Cayuse descent (such as Cayuse and Nez Perce) became full-blooded Cayuses. There was a unique blend with the Walla Wallas and Palouses, however, because they all became known as full-blooded Walla Walla Indians, regardless of their true genealogical backgrounds. This was vitally important, since the BIA had to link this blood-quantum concept to the provisions of the Dawes Act. Once the communal land base on the reservation was divided into individual allotments, the enrollment criterion was used to mark the passing of one generation and the beginning of another. In this way, with each passing generation, the land allotments would become further subdivided among a person's heirs.

Senator Henry L. Dawes, the principal proponent of the Indian General Allotment Act in 1887, was blunt about it. "Indians," he said, "had to become selfish." The Dawes Act, as amended in succeeding years, set up procedures that resulted in

Blood Quantum and Determining Indian Identity

Blood quantum laws were enacted to define membership in tribal groups. "Blood quantum" refers to attempts to calculate the degree of racial inheritance for a given individual or the total percentage of one's blood that is tribal due to bloodline. All tribal nations today use blood quantum as a requirement for membership. Usually, this is detailed on a Certificate or Degree of Indian Blood (CDIB) Card issued by the United States government. There is variation in blood quantum requirements from tribe to tribe, and many tribes may have additional requirements for membership.

The Dawes Act, also known as the General Allotment Act, was part of a federal initiative to "civilize" the Indians by forcing them into Western cultural and legal practices. The strategy of this Act was to take lands held in common by tribes as reservations and break them up into individually-owned parcels. Parcels of land were given to individuals who could prove that they were members of the tribe who owned the land, and the remainder was often opened for white settlement. Tribes set their own membership requirements, and many used blood quantum as part of the necessary qualifications.

Many Indian tribes continue to employ blood quantum in their own current tribal laws to determine who is eligible for membership in the tribe. These often require a minimum degree of blood relationship and often an ancestor listed in a specific tribal census from the late 1800s or early 1900s. . . .

Critics of the laws say they have been used to discriminate against . . . Native Americans and deny them their civil rights as well as pre-empt the right of tribes to determine themselves who is and who is not a member. Contemporary defenders point out that U.S. tribes set their own rules to determine tribal membership, and that they can decide on their own whether or not to employ blood quantum.*

*Reprinted from "Blood Quantum Laws," Wikipedia, The Free Encyclopedia, http://en.wikipedia.org/w/index.php?title=Blood_quantum_laws (accessed July 4, 2006).

the transfer of some 90 million acres from Indian to white owners in the next forty-five years.[56] In the end, the Dawes Act was used so effectively that it reduced Indian landownership to about 50 million acres. With the land disappearing at a rapid rate, so went the sovereign powers of Indian nations, for the native people could not expect to survive without the care of their Earth-Mother.

On the Umatilla Reservation, the diminishing land base became evident. After the Treaty of 1855, the 245,699-acre reservation was reduced to 157,982 acres in 1887 and was further reduced to 85,322 acres in 1879. It was in this way that the Umatilla Indian Reservation became the model of a "checkerboard" reservation.[57]

In 1855, Governor Isaac Stevens had told the chiefs that no white man would be allowed to enter the reservation without their consent. First, however, the Indian populace was encircled and confined. Second, the U.S. government made the bold move to breach the Treaty agreement and promises, and the Dawes Act created surplus lands that eventually fell into the hands of white farmers and ranchers. If the Indian lands were poor and arid, then this probably would not have happened, but the reservation lands were rich and fertile — prime farming, grazing, and timber country — and the U.S. government wanted them.

Because the Indians were considered wards of the federal government, it was reasoned that they were incompetent, especially when they lacked the skills to farm or had no notion of private landownership. That placed them in peril, because "when [the 25-year] trust periods expired, they were forced to sell or lease their lands to non-Indian farmers and ranchers, which increased the reservation's grid or checkerboard, . . . increasing the growing tribal population's already heavy demands on shrinking timber and grazing lands."[58] On the Umatilla Reservation, upon the issuance of fees for a 25-year period and when they could not farm and produce crops, the government labeled the Indians incompetent and took their lands. Not too long after the Dawes Act went into effect, the Tribes lost about 87,000 acres. As a result, many tribal members became landless and economically depressed, with no place to go.

As early as 1910, tribes across the country were picked for termination. The government monitored cultural change in simple acts of cutting hair, wearing shoes instead of moccasins, and wearing Euro-American clothes. The goal was to sever any ties that distinguished a tribal-U.S. government-to-government relationship and let tribes blend into American society.

BIA Efforts to Ban Traditions

At the turn of the twentieth century, the Indians of the Umatilla Reservation faced new challenges, but they managed to carry on their old ceremonies, traditions, and customs. In 1891, the federal government, through the BIA agent, formally abolished traditional tribal chieftaincies of the Umatilla, Walla Walla, and Cayuse; they were

Memories of Wild Horse Roundups
Louie Dick, Jr.
Interview, May 13, 2004, by Marjorie Waheneka

I come up with my mother and father who rode up from Red Elk Canyon. It's about an hour and half ride. I come up in a *teekash* (babyboard) strapped to a saddle horn. I was asleep, my head was bouncing around. Yeah! After Red Elk died then it went to the whipman *"Paax it tuh moot sut"* Five Ridges, that was Tom Johnson. He became the corral boss on Telephone Ridge. Then after he died, a fella named Wocatsie took it over, and then after Wocatsie in the 'forties when I was up there with Tom and Charlie and then after those then I don't know who.

Those were the corral bosses. Corral bosses rode near the end. They would give the individuals horses, colts. The ones I remember being there was Lee and Raymond Totus. They used to ride. Bob Williams, Goose Williams, and Victor, Charlie and Arlen Franklin was there. Yeah. Jim Bronson, Ted Bronson, and what's his name, I remember him, George Fletcher. I remember a big tall fella, Clarence Burke's brother, George Burke. But anyway I remember going in the dark, you know. You think about that now, it's pretty unique. I'd ride from Cayuse up the ridge. I'd get halfway and the sun was coming up, and then I'd go up the rest of the way. But one time they went from where the corral is on Telephone Ridge and went over to Boiling Point. I was late and anyway they'd already gone. I didn't know where they went. At camp, the ladies told me "follow their tracks." I never done that tracking before. I went over and sure enough you could see where there was about eight horses going, so I followed them and got caught up with them about halfway to Boiling Point. . . .

The procedure was, one guy would take the ridge, and that's where we held them, and then us kids and the older ones would kind of line up about four, five people there and that was our job. . . . We would stay there but we would kinda get in single file and get out maybe three hundred yards or something, like run them into the corner and then one person would get on the ridge and whatever he got on the high point, like at Buckaroo, he would chase them down to the point and then we would quit and he'd go back to the top of the ridge and then anything that went within the ridge, well, he'd run them down. And then we had one individual at Buckaroo down in the bottom, anything that came down considered public authorities who were in conflict with federal wishes. For the Tribes, however, there was still an emphasis on traditional forms of chieftainship, the languages spoken, and the seasonal rounds of food-gathering activities in the Blue Mountains and the Grande Ronde and Wallowa valleys. This included horse roundups at places such as Telephone Ridge, Johnson Ridge, and McKay Creek. From 1909 to 1924, the assimilation policies, as enforced by the BIA, began to erode the cultural practices of the reservation inhabitants, even though the Tribes were now happily participating in the Pendleton Round-Up and had won the right to become American citizens in 1924.

In many ways, the Indians tried to live their lives according to the old ways, but children who were forced to attend government and parochial schools began to drift away from the oral teachings of their elders. Indians were placed in a reservation laboratory of sorts, whereby the BIA could closely observe how they responded to the educational initiatives forced on them and, based on that, how they shed their traditional teachings and adapted to the influences of white civilized society. The Meriam Report of 1928 helped usher in a brief reformist period in the 1930s, but it had also revealed child abuses in govern-

one side he would run them up the other side and just head them in that direction. It was relay all the way around. Yeah. When I was little we got, oh, 75 to 150 head. It was quite a substantial amount to run in there, and then the stallions would get together and they'd fight. . . .

When we branded them, we got the opportunity to ride the horse. When I was in grade school I got bucked off pretty quick and easy, but I didn't know it until I grew up a little bit later and my legs got longer that I could stick my legs underneath their armpits and, yeah, I stayed a heck of lot longer. Thought I was quite a bronc rider. All you could hold on to was their mane and stick your feet in there. When they bucked straight away I wasn't too bold, but when they start to turn that was when you ran into problems. Yeah. Then you had to hold on. Yeah. Then we kind of raced to see who was gonna ride, you know. . . . I got slammed on the fence. I'll tell you that really hurt, you know. "Ahh get up. You're all right." [laughter] "Get up. You're tough." [laughter] I could have had a broken bone. Yeah. . . .

On Kanine Ridge, sometimes they would have so many horses they would be only 150 or thereabouts. It was kind of fun to take them out of the corral, and ment-operated schools. The report recommended that something be done about the federal government-Indian relationship, because the Indians were becoming too dependent on the BIA. With a "civilized" lens, the BIA paid close attention to the Indians' social and economic conditions as they related to the development of their natural resources. The Bureau conducted the acculturation studies to measure a given tribes' "cultural retention," that is, whether they retained cultural values. In 1930, for example, the Indians of Kansas retained one-tenth of their traditional cultural heritage, the Indians in the Southwest retained seven-tenths, and the Indians in Oregon retained almost three-tenths.[59]

At the onset, the Columbia River Sahaptin, as the Tribes were referred to due to their language family, people retained about 53.33 percent of their cultural values. Then, in 1930, it was reported that the Sahaptin retained about 38 percent of their tribal culture. As time progressed, in 1947, the Umatillas received a cultural retention ranking of almost 31 percent, with the number "2" written above to indicate that they would be ready to terminated within ten years. To substantiate the acculturation field-survey ratings and findings, William Zimmerman, the assistant commissioner of Indian affairs, presented to Congress a priority list of tribes that were ready to be terminated. This "hit list" helped kick off the

then we would go down the ridge on about a mile from where the corral is. Some places where they would have dips in the ground. I don't know where they come from, but they had water in there. We'd go and let them drink water. . . .

I remember Mrs. Wocatsie and Molly and Smitty. They used to go out and dig roots and then they took the gentle horses out and they requested the men to be with them, but the men never went. It's a throwback from long time ago when it was protection from Bannocks, but then when we had horse round ups it was protection from the stallions. Sometimes the women would ride a mare and the stallions would come and run the mare out saddle and all. . . . On Telephone Ridge the ones that camped there had six tents. . . . They had a sleeping tent and a cook tent and they had two meals there. The Wocatsies had theirs and Tom Johnson had theirs. They kinda had another tent where all the cowboys would stay. The Totuses, they had two or three tents. I remember seeing Dorothy, Raymond, Lee and Mose Lloyd and then they had a tent and there was another group there but I can't remember who they were. Quite a lot of folks you know. . . .

assault on tribal sovereignty as represented by the Termination Policy. The tribes were divided into three groups, with the ones at the top of the list ready to be terminated immediately, the second group facing termination in ten years, and the third group considered for termination beyond ten years. Zimmerman explained the criteria: "The first one was the degree of acculturation; the second, economic resources and condition of the tribe; third, the willingness of the tribe to be relieved of Federal control; and fourth, the willingness of the State to take over."[60] This was a strategic move by Congress to settle Indian claims and turn the responsibility for providing services to tribes over to the states. It was also an unjust move to force American Indians into mainstream America.

The federal government, through the BIA, was persistent in terminating the Umatilla Confederated Tribes well into the 1960s, when termination was supposed to be suspended with the passage of the Indian Reorganization Act in 1934. At the time, the BIA reduced the Umatilla Agency to a subagency and moved the tribal governing body office off the reservation and into downtown Pendleton. The Bureau also shifted its main operations for the Umatilla Tribes to the Warm Springs Reservation in central Oregon. During this time period, the U.S. government's efforts to terminate us was very evident, especially since we were rich in timber, agricultural, and grazing lands. Even though we were encouraged to adopt a tribal constitution, the govern-

ment never intended for us to last very long. Ultimately, the government's position in the 1930s did not significantly depart from either the assimilationist focus of the early twentieth century or the official termination policy of the mid–1940s and 1950s.

Indian agency superintendents, for the most part, were even more aggressive in displaying a "pro-assimilationist" attitude or mind-set, and it appeared that they were well-trained in maintaining a superior role in not only managing but also controlling Indian affairs at the reservation level. According to our elders, the superintendents were the ones who set the agendas and then summoned the tribal members to the General Council meetings. Superintendent Henry Roe Cloud (1930-1949), for example, was a Winnebago from Nebraska. He coordinated General Council meetings, made sure the meetings were well attended, and bussed tribal members to the BIA campus grounds. As for the chiefs, Roe Cloud made it clear that he, not they, had sole authority in dealing with tribal matters.[61]

Seasonal Rounds

Even with all of this external pressure to assimilate, much of Indian life continued as normal. In the 1930s and 1940s, the Indians living on the Umatilla Reservation moved about the land as fishers, hunters, and food gatherers; but since they lived in two worlds, they not only carried on their tribal traditions but, being economically depressed in the white Euro-American sense, they became employed as seasonal farmworkers. As related to their traditional food-gathering activities, the people held on to their old ways and traveled by horseback to their old family haunts in the mountain streams and valleys that surrounded the reservation. The extended families sought employment picking strawberries at Gresham, Oregon, cherries and apples at Milton-Freewater, Oregon, potatoes in the Blue Mountains, and hops in the Yakima Valley in Washington. Many families traveled to Celilo Falls to harvest the fall Chinook run and prepare and store food for the winter months.

For the Indian people, there were two important times of the year — the winter solstice and the summer solstice. As the Earth-Mother moved in that counterclockwise circular motion and the seasons began to change, December 21 marked the shortest day of the year and people took the time to honor the twelve lunar phases of the moon. Thus, there were two parts to the peoples' cultural universe.

In oral tradition, Coyote and Bear made an agreement, with Bear telling Coyote that he was going to sleep and for Coyote to wake him up before the sun disappeared over the horizon. With that, Bear went into his den and went to sleep, and he was sleeping so soundly that Coyote could not wake him up. As the sun began to arch across the sky, Coyote began to panic and shook Bear over and over again, and just when the sun was about to disappear, Bear finally woke up and that's how the sun came back.[62] As the Earth continued to rotate, June 21 emerged as the longest day of the year.

The First Part

In celebrating the Indian New Year, which occurs on the winter solstice, the old people put up a big tent in the upper reaches of the Umatilla River and held their own gift-giving ceremony. That was when the elders and family heads gathered and brought forth gifts and lined up facing each other in the big tent, and the elders gave speeches about their friends and relatives and presented them with gifts. This went on into the night until all of the gifts were handed out. Then everyone sat down for a "holy" meal.[63] After that, it was a time for spiritual renewal, and the people prepared themselves for the winter spirit dances. In the first part, certain families put up big tents, and the *tewats*, or Indian Doctors, would sing their spirit songs or bring out new spirit songs. The people attended not only to witness but to be worked on by the Indian Doctors.

In one story, there was a big tent put up on the north side of the Umatilla River, across from the Indian Agency, where the *tewats* came with bundles in hand. The men and women doctors took turns singing, and the young boys who were there had to dance for them. There was a "second" who held on to the doctor's body as the spirit came and worked on the people through her body. This was how the Indian Doctors sang the songs to summon the spirits and went into a trance; most often, that's when the spirit was present and worked on the people.[64] In the old days, these spirit dances or Medicine Dances, represented a strong tradition and were usually held during the winter months, from December to March. The last ones known to be held on the Umatilla Reservation took place in the 1950s at George Spino's home at McKay Creek and at Alice Barnhart's place east of Mission toward Pendleton.[65] Today, the Medicine Dance is being revived on the Umatilla Reservation and elsewhere across the Plateau. There was also a time when the white farmers would ask the local Indians to perform a Chinook (Wind) Dance to bring the warm wind and cause the weather to break to end a bitter cold spell.[66] Up and down the Umatilla River and across the reservation, many tribal elders maintained strong contact with spirit helpers, and that was why during funerals and special gatherings children were instructed to keep their distance from the elders for fear of being spiritually "hit." (Before a funeral took place in the 1950s, family elders told this co-author and his cousin to refrain from crossing in front of or in back of the women elders, because they were strong Indian Doctors.)

As the Chinook winds began to blow, the weather turned warm and the first plant-food showed itself — *latitlatit*, or Indian celery. On the Umatilla, at McKay Creek, or in our language, Háwtmipa, 'the heavenly place', the elder Charlie Toy Toy put up a big tent to honor the Indian celery. According to oral tradition, old Toy Toy had a special kinship with celery because it represented his spirit medicine power. When he danced to honor the new food, one elder said, "As old as he was, he appeared to float or glide around the floor with ease."[67] When old Toy Toy passed away, the Celery Feast celebration went with him, but it was later revived at the Umatilla Longhouse in the 1970s. According to custom, the women and young girls gathered together and traveled to the lava buttes in the local area to search and dig for celery. On such occasions, an elderly woman accompanied the younger women to sing and pray for the new food. Once an adequate supply was gathered, the women headed back to the longhouse. They lined up on the east end of the longhouse and, upon entering, were greeted by the men. They carried the celery-bags around the earthen floor in counter-clockwise fashion. After that, the men would sing a song, and the women would speak. The elder who had led the young women ended the speeches with a song. The new plant-foods were then taken and cleaned and made ready to be served on Sunday for the first plant-food celebration of the new year.

As the snow melted and the days grew longer, that signaled the time for the *kawsh* (lomatium root) and *piyaxi* (bitterroot) to show themselves. They both grew extensively in the area, with the *kawsh* blossoming in the bottomlands and higher elevations of the Blue Mountains. But the people were not allowed to dig for the roots until the feast was held. At Cayuse, for example, the men traveled to the mountains to hunt for deer and, upon

Memories of Lydia French Johnson, age 85

I was born in 1920. My grandfather was Joseph Craig. He was the tribal interpreter in the 1910s and 1920s and went to Washington, D.C. He died in the 1930s. There used to be a group photo with him in the tribal museum. He never looked directly into the camera. He wore a hat and braids. After he was no longer an interpreter, he had a second family. He was a quarter Scot and was a grandson to Colonel William Craig, a non-Indian who was involved with the Whitmans. But he was Catholic so he was not too involved. He married Isabelle, the chief's daughter.

First foods: No picking was allowed before feast. The foods were too scarce. Once, when I was twelve, she went in a buggy with the Minthorns and my cousin, Amy Johnson. We went up and couldn't find any. We must always leave some for the animals and to come back.

Schools: The Catholic religion and mission at St. Andrews was the main source of education for Catholic Indians. There was a boarding school run by the Franciscan sisters. The other main religion besides the Catholic was the Presbyterian with a church at Tutuilla and a hall beside it. Students were also sent to government schools, at Cushman Indian school in Tacoma, Washington, Chemawa near Salem, Oregon, Sherman Institute in Riverside, California, Haskell Institute in Lawrence, Kansas, and Carlisle in Pennsylvania. To civilize the Indians, their Indian language was forbidden. My mother, Isabelle Craig French, said that at St. Andrews, the French breeds could speak French but the other Indian children could not speak their language, especially in the 1910s to 1920s and before that.

Indian religion: The longhouse religion was practiced quietly during the 1920s and 1930s. They were able to preserve the language because some of them refused to be sent to school. On the Yakama Indian Reservation, the children were hidden when it was compulsory to attend the government school at Fort Simcoe. The prayer songs were sung at the feasts and at funerals and so were preserved.

Indian celebration: Indian "celebrations" were continued and, I believe, encouraged by the founders of the Pendleton Round-Up, which was the big event of the year with the Indians coming from Yakama, Colville, and Nez Perce reservations to take part in the fun. "Happy Canyon" was held in a building on Main Street in downtown Pendleton with the pageant held first and a dance in the hall afterwards. The music was provided by good bands, who did not always necessarily play western music. The Indian participants have always worn their own Indian-made outfits in the pageant.

The national and religious holidays provided a reason for Indians to get together and have a celebration. The word "pow wow" came into vogue around the 1960s when the celebrations became larger with more money to use for contests so that today there is no "pow wow" unless there is plenty of money for prizes.

Language: The languages spoken on the Umatilla Indian Reservation were Nez Perce (by, it seemed, most everyone when I was young), Walla Walla, and Umatilla. My grandmother, Sistine Craig Cowapoo, former wife of Joseph Craig, was the last person on the reservation to speak the whole Cayuse language — so it is a lost language now.

Dress or fashion: Most everyone who had attended school wore the clothes of the time except some of the older ones. Among the women in the 1930s and 1940s, Molly Penney Hays, my mother, Isabelle Craig French, Rose Thompson, Amy Webb, Gertrude Williams, and Mary Halfmoon, all wore their hair in braids and wore specially made kerchiefs made of rayon or silk on their heads. They wore shoes, plain dresses, and shawls until about the 1940s, when they wore coats and sweaters and jackets when needed. My grandmother, Sistine, however, who would never speak English (I never knew if she could), always wore kerchiefs on her head, wing dresses with the undergarment, yarn belts, moccasins, and shawls. At home, when she was working, she would wear an old shawl around her waist as an apron.

The men wore the men's clothes of the time with an added silk scarf at the neck, and in the 1920s, during the time of the Rudolph Valentino era, white shirts, black pants, and sashes around their waists. They looked very nice. Maudie Craig's brother, Johnny Craig, looked a lot like Valentino and dressed like him.

The Indian men of those times took great pride in their appearance. Of course, the women did too. The older men wore wide hats with a scarf as a hat band.

Transportation: The train was used a lot by the Indians at one time because they could ride for free. In the Northwest, where the reservations had white inhabitants, the Indians probably got cars as soon as their white neighbors did. My mother was the first Indian woman on the Umatilla Reservation to own a car.

Diet: Besides beef, pork, and other staples such as beans, rice, macaroni, spices, sugar, tea, and coffee, the Indians had several roots (like *kawsh*) that they dug for in the spring. Salmon came from the Columbia River at The Dalles and the Umatilla River. Deer, elk meat, chokecherries and huckleberries were plentiful. The women were good cooks and seamstresses and provided good food for their families. The food was simple. The women sewed their own wing dresses and other clothes, made tepees for the Round-Up and camping, made moccasins, and did beadwork. They also made yarn belts for their use and for the children. They also made horse trappings for their horses for parades.

Wartime: The men cared for their horses and some, I'm sure, utilized what they learned like carpentry, from the schools they attended. Much of the land (allotments) was rented for grazing or wheat farming by white farmers at a very low rate, which was 25 cents an acre for years. During World War II, when there was a shortage of laborers for the wheat farms, the Indian women drove trucks for the farmers.

The Indians are very patriotic and when World War II was declared, the men enlisted in great numbers. Women also joined and some became nurses during the war. Veterans are always honored at feasts and celebrations and the veterans and their close relatives now belong to the VFW and American Legion posts.

Music: The music of the early 1900s, 1920s, 1930s and 1940s was also part of the scene and people learned the dances of the times. These were learned at the various schools — government or public and religious schools. I remember that Joe Johnson played with a band on the Umatilla Reservation. Duane Conner played the piano at the Presbyterian church at Tutuilla.

Sports: Baseball and, later, basketball was an important sport on the reservation. At the schools, local Indian boys were good football players such as Duane and Cecil Conner.

Housing: Most homes were made of wood with one or two stories. A one-story house had a living room, kitchen, with dining area and one or two bedrooms on the main floor. Better housing did not happen until after World War II. For several decades, a lot of homes had tepees outside of their homes made of old flour sacks and gunny sacks. These were used to dry or smoke deer meat in. My grandmother had two of them and we used to like to play inside them. There were several layers of material that withstood rain or snow.

The homes did not have electricity or running water until the late 1930s or early 1940s. The homes had wells with outdoor pumps to get water. We had wood stoves to cook on. My father had a sweathouse to keep clean with. If they lived by the river or creeks, they had a sweathouse and the children swam during the summer to keep clean.

Washing clothes was done with the washboard just like the rest of society until electricity was put in the home. My mother bought a gas washing machine in 1932. Our home did not get electricity until 1939.

Health: The flu epidemic of 1918-1919 caused the death of many Indians including two of my baby brothers, who were born before and during that time. Tuberculosis was also quite prevalent. Sorrow over the loss of loved ones or other loss, poor diet, and exposure to the TB germs, I believe, is the cause of tuberculosis.

Before the 1940s, treatment for TB was bed rest in a sanitorium or possibly surgical removal of the affected lung or pneumothorax (collapse of the lung to give it rest). When I was hospitalized in 1950 for minimal TB, after having worked as a registered nurse in Tacoma on the TB ward for several months, I had only bed rest. Isoniazid and streptomycin were the TB treatments by then. Streptomycin could cause deafness. In the 1920s, 1930s, and 1940s, Indian TB patients were sent to sanitariums in Lapwai, Idaho, Toppenish, Washington, and Tacoma Indian Hospital, also called "Cushman." The Tacoma hospital was fairly new and large and was kept open until the 1960s. Toppenish Hospital was closed as an Indian hospital and became the Yakima Indian Agency in the 1940s. The Lapwai one was closed around that time.

Health care was minimal before the 1970s and hospital care was by contract with the hospitals. The clinics were small. There was usually only one public health nurse and one doctor. Health care has greatly improved since about the 1970s.

Storytelling: All of the tribes had or still have Indian legends. Grandmothers taught the children during winter evenings with stories of animals, fish, and birds. My mother used to say the stories were about "when the animals were people." Human characteristics taught were humility, generosity instead of greed, and other good manners. Instead of "shooting first and asking questions later," strangers were greeted kindly until they proved to be unworthy of respect. The stories were told with sound effects and action so the children learned to be good mimics.

returning, cut and dried the deer meat. After that, they transported the meat to Celilo to trade for dried salmon for the feast.[68] An elder related a time when two Walla Walla chiefs provided food for the Cayuse feast, where one brought food for one setting and the other took care of the other setting. The food was set in two long lines that paralleled one another in the big tent.[69] It is not certain when the Cayuse first food rites ended, but the big Summer Cayuse Celebration ended in 1924.

In that same year, the tribal elders dedicated the use of the Celebration Grounds, located due east of the Umatilla Agency, to the Indian veterans.[70] In the month of June, tribal members traveled to the Blue Mountains to cut teepee poles, because it was during that time of the year that the sap was running and the poles were easier to peel. Families cut teepee poles from the fir-tree stands that surrounded the old Johnson Ridge lookout tower. The great circle of teepees at Cayuse may have disappeared, but it moved down to the Celebration Grounds at Mission. It, too, disappeared sometime in the early 1950s. From there, in the later part of July, the people traveled to the Wallowa Valley and moved into the Indian encampment at the Chief Joseph Days rodeo; and in early August, some Palouse descendants traveled and put their teepees up at the rodeo in Omak, Washington. Then, in early September, tribal members either attended and moved their teepees to the Ellensburg rodeo or to the Walla Walla fairgrounds. Finally, the great September event

included tribal members and their Sahaptian-speaking neighbors, who moved their teepees into the Indian Village at the Pendleton Round-Up.

Schooling and Church Life on the Reservation

The Treaty had many guarantees, and education was one of them. We had to adhere to a U.S. law to send our children to school. Most children were sent to the Catholic school on the reservation. In the early years, the missionaries competed for Indian converts; but because many tribal members remained loyal to their oral traditions, the elements of Christianity were blended in with the elements of Indian religious teachings. This unique blend of cultures took place at St. Andrews Catholic church, located in the foothills of the Blue Mountains, and at the Tutuilla Presbyterian church at a place called Shishnimishpa, the place of the thorns, on the western part of the reservation.

At St. Andrews Mission, the old church was constructed with a traditional Indian longhouse type of structure on its north side. A traditional service was held in that longhouse, although the tradition of facing toward the light from the east was not enacted. There were single-room houses for tribal members on the north side of the church as well, and a large congregation of enrolled members attended church there.[71] In the old days, the children were rounded up along the Umatilla River and forced to attend school there. In observing what was unique about the

This is the second site of the Presbyterian mission at Tutuilla, or Shishnimishpa, on the Umatilla Reservation, photographed by Lee Moorhouse.

Catholic church, there was a strong group of elderly women who sang and prayed in the Lower Nez Perce language.[72] Some of the songs came to them in the old way, through their dreams. At the church, there was a great deal of ceremony when a tribal member passed away, because the priest, along with the altar boys bearing church banners, led the congregation and the body to the cemetery a short distance away.

At the Tutuilla Presbyterian church, Sunday school lessons were taught in the Umatilla language and church songs were sung in the Umatilla and Lower Nez Perce languages. On Sundays and for other special events, the women wore traditional wing dresses and prepared traditional meals for the people. The wing dress was adopted from the traditional buckskin dress. With the introduction of cloth from traders, women wore trade-cloth cotton as an alternative that was easier to care for than buckskin. The sleeves were cut in a shape similar to a bird's wing, replicating the traditional style of the buckskin dress.

With all of the sermons delivered in the Indian language, the big event of the year took place in the spring. It included a

In "Whistling for Thornhollow," Lee Moorhouse photographed traditional camps, a tilled field, a steam locomotive, and native vegetation along the Umatilla River.

large evangelistic gathering, where teepees were put up for the visiting delegations. In later years, small homes were built between the church and cemetery to house tribal members. There, too, a large building was moved in that served as a gathering place. The church members gathered traditional foods, and large feasts were held on Sundays. At Christmas time, both churches sponsored plays and gave out presents, especially at Tutuilla and at the Old Barn at the agency grounds, where large Christmas trees were put up and tribal members brought their Christmas presents to be distributed. The first settlements on the reservation were single-story houses built next to the two mission churches. Soon afterwards, baptizing became a regular practice. There are still strong Catholic and Protestant families here today, but many never gave up the traditional Indian religion completely.

The Second Part

The summer solstice marked the longest day of the year, and this became the second part of an important time of the year for tribal members. People usually traveled together to attend celebrations. According to custom, early July was the time of year when tribal members began to hunt, and the two-point buck was the prized game animal. Hunting and shooting this particular game animal would bring the hunters good luck for the rest of the season. Often, the people referred to the two-point buck as the "Big Doctor." Some elders say that the buck was special because of its forked horns, which were shaped like parts of stars.[73] It was during the heat of the summer months that the women soaked, scraped, and tanned deer hides. In the old days, it was during the summer months that the family members moved to the Blue Mountains to hunt deer and dry meat, with many families staying in the mountains until August.

In late July and early August, the huckleberries began to ripen, and that was when the tribal members went to their favorite berry-picking places along the Imnaha River, at Johnson Creek (south reservation), near Spout Springs, and at Motet Springs in the Blue Mountains, with other families traveling to Mount Adams. The season was changing, and it was a time when the first rainfall crossed the Umatilla Valley. According to an elder chief, it was a good time of the year, because the berries were harvested and the wheat was harvested as well. This led to the start of the Pendleton Round-Up, where both Indians and whites gathered to celebrate their bountiful crops by staging a rodeo and Indian encampment.[74]

Toward the end of August or in early September, the tamarack or western larch trees in the Blue Mountains began to change to gold, and that signaled the start of the elk-bugling season.[75] As the season

began to change and with the weather growing colder, the people began to prepare themselves for the fall hunt. For the men, hunting for deer and elk was a religious and sacred event. The men would go to the mountains and build a sweathouse and sweat for seven days straight to purify and prepare themselves for the hunt.[76] Then there is the story of the elderly men who disrobed themselves in dressing out a big buck so as not to contaminate the meat.[77] According to the oral teachings, a hunter, when packing out deer or elk meat, must never let the meat touch the ground or, for that matter, handle the meat in a rough manner.[78] The hunters must always show respect to the game animals for showing and giving themselves to the people. They were taught not to hunt beyond the month of November, because the weather gets colder and that makes it more difficult for the big game animals to survive the winter months. Usually, when the third snowfall fell across the Blue Mountains, it was a time when the old people gathered their dried meat together, along with other food supplies, and made their way back to the reservation. In the early years, the old people traveled to hunt deer and elk in places such as the Imnaha River, the Walla Walla Mountains, the Grande Ronde River, Johnson Creek, and on the North Fork of the John Day River.

Thus, putting the two solstice parts together, represents a full cycle of food-gathering activities for the tribal members living on the Umatilla Reservation.

Dusk falls on the Indian Village at the Pendleton Round-Up.

Where We Gathered

In the 1940s, all of the tribal celebrations, ceremonies, and other social functions took place in the Old Barn that was located on the floodplain between the BIA Agency grounds and the old cemetery on the hill. The Old Barn was a gathering place for tribal members, and a host of social and cultural activities were held there, such as the Christmas War Dance celebration, talent shows, modern dances, and the spring Root Feast.

All across the reservation, the tribal members had their homes built on family allotments, with some small family homes constructed at Mission, Cayuse, Thornhollow, and Gibbon. There was an old trail on the north side of the Umatilla River that tribal members used to travel from Mission to Cayuse and Thornhollow. Later on, dirt roads crisscrossed the reservation. Then the paved U.S. Highway 30, which followed the route of the Oregon Trail, cut across the heart of the reservation, extending from Pendleton to Mission, up the hill to Boiling Point, and from there to Emigrant Springs, Meacham, and across the Blue Mountains to La Grande.

Because Mission was at the heart of the tribal community, a prominent non-Indian named Frank Bowman, who was a friend to the Indians, had a store and gas station built directly across the highway from the BIA Agency. The elders lived in small, single homes built there, and across the dirt road some tribal members lived in an L-shaped apartment building. Across from the Bowman store, Joe Miller had a store built, too, with his home situated behind the BIA superintendent's house. It was Joe Miller who sponsored the Mission Indians baseball team and had sweatshirts made for the team players with the words "Texaco Chiefs" written across the front.

They Come for Round-Up

September was the time for the Indian and cowboy rodeo, the Pendleton Round-Up. The people moved into the Indian village at the Round-Up grounds, and each family group had their own camping spots. Sadly, as the elders have passed away, many in the younger generation no longer carry on the tradition of moving into the Indian Village to take part in the Round-Up activities.

In the early years, the people held onto their traditions and practiced them at the Round-Up grounds and Indian Village. The men made sweathouses along the Umatilla River and sweat every morning. The chiefs held big dinners at the Indian village for friends, visitors, and relatives.[79] In the 1940s, a wooden fence surrounded the Round-Up Indian Village; and open pathways, running east, west, north, and south, divided the village into quadrants. That was also the time when the camp crier Andrew Allen, dressed in a dark outfit and wearing a war bonnet, rode around the village in counter-clockwise fashion on a white horse, echoing the words of the chiefs as he went. The War

Dances sponsored by the Pendleton Woolen Mills were held on Friday nights on the south end of the Round-Up grounds, with whipman Tom Johnson there to help coordinate the dances. (The co-author was a boy when Andrew Allen rode around the campground and was there when Tom Johnson served as whipman in the 1940s.)

In 1911, Pendleton Mayor Roy Raley wrote the Wild West show for the evening entertainment called the Happy Canyon Pageant. The story was loosely based on the history of the region but was romanticized to the point of being unrecognizable, complete with an Indian love call and a shoot-out with an Indian falling over a cascading waterfall. The story told of the emerging town was also rife with stereotypes, yet efforts to update the show have been thwarted. The pageant in its original form is still held dear to many, giving all who participate a chance to laugh at themselves once a year. The Indian participants know their roles just like people remembered their camping places in the Indian Village, and those roles have been passed down to the younger generation when the elders either got too old to perform or passed away. The wagon-burning scene used to be staged everyday during the Round-Up, across the Umatilla River on Pendleton's north hill, but that colorful event has long since ceased to exist. In the evenings at about six o'clock, three or four trucks parked at the southeast part of the Village blared their horns for the Happy Canyon participants to come and load up. Then they were taken for a ride through Main Street to advertise the evening show. That used to be a big-time fun event that does not take place anymore.

In the old days, the young Indian cowboys from the reservation were paid a dollar a head to try out the bucking stock.[80] At the end of the week, the family groups stored their Round-Up teepee poles under the wooden bleachers, which were reserved for Indian participants. The poles were stored all year long until Round-Up came again. No one bothered them.

Other forms of local social interaction reinforced representations of cowboys and Indians in the Old West. By 1920, several photographers had set up shop in Pendleton. The more famous among them was Major Lee Moorhouse, who produced thousands of glass plates of Indian people and local Pendleton interests, such as the Round-Up, to be made into postcards. As the U.S. government was pressing forward on assimilation policies, photographers were capturing people in traditional regalia, occasionally posing them at scenic locales around the homeland.

Tribal members made light of all of this local color they were involved in, and still do for the most part. Even Hollywood

Traditional Role of Camp Crier

There is a story told by William Minthorn, the late Chief Blackhawk, about the chiefs who would meet at Tutuilla, which was called Shishnimishpa. He met the Cayuse chief from upriver at Tutuilla when he was a young boy. It was a custom for him to be the "crier" for the upriver chiefs. He would welcome the other chiefs, who were most likely from Umatilla, McKay Creek, and elsewhere around here. Young Bill Minthorn would relate the information to the people. One day, old Amos Pond told him "to sit down, that he was just a boy and he didn't have a right to speak." But even at the age of ten or twelve, he would travel from place to place to do business.

Of the role of the crier, anthropologist Helen Schuster writes: "Each village headman had an assistant or spokesman who repeated the details of a headman's speeches in a loud voice for all to hear." This status also included the role of "village crier . . . who went through the village each evening announcing the news of the day and activities planned for the next day." An extension of this role can be seen today in the status of the "interpreter" at religious dances, who announces to the assembly the import of a message "spoken out" by individual participants or leaders. There were also messengers to carry news and announcements to other villages.*

came to call on the reservation in the mid-1940s. Two Westerns were filmed in the foothills of the Blue Mountains, featuring many tribal members and herds of Indian-owned horses. The sting of having to dress up as Indians in braided wigs and dark makeup was relieved in part by the pride shown in the vast herds and horsemanship that tribal members displayed in the films.

Traditional Leadership

It must be clearly understood that the Euro-Americans have always remained ignorant of the true meaning of tribal leadership. Indians have conformed to the white peo-ple's usage of the term "chief," for example, which for them is a person who maintains absolute control over the people, like a foreign monarch. For the Sahaptian-speaking peoples, such a person does not exist; but because the term has been used so frequently in Indian-white relations, the Indians have conformed to its usage. For the Indian people, the term "chief" may be spoken as *mayux* or *miyoxat* in Umatilla or Nez Perce. The term more accurately denotes "leadership," whereby such a person, whether man or woman, is vested with the responsibility of seeking and promoting the will of the people.

Hereditary leadership was in place when Andrew Allen was the crier, but no one stepped forward to take his place. By the time Andrew was too old for the part, everyone spoke English and announcements at Round-Up were taken over by loudspeaker. His nephew Kenny Allen wanted to claim the place (he lived in Idaho on the Nez Perce Reservation, but he was enrolled here). He had a severe case of diabetes and passed away many years ago. There is an urgency about some of the descendants who inherit those roles, that they have a right to step forward and take them. Bill and Andrew were two primary figures. It is important to relate that we had a sovereign image that predated "discovery" by Lewis and Clark.

As sovereignty was practiced in a traditional sense, leaders were bound with a responsibility. People gathered to talk about essential things, such as politics and celebrations. The people needed to stay focused on working together, especially since the artificial boundaries of the reservation were set down. The 1950s proved to be a critical point where change was concerned. When the chiefs such as Kanine and Wocatsie passed away, the crier role passed away, too. No one encouraged the next generation. Elders used to encourage the roles to continue. The role of encourager was the elder's role.

*Helen Schuster, "Yakima Indian Traditionalism: A Study in Continuity and Change" (Ph.D. diss., University of Washington, 1975), 54.

The Great Sioux Uprising was filmed in the Blue Mountains using local Indians as actors and their horses. Chief Clarence Burke is seated third from right.

Such leadership contained the elements of the inherent sovereign powers that were passed on through the generations since time immemorial. After all, at the Treaty of 1855, the principal negotiators said that the Umatilla, Walla Walla, and Cayuse people would be recognized, from that time on, as the Umatilla Nation. Not so, because in modern times the three principal bands developed a tribal constitution and became known as the Confederated Tribes of the Umatilla Indian Reservation. Unlike a nation, a confederation conformed to the wants and needs of a predatory nation, the United States government. In the assimilation process, the government officials found that the so-called Indian chiefs, religious leaders, and other prominent people stood in the way of the government's aim to "Americanize" the Indian people.

Plateau leadership was premised on a strong religious value system that recognized an all-powerful Supreme Being, with the land as Earth-Mother. An Indian leader was not a leader until he or she absorbed the teachings from the elders at a young age. For example, water was sacred, and the young children were sent to bathe every morning at the dawning light. In the early morning hours, the elders lit the fires for the sweathouses, and everyone took the time to pray to the Creator, give thanks for a new day, and pray for the people. Along the Grande Ronde River and other places, once the men chose a place to camp the first thing they did was build a sweathouse. That was when the horsemen took the fur-skin saddle blankets off their horses and placed them over a domelike wooden frame and proceeded to "make sweat."[81] This was something that the white people never understood, because it was non-Christian. Therefore, it was stereotyped as an evil practice. Leadership began as the children learned how to physically and spiritually cleanse themselves before the Creator, in a chapel in the wild, through song and prayer. Through the sweathouse, the Plateau people always lived a clean life.

The three principal bands, although forced to live on a reservation, managed to carry on their traditional forms of leadership. Due to the BIA's efforts to wipe out tribal traditions, however, very little information has been found about chieftain leadership. As for the Walla Walla line of chiefs, "Meanatete" or "Pierre" was listed as "head chief"; "Homli" was listed as "peace and war chief."[82] It was not known when Pierre was born or when he died. Homli was born on 1820, but with no date listed when he passed away. As it appeared, Pierre was favored by the Bureau officials, and Homli was treated more like a troublemaker because he continued to follow the ancient religious belief of his forefathers.

Chiefs were chosen based on their ability to promote traditions, especially that of carrying on the Seven Drum religion. That may not have been a strict rule, but the Jefferson Peace Medal gifted by Lewis and Clark to a tribal leader may not have survived into the twentieth century if it had not been passed on to such capable leadership, from chief to chief. As for the Umatillas, there were Chief Peo and Chief Amos Pond, with Pond succeeding Peo. The chiefs lay buried in the Tutuilla church cemetery. Captain Sumpkin was recognized as a Umatilla war chief, too. As for the Cayuses, there was Chief Red Hawk and Chief Luke Cowapoo. Chief Umapine was a Cayuse war chief, and Charley Whirlwind was a Cayuse Indian Doctor. In speaking about Cayuse and Umatilla leaders, this has proved to be problematic for the historical record, because very few studies have been conducted. Now it is made worse with the peoples' oral traditions diminishing.

The chiefs were very compassionate toward the younger generation, because they always made sure that future generations were cared for. For example, active leaders in the allotting question in the late months of 1916 were Billy Joshua, Umapine, Amos Pond, No-Shirt, Wanako, and Otis Halfmoon, who were later joined by James Kash Kash. They decided to send tribal delegates to Washington, D.C., to represent their cause. In 1917, Billy Joshua and Otis Halfmoon were the chiefs' messengers, and they presented a bill to the congressional lawmakers about the children who were not allotted lands on the reservation. As Halfmoon voiced and advocated the chiefs' concerns, the congressmen were impressed at how well-organized the delegates were in arguing their case. With that, this proved to be a major victory for the chiefs, as the Senate and House approved the bill and ruled in favor of allotting lands to the children enrolled on the Umatilla Indian Reservation.[83]

Chiefs in the Period of Transition

To many Indian people, especially those who have knowledge of their traditional tribal value systems, democratic elections more often than not create artificial elites who then rule more or less in an arbitrary manner.

— Tom Holm, "The Crisis in Tribal Government"[84]

The Tribes held onto tribal traditions even while a business council was being formed which held the responsibility of developing a modern tribal constitution. There were a number of chiefs of the three bands as late as the first half of the twentieth century. All were involved in decision making just before the 1949 Constitution and By-Laws were developed. In the early 1900s, the chieftainship was strong, and all of the leaders used to meet on a regular basis. A trust relationship existed between the government and Indian people that was parental in nature. This dynamic led most people to assume that there was no prior organization among the Indians, but in

reality the chiefs had real authority and concern for the people. The chiefs of the Tribes during this time period conducted and managed tribal affairs. Indian religion was also at the center of our cultural lifeways, as reflected in the 1855 Treaty. Chieftain leadership began to be threatened during this period. The traditional roles were not recognized in the tribal constitution. Every tribe in the nation was faced with developing a constitution, and that affected the traditional roles. The U.S. government did not allow for the traditional roles to continue as part of the constitutional process.

With the development of the Business Committee, the stage was set for the adoption of the tribal constitution in 1949. Conflict with traditional leadership came into play at that time and holds true to this day. Chieftainship became arbitrary. The effect of modern governance took away the traditional base of knowledge. In 1949, a news article appeared in a local newspaper: "Rule by Chiefs Is Ending: Indians Adopt Constitution." The article gave a brief account of how the Tribes made the move and took the necessary steps to develop a Constitution and By-Laws. It was mentioned that the Tribes had developed a new form of government that replaced the older forms of tribal governance based on chieftain leadership.

In the realm of traditional leadership, the chiefs were bound by unwritten laws and were obligated to pass on their knowledge to the younger generation through oral traditions. Contrary to popular belief, the people represented the sovereign status of a nation and the chiefs only echoed the voice of the people. This was particularly the case in caring for the needs of the children. It was the chiefs who often said, *"Inmímam miyánashma"* or *"Naknúwishaash inmi miyánashma"* — 'Watch out for the children'. The newspapers also mentioned that two years before, in 1947, efforts had been made to revive traditional forms of chieftainship, but they had failed. It was said that a council was created to take the place of the chieftain leadership, but a council forum had always been a part of the Tribes' governing system.[85]

Indian Citizenship and a Non-IRA Tribe

By an act of Congress, tribal members enrolled on Indian reservations became U.S. citizens in 1924, with the right to vote for the first time. For some, this may have been heralded as a major victory, but the underlying truth was that the federal government, through Congress, wanted to place the Indian people on the threshold of "civilization." It was the determined effort of Congress to solve the Indian problem by granting citizenship and, by that, having the Indians abandon their reservation home bases and become absorbed into mainstream American society.

In 1934, Congress passed the Indian Reorganization Act to reestablish tribal governments and tribal societies under reformist Indian Commissioner John Collier. The same year, Congress passed the Johnson O'Malley Act to provide funds to public schools for the education of Indian students. The next year, a tribal referendum rejected the Indian Reorganization Act of 1934 by a vote of 299 to 155. The total reservation population at the time was 1,140, with 681 eligible to vote; 454 voted on the issue. After the IRA was enacted into law, the BIA officials traveled from reservation to reservation to impress on the Indians that they should accept and implement the act's provisions to adopt a formal means of governing themselves. There existed some misgivings about their proposals, however, because it meant that tribes would have to give up their old ways and draft and adopt a tribal constitution. In most cases, the BIA coerced Indian tribes into adopting "template" constitutions that purposely left out traditional forms of leadership. As a result, "BIA records indicate that 181 tribes voted to accept the IRA and 77 tribes voted to reject the IRA."[86]

What is an "IRA tribe"? The IRA tribes have committed themselves to be more accountable to the federal government through the secretary of the Interior, especially in adopting tribal resolutions, where it is indicated that such resolutions are subject to secretary of Interior approval. This gave BIA officials veto power over important tribal government decisions made by resolution. With the lawmakers promoting termination, the federal government maintained a paternalistic grip on every action taken by tribal governments.

Traditions Lost and Found

The July Celebration encampment would last a week as people camped together on the July Grounds, where the tribal offices stand today. While centered around the veterans' honor ceremony, there were also games, horse races, songs, dances, and serenading at night. Today, they are held on the Fourth of July, not in keeping with America's Independence Day but simply as a convenient borrowing of that date. As the July Celebration began to fade in the early 1950s, it was a pivotal point in history for the three principal bands, because the old leaders were passing away. Noted leaders of that time included Wilfred Minthorn, Joe Thompson, and Amy Webb, who were in charge of give-aways; whipmen, Tom Johnson and Mitchell Lloyd; and whipwoman Magaret White–Wilkinson. In the early 1960s, Annie Johnson put on a big dinner to reaffirm the line of whipwomen roles for the Tribes, making sure that the whip was passed on to Janie Wilkinson Pond.[87] Other noted leaders were Tom Joe, George Spino, and Louise Long Hair. Chiefs played a prominent role in carrying on traditions, and they were supported by a circle of elders on the reservation.

At the summer solstice, the people gathered for a large encampment, where a memorial horse parade, rejoining, Indian namings, and give-aways took place. According to an elder, that marked the time of the year when the people in charge of give-aways began to keep count of the ones who had passed away after the summer encampment. From that point on, and when a whole year had elapsed and the summer solstice came again, the leaders in charge of the give-aways consulted with each of the families who had lost loved ones during the year and made preparations for the big memorial event. It was a time for grieving, yet also a time for happiness and joy. If a respected lady elder had passed away, for instance, the family selected someone to wear her regalia during the horse parade, and that was when friends and relatives shed tears and then rejoiced and showed respect for her accomplishments in life.[88] Tribal elder Dan Motanic, now in his nineties, said that those old people chose the summer solstice because it was the longest time of the year. This holds two important points. On the day of the sun, the longest day, those people who pass away after that time, the families are recognized first. When people leave that circle in the past year, they have priority.

Through assimilationist policies, the government discouraged such important tribal ceremonies, not knowing that the people were showing respect to the ones who had passed on before them. On the importance of the annual event, one elder said: "When you dance, you dance with pride because you're showing yourself and dancing for the Creator and giving thanks for everything that you have."[89]

When we have the July Celebration and we parade around, according to elder Ike Patrick, what we emulate in this revitalization is warriors coming back from somewhere. The warriors would stop a mile from camp and ride in bareback. They always brought an empty horse to symbolize the warriors who did not return. A rider would go ahead and inform the crier, who would disseminate news of the battle. They also sang when they left and when they returned. The singer was at the front. The *papuu* song 'the little owl that burrows' shows how closely related we were when the Nez Perce War broke out. They sang the song there, too. There was a little boy who communicated with the owl, and the owl gave him his song. It was the owl's war song.[90] Honor in the warrior culture and pride in our veterans has never ceased from the traditional times to now. In 1941, for example, following the attack on Pearl Harbor, many enrolled members volunteered or were drafted for military duty. So many reservation men were part of the war effort in World War II that when they returned home, deer and elk were crossing the reservation roads in their plentifulness.

In the face of so much loss, there were interesting ways of making sure that we still promoted our own culture locally. Traditional roles were still practiced but in new contexts, such as at the Pendleton Round-Up, where serenading often took place in the village. The chieftainship was still honored even after the establishment of the tribal modern government. At the Round-Up, we still had the camp crier, which was a traditional role. We still had the July Grounds celebrations and honored the warrior tradition there. We still

had our ceremonies, and the practicing of the Indian religion began again. Simultaneously with the effects of assimilation, traditions stayed strong. Reminiscences of the past regarding horse roundups and traditional gathering places in the Blue Mountains are prevalent in our oral histories. Our story is similar to that of every other Indian tribe in the country. They all went through many of the same things. Some suffered more, and their traditions were affected far worse. We are fortunate that we retained what traditions we now have.

Conclusion

Consistent with the circle-of-life theme central to tribal culture, the Tribes have given new life to the Treaty and the promise of a tribal homeland. The second century of the Treaty of 1855 is one dedicated to the restoration of its original promise. The Cayuse, Umatilla, and Walla Walla Tribes adopted a constitution for its government on November 4, 1949, and the purpose of that government is clearly established in Article 2:

The purpose and powers of the Confederated Tribes shall be, within law, to exercise and protect all existing and future tribal rights arising from any source whether treaty, federal statute, state statute, common law, or otherwise; to achieve a maximum degree of self-government in all tribal affairs; and to protect and promote the interests of the Indians of the Umatilla Indian Reservation.

The new tribal government faced a difficult challenge — how to restore the reservation land base, the water, the fish, and other resources that had been reserved by the Treaty but had been taken away. Familiar with and respectful of their ancestors' commitment to the Treaty, tribal leaders have relentlessly pursued the homeland and the resources the Treaty reserved.

There is an innocence as well, in the sense that the three bands are an extended family. We all had responsibilities for the children. We all had a hand in it. We are three large families bound together to care for one another. This was evident in our grandfathers' time. Sadly, the churches are no longer filled since the elders have left us. A large number of our people no longer worship. The longhouse is there, but the moral values are not being impressed upon the young people. Yet, things have remained. Many people have been taken in and mentored by distant relations. Sometimes it is the simplest traditions that are passed down, such as you always make sweathouse for the woman folks; you don't just do it for yourself. Men sweat first but make sure there are enough rocks for the women. The Indians had to resolve these things spiritually. We had a Creator. Most tribes had one powerful Supreme Being. People had a way of preparing themselves. They have inherited the *wéyekin* and *šúkwat* 'spiritual knowledge'. When you have an Indian name, you are grounded. You are never too old to learn, and it is never too late. That is what the old people would tell me.

For generations, there was a system to who we were and how we were grounded. It was displayed in the leadership and shown even in the long-term efforts by the federal government to change us. It is a miracle that we have survived. Congress was on a mission to determine which tribes were progressive and ready to sever ties with the government. The BIA had a goal in mind — to deal with what they called the "Indian Problem." The thinking was: "We have their land now, so how do we force them into the mainstream?" Farming was one way. In our Treaty, there were supposed to be mills and tracts for farming.

The government wanted to wash their hands of the "Indian Problem." One reason we have so many social problems is because we came so close to losing our identity. Our leadership was intact and communicating their protests, but the non-Indians did not listen to them. Indians are very reserved. They were not going to scream and yell about it. They say things only once. Maladies are in Indian communities, and they are directly tied to the social problems of the twentieth century. We hope to have shown cause and effect, which will bring this to light.

Indians live by signs. Signs are the messages that are there, whether in coyote or other animals. The elders could talk freely about these things at one time. We have to reassert who we are as Indians, become involved in the traditions, and listen to those signs.

Notes

1. 18 U.S.C. §1162, 28 U.S.C. §1360.

2. Charles F. Wilkinson, *Blood Struggle: The Rise of Indian Nations* (New York: Norton, 2005), xii.

3. James E. Falkowski, *Indian Law/Race Law: A Five Hundred Year History* (New York: Praeger, 1992), 100.

4. Wilcomb E. Washburn, *The American Indian and the United States: A Documentary History* (New York: Random House, 1973), 119.

5. Judith Nies, *Native American History: A Chronology of the Vast Achievements of a Culture and their Links to World Events* (New York: Ballantine Books, 1996), 222, 223.

6. Diane Mallikan, National Park Service, conversation with the author, 2004.

7. Russell Thornton, *American Indian Holocaust and Survival: A Population History Since 1492* (Norman: University of Oklahoma Press, 1987), 43.

8. Jeff Zucker et al., *Oregon Indians: Culture, History and Cultural Affairs* (Portland: Oregon Historical Society Press, 1983), 100.

9. Zucker et al., *Oregon Indians,* 82.

10. "Oregon Indian Profiles," insert in ibid.

11. *Missouri v. Holland*, 252 U.S. 416 (1920). This Supreme Court declaration did not arise in a case where an Indian treaty was at issue. The case involved the State of Missouri's challenge of the United States' enforcement of the Migratory Bird Treaty Act, which enforced a treaty between the United States and Great Britain executed on December 8, 1916, to protect birds whose annual migrations traversed the United States and Canada.

12. In *Lone Wolf v. Hitchcock*, 187 U.S. 553 (1903), the Court held that when "treaties were entered into between the United States and a tribe of Indians it was never doubted that the power to abrogate existed in Congress. . . ."

13. 1860 Report of Commissioner of Indian Affairs, 177.

14. 1862 Report of Commissioner of Indian Affairs, 258.

15. 1860 Report of Commissioner of Indian Affairs, 176.

16. 1861 Report of Commissioner of Indian Affairs, 24. The agent's reports did not describe all three of the tribes in the same way. The agent spoke very highly of the Cayuse and Umatilla Tribes, but was less laudatory of the Walla Wallas, which the agent described in the 1860 Report as "much deteriorated by vicious indulgences."

17. 1860 Report of Commissioner of Indian Affairs, 259.

18. 1860 Report of Commissioner of Indian Affairs, 177. The agent also expressed concern about the "predatory forays of the Snake Indians."

19. 1866 Report of Commissioner of Indian Affairs, 87.

20. 1868 Report of Commissioner of Indian Affairs, 68.

21. Ibid.

22. Beginning in 1869, the agent reports on mining, and gold mining in particular, as attracting more settlers. See 1869 Report of Commissioner of Indian Affairs.

23. Terence O'Donnell, *An Arrow in the Earth: General Joel Palmer and the Indians of Oregon* (Portland: Oregon Historical Society Press, 1991), 206.

24. Ibid., 138-9.

25. The City of Pendleton was named after Senator George H. Pendleton of Ohio, who was the vice-presidential candidate on the Democratic Party ticket in 1864, which was defeated by the Republican incumbent President Abraham Lincoln. See www.pendleton.or.us/history.

26. Mildred Searcey, *Way Back When* (Pendleton: East Oregonian, 1972), 50.

27. A Petition of the Citizens of the Town of Pendleton, Oregon, March 29, 1870, forwarded to A.B. Meacham, superintendent of Indian affairs, by Boyle of Umatilla Indian Agency.

28. Letter, May 16, 1870, from E.S. Parker, Commissioner of Indian Affairs, authorizing Indian Affairs to grant requests in LaDow, et al. Petition.

29. Letter to citizens of Pendleton from E.S. Parker, Commissioner of Indian Affairs, Department of the Interior, May 16, 1870; referenced in 1885 Umatilla Allotment Act.

30. 1870 Report of Commissioner of Indian Affairs, 50. This Umatilla Agency report was filed by Acting Agent Lt. W.H. Boyle, United States Army.

31. 1871 Report of Commissioner of Indian Affairs, filed by Umatilla agency Indian Agent N.A. Cornoyer, 313.

32. Act of August 5, 1882, Chapter 392, 22 Stat. 297 [hereafter 1882 Act].

33. 1882 Act, Section 7.

34. Senate Report 234, 48th Cong., 1st sess., February 27, 1884. The House Committee on Indian Affairs issued a similar report on the House Bill, H.R. 1290, H.R. 387, 48th Cong., 1st sess., February 20, 1884.

35. The heart of the General Allotment Act may be found at 25 U.S.C. §331. The loss of Indian lands was estimated by John Collier in a memorandum submitted to the House Committee on Indian Affairs in connection with H.R. 7902, 73rd Cong., 2d sess. (1934). He summarized the loss of Indian lands as follows: "Through sales by the Government of the fictitiously designated 'surplus' lands; through sales by allottees after the trust period had ended or had been terminated by administrative act; and through sales by the Government of heirship land, virtually mandatory under the allotment act: Through these three methods, the total of Indian landholdings has been cut from 138,000,000 acres in 1887 to 48,000,000 acres in 1934." Collier's memorandum was cited in David H. Getches et al., *Cases and Materials on Federal Indian Law* (St. Paul, Minn.: West Publishing, 1979), 74.

36. Senate report, S.B. 66.

37. Ibid., Section 5.

38. Order of Secretary of the Interior, December 4, 1888, defining boundaries of Umatilla Reservation, Oregon.

39. The amendment to the Umatilla Allotment Act was provided by the Act of June 29, 1888, Chapter 1186, 25 Stat. 558 [hereafter 1888 Amendment]. This Act was principally designed to grant a railroad right-of-way through the Fond du Lac Indian Reservation. In section 8 of the Act, however, the Umatilla Allotment Act was amended.

40. In the Secretarial Order, which comprises just two pages, the term "diminished reservation" is used nine times.

41. 1890 Annual Report of Commissioner of Indian Affairs, l, li.

42. 1891 Annual Report of Commissioner of Indian Affairs, 379.

43. Act of May 29, 1928, Chaps. 9 and 12, 45 Stat. 1008.

44. Act of August 10, 1939, Chap. 662, 53 Stat. 1351.

45. Secretarial Order No. 8383, Order of Restoration, Umatilla Reservation, Oregon, signed by E.K. Burlew, Acting Secretary of the Interior, March 20, 1940. The Secretarial Order states that "all lands which are now, or may hereafter be classified as undisposed of surplus open or ceded lands of the Umatilla Indian Reservation, Oregon, are hereby restored to tribal ownership for the use and benefit of the Indians of the Umatilla Reservation, and are added to and made a part of the Umatilla Indian Reservation. . . ."

46. *Winter v. U.S,*. 207 U.S. 564 (1908); Article 1, 12 Stat. 945.

47. Article 1 of the Treaty states "That the exclusive right of taking fish in the streams running through and bordering said reservation is hereby secured said Indians, and that all other usual and accustomed stations in common with citizens of the United States. . . ." See Treaty of 1855, Articles 2 and 3 (payment of federal funds to the Tribes for ceded lands to be expended by the president for "opening and fencing farms, breaking land, purchasing teams, wagons, agricultural implements and seeds, for clothing, provision and tools, for medical purposes, providing mechanics and farmers . . .") and Article 4 (United States agreed to erect a saw mill, a flouring mill, one blacksmith shop, one building for wagon and plough maker, dwellings for a miller, farmer, superintendent of farming operations, blacksmith, and wagon and plough maker). Other references to an agricultural purpose in the Treaty are found in Articles 5 and 6.

48. See, for example, *Arizona v. California*, 373 U.S. 546 (1963), decree entered 376 U.S. 340 (1964), supplemental decree entered, 439 U.S. 419 (1979); *In Re* Rights To Use Water In Big Horn River, 753 P.2d 76, (Wyo. 1988), aff'd by an equally divided court, sub nom., *Wyoming v. United States*, 492 U.S. 406 (1989). See *United States v. Adair*, 478 F.Supp. 336, 345 (D. Or. 1979); aff'd 723 F.2d 1394 (9th Cir. 1984) cert. denied sub nom., *Oregon v. United States*, 467 U.S. 1252 (1984); *Colville Confederated Tribes v. Walton*, 460 F.Supp. 1320, aff'd, 647 F.2d 42 (9th Cir. 1980) cert. denied, 454 U.S. 1092 (1981); enforced, *Colville Confederated Tribes v. Walton*, 752 F.2d 397 (9th Cir. 1985); *United States v. Anderson*, 736 F.2d 1358 (9th Cir. 1984); *Kittitas Reclamation District v. Sunnyside Valley Irrigation District*, 763 F.2d 1032 (9th Cir. 1985), cert. denied, 474 U.S. 1032 (1985); *Muckleshoot Indian Tribe v. Trans-Canada Enterprises*, Ltd., 713 F.2d 455 (9th Cir. 1983), cert. denied, 465 U.S. 1049 (1984); *Joint Board of Control of the Flathead, Mission & Jocko Irrigation District v. United States*, 832 F.2d 1127 (9th Cir. 1987). *In Re* Rights To Use Water In Big Horn River, 753 P.2d 76, 99 (Wyo. 1988), aff'd by an equally divided court, sub nom., *Wyoming v. United States*, 492 U.S. 406 (1989). Ibid.; *Arizona v. California*, 376 U.S. at 344; *United States v. Powers*, 305 U.S. 527, 533 (1939); United States v. Walker Irrigation District, 104 F.2d 334, 340 (9th Cir. 1934); United States ex rel. Ray v. Hibner, 27 F.2d 909, 911 (D.C. Idaho 1928); Conrad Investment Co. v. United States, 161 F. 829, 831-32 (9th Cir. 1908).

49. Jeffrey Charles Reichwein, "North American Response to Euro-American Contact in the Columbia Plateau of Northwestern North America, 1840 to 1914: An Anthropological Interpretation Based on Written and Pictorial Ethnohistorical Data" (unpublished manuscript, 1988), 30.

50. Memorial of the Legislature of Oregon, Senate Misc. Doc. No. 53, 43rd Cong. 2nd sess. The memorial was referred to the Senate Committee on Indian Affairs on January 25, 1875.

51. *East Oregonian*, December 22, 1877, cited in Robert H. Ruby and John A. Brown, *The Cayuse Indians: Imperial Tribesmen of Old Oregon* (Norman: University of Oklahoma Press, 1972), 279.

52. 1878 Annual Report of Commissioner of Indian Affairs, filed by Umatilla agency Indian Agent, N.A. Cornoyer, August 23, 1878, 123.

53. Ibid., xxxvii.

54. House Report, 1953, 628

55. Sam L. Rogers, *Indian Population in the United States and Alaska* (Washington, D.C.: GPO, 1915), 95. See other population figures and economic conditions on the Umatilla Reservation in the BIA Investigation Study.

56. D'Arcy McNickle, *Native American Tribalism: Indian Survivals and Renewals* (1973; reprint, New York: Oxford University Press, 1993), 82, 83.

57. Zucker et al., *Oregon Indians*, 100.

58. Ibid., 101.

59. House Report, 1953, 158–9.

60. House Report, 1953, 159, 160, 164.

61. Elzie Farrow, Oral Story, as told in the 1990s, in Ron Pond's collection.

62. Bob Perry, Oral Tale, Mission Long House, 1980s, in Ron Pond's collection.

63. Isaac Patrick, Oral Tale, early 1980s, in Ron Pond's collection.

64. In the 1970s, this story was told at the sweathouse by the co-author's maternal uncle, Charley Wocatsie, in Ron Pond's collection.

65. The co-author's father Walter Pond attended the Medicine Dances because he was related to both the respected elders.

66. Isaac Patrick, Oral Tales, 1970s, in Ron Pond's collection.

67. Marvin Patrick, Oral Tale, as told at the sweathouse in the 1980s, in Ron Pond's collection.

68. Cyrus Wilkinsen, Oral Tale. Wilkinsen was an enrolled Nez Perce but married Margaret White-Wilkinsen, who was an enrolled member of the Umatilla Tribe. In Ron Pond's collection.

69. Elizabeth Wocatsie-Jones, Oral Tale, as told in the 1980s, in Ron Pond's collection.

70. Bill Minthorn, a.k.a. Chief Blackhawk, Oral Tale, as told in the 1980s, in Ron Pond's collection.

71. Patrick, Oral Tale, 1970s.

72. Chief Raymond Burke, Oral Tale, as told in the 1980s, in Ron Pond's collection.

73. Isaac Patrick, Charley Wocatsie, and McKinley Williams, Oral Tales, as told from the 1960s to the 1970s, in Ron Pond's collection.

74. Chief Clarence Burke, Oral Tale, as told in the 1970s, in Ron Pond's collection.

75. Henry Whitestone, A Sweathouse Story, as told in the 1970s, in Ron Pond's collection.

76. Isaac Patrick, A Sweathouse Story, as told in the 1970s, in Ron Pond's collection.

77. Whitestone, A Sweathouse Story.

78. Charlie Wocatsie, Oral Teaching, as taught from the 1950s through the 1970s, in Ron Pond's collection.

79. Burke, Oral Tale.

80. Patrick, Oral Tale.

81. Patrick, A Sweathouse Story.

82. Alexander Gunkel, *Culture in Conflict: A Study of Contrasted Interrelations and Reactions Between Europeans and the Wallawalla Indians of Washington State* (Dept. of Anthropology, Southern Illinois University, Carbondale, 1978), 55.

83. "Halfmoon Remembers Success In Capital," *East Oregonian*, January 1, 1947.

84. In Michael K. Green, ed., *Issues in Native American Cultural Identity* (New York: P. Lang, 1995).

85. Jim B. Anderson, "Rule by Chiefs Is Ending: Indians Adopt Constitution," *Walla Walla Bulletin*, November 27, 1947.

86. See Arlene Hirschfelder and Martha Kreipe de Montano, *The Native American Almanac: A Portrait of Native America Today* (New York: Prentice Hall, 1993), 74.

87. Anna Jane Pond, Oral Tradition, as told in 2005, in Ron Pond's collection.

88. Elizabeth Jones, Oral Tradition, as told in 1992, when the Memorial Horse Parade was revived, in Ron Pond's collection.

89. Isaac Patrick, Oral Tradition, as told in the 1970s, in Ron Pond's collection.

90. Marvin "Wish" Patrick, Oral Tale, in Ron Pond's collection.

Indians Then and Now

I do not recite these incidents to build sympathy for my people; rather that you may understand and realize how all-embracing was the catastrophe that had fallen upon our people and how shattered they were. This is the story of every tribe. Their histories are the same — loss of homelands, enforced emigration, enforced idleness, poverty, segregation, defeat. Indian economies were completely destroyed, which consisted of hunting, fishing, and gathering of wild fruits and roots. This was replaced by their total subsistence with limited farming operations on lands the white man didn't want.

To add to the misery and subjugation of this so-called past history, fallacious beliefs hold that the Indian clings so stubbornly to his established way of life because of some innate racial defect or character deficiency that renders him unable to attain standards of white culture. Social delinquencies, excessive drinking, shiftlessness — where these exist, are often termed as racial weaknesses, rather than for what they are: symptoms of conflicts in any human race. Forcing a sense of inferiority upon us has held us in bondage more securely than prisons or bars. Pressure from every side has been exerted upon us, pressure that has injured our pride and racial heritage and, by implication, has weakened confidence in our own abilities. We have seen our people overwhelmed by the most grievous poverty and pauperized by enforced dependence, degenerated because of race and color. Today science tells us there are no superior races, that the color of one's skin is no mark or distinction of superiority. In short, blood in one's veins is but a moment's flow.

Let us now examine the record of how the U.S. government has discharged its responsibilities and fulfilled obligations to the letter as they claim. You must be the judge. The Bureau of Indian Affairs, since its foundation, has been a closed corporation. Its functions have never been guided by the Constitution or Bill of Rights in the management of our affairs. Contrary to early predictions and policy that the Indians were a dying race, today there is an estimated 450,000 population in the U.S. and Alaska whose affairs are the concern of the federal government. The dominating factor of Indian reservation life has been the federal government expressed in terms of hundreds of Indian Agents and thousands of field staff employees appointed by the Secretary of the Interior and the commissioner of Indian Affairs. For no other citizens or groups has the government in such magnitude intruded so completely into all aspects of life, property, private life, and even personal affairs than that of the Indians. From this has emanated vicious and unfounded insinuations that the government doles out monthly cash grants to the Indians. This has created unnecessary ill feeling because many believe we get many things for nothing at the taxpayer's expense.

Today the U.S. government, who accepted the obligations and responsibilities of the Indians through treaties, is ready to withdraw, and wants termination of trusteeship of the Indians. This government advocates its termination under the guise of "freeing" the Indian, without explaining that freedom. More than one-quarter of the Indian population haven't one square foot of land, the sole means of their livelihood. More than 400 years of despoliation have left the majority landless. The freedom the government advocates for the Indian means in truth the destruction of reservation community life, and will more completely destroy and remove all safeguards provided by treaty and law, which now protect Indian property and civil rights. It will further deprive us of all protection and assistance by the government. Under the new policy of this so-called freedom, our agents urge us to sell our fractionated inherited lands as the only solution, which they have never

attempted to settle under any means so the land could be reserved to the heirs. Oil and rich minerals have been discovered on Indian lands today, bringing sudden wealth which they are unable to competently manage. Termination of federal trusteeship will in truth put the remainder of Indian lands on the market for sale. Lands will be taxed as another means to force us to sell. We were given begrudging citizenship in 1924 with the right to vote as any other citizen. As registered voters in our respective counties we have voted for congressmen and presidents hoping for some consideration. We have helped better conditions for others with neglect of our own, by trying to be good citizens. Congressmen yield blindly to the importunities of voters concerning Indians, without knowing facts and reasons why Indians oppose termination of federal wardship. The government informs the public of the high cost of support to the Indians. Yet it has a bottomless purse for help of foreign nations. Our Indians have gone to Washington, and pathetically pleaded for aid and for a better deal for their people. The answer is always a cold, "Uncle Sam has no more money for the Indians," but lets Nehru come over and he is royally received and the answer to his begging is always an empathic yes. We have attained none of the freedom and equality for which thousands of our Indian sons have fought and died for. Veteran's privileges are limited to the Indian ex-service man. We have thousands of young men today in every branch of the armed forces. Disregarding discrimination they suffer, they are ready to serve their country, not only for the Indians but also for all American citizens. They are neither bitter nor prejudiced, but they believe that the preservation of freedom and equality for themselves, their Indian people, and neighbors is worth fighting for.

Unfounded insinuations that we receive monthly cash gifts and rations from the government as treaty obligations have created unnecessary prejudice by an uninformed and uneducated public. Indians receive monthly checks only if they own property. Income placed in the agencies comes from lease rentals and other resources individually or tribally owned, and not government. The government has given limited assistance in welfare, education, and health, which no longer exists because they have been transferred to state and county departments where reservations exist. The federal government buys nothing for the Indians; all personal property is bought the same as you buy, for cash or on contract. If we pay we keep it; if we fall behind maybe we lose it just as you do. We pay taxes of every type even on income, our only exemption is our lands held in trust, and if taxed would absorb all the income in rentals from them. These lands are held in trust, an obligation arising from our treaty and have been guaranteed to us to remain tax-free forever in consideration for all other lands we have and were forced to give up.

Our hunting and fishing rights granted by our treaty are being contested today. Indians have observed laws of game conservation for generations before the white man set foot on this continent. Where game has been depleted has been no fault of the Indian. They never kill for sheer sport. On March 10, 1953, we signed another agreement taking away the last link of our forefathers for a cash settlement of $4,198, Celilo Falls, the ancient fishing site used for centuries by our people. Giving up these rights, agreeably though reluctantly, has in no measure protected us from being stripped of others without our consent or agreement.

Maudie C. Antoine, Chairwoman, Board of Trustees, Confederated Tribes of the Umatilla Indian Reservation. These remarks were made at the 1855 Treaty Centennial observance in Walla Walla, Washington, June 11, 1955.

The Beginning of Modern Tribal Governance and Enacting Sovereignty

Charles F. Luce and William Johnson

Just prior to the middle of the twentieth century, the internal governance of the Confederated Tribes of the Umatilla Indian Reservation was little changed from what it had been fifty or seventy-five years before. The world outside the reservation, however, had gone through dramatic change, and those changes were presenting daunting challenges to the members and the government of the Tribes. In response, the Confederated Tribes would go through dramatic changes of our own. In some cases, we would score astonishing successes. Others would leave our tribal membership divided and demoralized. Yet, the ultimate consequence of this period was to leave the Tribes singularly qualified to capitalize on the opportunities that would be presented by the era that would follow — the era of self-determination.

Part I: The Early Years

Charles F. Luce

In 1946, as America's wartime economy adjusted to peacetime, things on the Umatilla Reservation were about the same as they had been before the war. Of the 1,200 or so enrolled tribal members, about 600 lived on the reservation. Some 80,000 acres of the reservation were rich farmland growing wheat or peas. Over the past fifty years, about half of this farmland had passed into white ownership. The remaining 30,000 to 40,000 acres were held in trust by the Bureau of Indian Affairs for Indian owners. The pattern of ownership was checkerboard; white and Indian-owned parcels of 160, 80, or 40 acres or less were interspersed. The Indian trust parcels often were owned by more than one individual, sometimes by as many as six or eight adults and children.

Almost all Indian-owned farmland was leased to white farmers who owned large ranches outside the reservation. The small size of Indian-owned parcels, the multiple ownerships of many of those parcels, and the high cost of farm machinery made it impracticable for tribal members to farm their parcels. Leases of Indian trust lands required approval by the superintendent of the reservation, Henry Roe Cloud. Roe Cloud was a Winnebago Indian who earned distinction as the first full-blood Indian to graduate from Yale University. He served on the commission for the Meriam Report of 1928 as a vocal proponent of Indian education. In the 1930s and 1940s, he worked in several capacities for the BIA. In 1947, he arrived on the reservation as superintendent of the Umatilla Agency, where he was met with a mixed welcome by a tribal membership that was leery of the Bureau even if it was headed up by an American Indian.

Roe Cloud was a model for Indians in higher education, but that reputation would actually work against him in this setting. The battle on the Umatilla Reservation at the time had more to do with fighting off potential land grabs by non-Indians. If Superintendent Roe Cloud did not require competitive bidding for new leases — and he did not — Indian owners of trust lands were at the mercy of the white rancher who held the previous lease. As a result, the owners were receiving scandalously low rent, as little as one-fifth or one-sixth of the rent that a white rancher would pay to lease white-owned farmland of equal quality. Superintendent Roe Cloud was assiduously courted by the white ranchers, many of whom were prominent citizens of Pendleton.

Tribal members who lived on the reservation eked out a living by their small rentals, hunting and fishing (especially salmon), government assistance, and such off-reservation jobs as they could find. A few held good-paying off-reservation jobs — printer, rural mail carrier, county highway department workers — but they were the exceptions. Most housing was of poor quality, scattered over the reservation, with no electricity or indoor plumbing.

Tribal governance resided in the General Council, which was simply a meeting held in a barnlike structure. There was little perceived authority in the Council to attract attendance, mainly the enrollment of new tribal members and the leasing of some six hundred acres of tribally owned farmland. That land, incidentally, was farmed by the Umatilla County sheriff who, when his lease was being voted on, sent his deputies out to round up tribal members to attend the Council. Voting was not secret (either by raised hand or by standing), and the superintendent usually attended the Council meeting. Tribal officers elected by the Council included a chairman, vice chairman, secretary, and interpreter. Proceedings often were conducted in the Sahaptian language.

Courtesy of the *Confederated Umatilla Journal*

Sam Kash Kash on the Umatilla Reservation in about 1974

The perceived lack of real authority in the Council, the infrequency and irregularity of its meetings, the small and varying attendance by tribal members, and the superintendent's surveillance of voting made the Council an ineffective body to protect and enhance the welfare of the people and to assert their Treaty rights. The actual governance of the reservation still lay with the superintendent.

Hiring the First Tribal Attorney

Nevertheless, winds of change were blowing across the reservation in 1946. Young tribal members, returning from military service, were unwilling to accept the status quo. A young man, David "Steve" Hall, was elected chair of the General Council, and he appointed a business committee of mostly younger members to function between meetings. Among other actions, they encouraged a newly formed electric cooperative in Eastern Oregon to build lines to serve their people. They also began to consider employment of a tribal attorney. Many other tribes, including the Warm Springs and Yakama, already had tribal lawyers. It was at an organizational meeting of the eastern Oregon Electric Cooperative that members of the Business Committee, including Richard Burke and Sam Kash Kash, met the Cooperative's attorney. I was explaining the terms of the

Cooperative's charter and bylaws and the procedure for obtaining a federal loan to build its lines. Before I had opened my law office in Walla Walla, Washington, in September 1946, I had studied law at the University of Wisconsin and Yale Law School, had clerked for U.S. Supreme Court Justice Hugo L. Black, and had worked as a junior attorney for the Bonneville Power Administration in Portland. I was twenty-nine years old.

A few days after the Eastern Oregon Coop meeting, Richard Burke and his wife Winnie Crane came to my office to employ me to try to renegotiate a lease of their trust land to a white rancher. Richard also asked me if I would be interested in meeting with members of the Business Committee to discuss becoming Umatilla tribal attorney. I said yes.

In February 1947, four members of the Business Committee — Richard Burke, Sam Kash Kash, David Hall, and Louis McFarland — called my office in Walla Walla to interview me as possibly their tribal attorney. They said their immediate concern was to raise the rentals on the tribal members' farmlands and that they were getting little help from Superintendent Roe Cloud. After I told them that I had no clients who farmed their lands and would accept no such clients if I were tribal attorney, Mr. Kash Kash explained that the tribes had only $40,000 or so of cash and asked what I would charge for his services. I suggested a retainer contract of five dollars per hour plus travel expenses. This being agreeable to the four tribal

committeemen, Mr. Kash Kash explained that an attorney contract must be approved by the General Council and the Bureau of Indian Affairs.

Before I appeared before the General Council for inspection at a meeting, I did a little research and found that many tribal members owned interests in rich farmland that ranchers were leasing for six dollars cash per acre to grow wheat and peas. Similar land if white-owned would lease on shares producing twenty-five to thirty-five dollars an acre. I met with Henry Roe Cloud, the superintendent of the reservation, whose approval was required for leases of Indian-owned land. He resisted showing me leases on file in his office and made it clear that he did not want the tribes to hire me.

At the General Council meeting, Sam Kash Kash greeted me by saying that his people would like to hear me make a speech. I was ushered to a platform facing a hundred or so members of the Tribes and Henry Roe Cloud. My extemporaneous speech was autobiographical and concluded with my pledge to get the rents on their farmland raised to the same level as the rents on white-owned farmland. Roe Cloud then rose to say that the Tribe had only $40,000 in its treasury, which should be saved for the members' children; that they could not afford to hire a lawyer and waste their children's inheritance; further, that it was unnecessary to hire me because all the Indian law was contained in a book which he had (he held aloft for all to see a blackbound Title 25, Code of Federal Regulations); that tribal members could ask him the law and he would read to them from the book; and that if they employed me all I would do was ask him the answers to their legal questions and repeat his answers to the tribal members. So there was no reason to employ me.

Thus challenged I had no alternative but to attack Roe Cloud's credibility. Superintendent Roe Cloud, I asserted, was no friend of the Umatillas; a friend would not allow ranchers to rob them by approving six-dollar leases; and his real friends were the ranchers and businessmen.

The Council members then debated in their native Sahaptian language whether to hire me. Speakers would point to me or to Roe Cloud, and neither I nor Roe Cloud had any idea what they were saying. The faces of the four men who had invited me to be tribal lawyer offered no clue. Finally, after several hours, the Council took a standing vote, 58 to 1, to hire me. Many Indians did not vote, perhaps because Roe Cloud was watching. My contract required the approval of the commissioner of Indian Affairs, and Roe Cloud did his best to block it.

The year-long struggle of the Business Committee to employ legal counsel over the determined opposition of Superintendent Roe Cloud — and the struggle of the Committee to assert more authority over other tribal affairs — is epitomized in the transcript of a Business Committee meeting held on February 9, 1948. Present were members Sam Kash Kash, chairman; David S. Hall, secretary; Richard Burke;

Charlie Johnson; Sam Luton; Ike Patrick; and Philip Guyer. Also present at the Committee's request was Superintendent Roe Cloud.

Under persistent questioning by Chairman Kash Kash, Superintendent Roe Cloud finally admitted he had recommended that the commissioner of Indian Affairs not approve my contract. He asserted that the Confederated Tribes could not afford *any* attorney; that my compensation (five dollars per hour up to a maximum of 1,000 hours per year) was excessive; that Mr. Luce was a young "green" man "inexperienced in Indian Affairs" and "unbalanced in his judgments"; that under his proposed contract he would "get into the organization of this tribe which is a duplication of work that the Indian Bureau is doing" and "into the administration of this reservation which is an invasion of the Superintendent and his staff."

Superintendents Bureau of Indian Affairs

1907–1909 — Arthur E. McFatridge

1910–1923 — Edward L. Swartzlander

1924–1925 — Bryon A. Sharp

1925–1939 — O.L. Babcock

1930–1949 — Henry Roe Cloud

1948–1950 — Rupert Anderson

Source: "CTUIR Treaty of 1855 Sesquicentennial Strategic Planning Symposium 2001."

The Business Committee was not persuaded to change its support for the attorney contract. Before the meeting ended, the committee members voiced disapproval of other aspects of the BIA's administration, including approval of leases of individual Indian's trust property over the objection of the owner, using tribal money to pay Round-Up policemen, and personal use of a government car. Three months after this meeting, on May 24, 1948, the commissioner of Indian Affairs approved my attorney contract. Superintendent Roe Cloud was soon transferred to Portland, where he served as the Bureau's regional representative.

The new superintendent, Earl Wooldridge, encouraged bidding on new farm leases. Edgar Forrest, Jr., a tribal member who leased an off-reservation wheat and pea ranch, began to bid for on-reservation leases. Word got around that only market-value leases would be approved by the superintendent. Within two or three years, the reservation-wide level of lease rentals increased by about $500,000. Mr. Forest successfully bid to lease the tribally owned 600 acres.

Formation of a Constitution

The Business Committee then turned its full attention to the improvement of tribal governance. It had some history to contend with. In 1935, the Confederated Tribes had rejected the Indian Reorganization Act of 1934 (IRA), passed by Congress to enable tribes to adopt a form of corporate government. The Warm Springs Tribes had accepted the 1934 act; the Yakama had not. In the debate at the Umatilla General Council, the older members expressed concern at the changes the IRA might bring about. They especially opposed a provision that Council proceedings would be governed by *Robert's Rules of Order*.

The Business Committee asked me, as tribal attorney, to draft a document that, if approved, would create a democratic representative government that could forcefully assert and protect tribal sovereignty and Treaty rights and improve the lives of all tribal members. In consultation with committee members, and after collecting other tribes' governing documents to be used as possible models, I drafted a Constitution and By-Laws for discussion by the committee. For more than a year, at meetings that sometimes lasted long past midnight, the committee worked over this draft, shaping and improving it to fit the needs of the Confederated Tribes of the Umatilla Reservation. Finally, on November 4, 1949, at a well-advertised election — the polls being open all day and voting being conducted by secret ballot — the membership of the Confederated Tribes approved the Constitution and By-Laws by a vote of 113 to 104 and elected the first Board of Trustees. Article 8 of the new constitution required that before it could take effect, it must be approved by an authorized representative of the secretary of the Interior. Assistant Secretary William E. Warne approved the new constitution on December 7, 1949.

The Constitution and By-Laws virtually vested all tribal powers in a nine-member Board of Trustees consisting of the chairman of the General Council and eight persons, eighteen years or older, chosen by tribal members by secret ballot. The General Council retained the authority to elect the Board of Trustees, to amend the constitution, to recall members of the Board of Trustees, to ratify a motion by the Board or remove one of the Board members, to schedule its own meetings, and to determine who was entitled to be enrolled as a tribal member.

The adoption of the new constitution effected a dramatic change in the governing power structure on the Umatilla Indian Reservation. Its adoption by a mere nine-vote margin virtually assured that a large number of tribal members would continue to be critical of the new form of government and attempt to reverse the changes brought about by the vote. Those efforts began almost immediately. On Monday, November 7, a delegation of tribal chiefs met with Superintendent Wooldridge to protest the election. According to Mr. Wooldridge, "They claim that the people did not understand the proposed constitution, that the method of voting [written ballots] was unfair, and that voting by Tribal members under the age of 21 [18–21] was unauthorized." On November 10, Sam Kash Kash also wrote a letter to the superintendent of Indian Affairs, urging the approval of the constitution. He characterized the dispute over the constitution as a dispute between young and old, with the young people supporting the constitution. He likewise emphasized that the permitted voting age had been publicized long in advance without dispute.

Thus organized, the Confederated Tribes began to act aggressively to protect and enlarge the rights of tribal members. In the decade of the 1950s, they filed in federal court and won two cases that established the right of tribal members to hunt and fish on the reservation without regard to state game laws and the right of tribal members to catch salmon at usual and accustomed fishing places outside the reservation, also without regard to state laws.

Protecting On-Reservation Rights

In 1955, the Board of Trustees asked the tribal attorney to establish a treaty right for the Umatilla Tribes to hunt and fish within the reservation during Oregon's closed hunting and fishing seasons. In conjunction with attorneys for the Klamath Tribes, I filed suit in the U.S. District Court – Oregon to obtain such a ruling. Judge Gus J. Solomon heard the case on stipulated facts in Portland and ruled in favor of the Umatilla and the Klamath. The Board of Trustees, having won the case, was concerned that unregulated hunting and fishing on the reservation not be abused and, therefore, enacted an ordinance that governed hunting and fishing by tribal members and required nontribal members to purchase permits to hunt or fish on the reservation.

Soon after Public Law 280 was enacted, the State of Oregon began asserting that this law gave the state authority to regulate on-reservation hunting and trapping by tribal members. The state told the Confederated Tribes that it would prosecute any tribal member caught hunting or trapping on the reservation without a state license. This was not an easy challenge to respond to. If the state prosecuted a tribal member, then the Tribe itself would not be a party to the case. The case would be heard in state criminal court. In other states, these courts have tended to be hostile to defenses based on treaty rights. Moreover, the facts in any particular criminal case might not cast the tribal cause in the best light. Consequently, the Confederated Tribes decided not to wait for the state to begin bullying tribal members. Instead, the Confederated Tribes filed suit against the State of Oregon in the U.S. District Court–Oregon, seeking a declaratory judgment that the state had no authority over on-reservation hunting and trapping by tribal members.

The Umatilla Indian Reservation was not the only place where the state had been making these threats. The same claims were made concerning the Klamath Reservation. Both the Klamath Tribes and the Confederated Tribes won their cases against the state, and the state did not appeal the decisions. Judge Gus J. Solomon of the U.S. District Court ruled that both tribes had the exclusive right to hunt on their reservations, free from state regulation.

Protecting Off-Reservation Rights

In 1959, when Oregon game wardens arrested tribal members for gaffing six salmon in Catherine Creek, off the reservation and out of season, the Board of Trustees asked me to defend them. I brought suit in the U.S. District Court to enjoin the Oregon Game Commission from enforcing its fishing regulations against the Umatilla, who exercised a treaty right to fish "at all usual and accustomed stations" outside the reservation. Settlement negotiations failed. The Game Commission interpreted the Indians' Treaty right to fish at such stations as no greater than any citizen's rights, because the Treaty spoke of the Indians' right to fish "at all usual and accustomed stations in common with citizens of the Territory." The Game Commission's interpretation, of course, rendered the Treaty fishing rights meaningless.

The case went to trial before Judge Gus Solomon in a courtroom in Pendleton, filled with older Indians from the Umatilla, Nez Perce, Yakama, and Warm Springs reservations. Many were dressed in smoke-cured deerskin and wore their hair in two long braids. The Game Commission conceded that the arrested Umatillas were fishing for subsistence, not for commerce. I called several old-time Umatillas to testify that Catherine Creek, a tributary of the Grande Ronde River, where the alleged offense occurred, had been a usual and accustomed fishing station of the Umatillas in 1855. Then, through adverse examination of the com-

The Trial of Claims Land 4, Indian Claims Commission, met in Washington, D.C., on March 17, 1958. From left are tribal member Gilbert Conner; tribal member Steve Hall; court reporter; court clerk; Verne Ray, anthropologist and witness for the CTUIR; tribal member Eli Quaempts; Walter Rochow, attorney for the United States; Charles Luce, attorney for the CTUIR; tribal member Sam Kash Kash; Robert Suphan, anthropologist and witness for the United States.

mission's fish biologist, I introduced a special study of the Columbia River salmon runs. I had employed a reluctant dean of the College of Fisheries at the University of Washington to make the study (Dean Richard Van Cleve was opposed to Indians fishing out of season). The study showed, among other things, that Oregon permitted an open season to catch salmon for sport on the Grande Ronde each year and that the previous year's catch from the Grande Ronde had been about six hundred salmon. I then introduced a copy of the Treaty of 1855 and rested the Umatilla's case.

The Game Commission's case consisted of the testimony of the same fish biologist who I had examined adversely. The fish biologist asserted that it was necessary for "conservation" to have a closed season on the Grande Ronde River and Catherine Creek so that salmon migrating upstream could spawn. He had to admit, however, that six hundred or so salmon caught by sportsmen on the Grande Ronde in the open season would have spawned if not caught. I asked him how, in view of this, he defined "conservation." He replied that "conservation" did not mean "no use" of a fish resource but meant "wise use."

The trap was set. I asked him whether the State of Oregon thought it a "wiser use" of spawning salmon to allow fishermen to catch six hundred of the fish for entertainment than to allow Indians with Treaty rights to catch a half dozen for their livelihood. As he defined "conservation," the Oregon fish biologist could not answer "yes." The state's lawyer objected to the question as argumentative, which it may have been. Judge Solomon asked me if I wished to restate my question. I declined, my point having been made. Judge Solomon ruled for the Umatilla Tribes and granted an injunction. On Oregon's appeal to the U.S. Court of Appeals for the Ninth Circuit, his ruling was affirmed.

It would be hard to exaggerate the importance of this case to the Confederated Tribes — and to Northwest tribal fishing in general. Judge Solomon defined the aboriginal territory of the Cayuse, Umatilla, and Walla Walla Tribes in the broadest terms advocated by the Tribes themselves and ruled that the members of the Confederated Tribes had treaty-reserved usual and accustomed fishing stations on the John Day, Walla Walla, Grande Ronde, and Imnaha Rivers. In an important precedent for future fishing and hunting rights cases, the conclusions of law and judgment ruled that the state could only regulate tribal-member fishing if doing so was "necessary for conserva-

tion" of the fish and then ruled that the state's current measures did not meet that standard.

We Seek Compensation

Another component of the termination laws passed by Congress in 1953 was the Indian Claims Commission Act. The purpose of this statute was to clear up, once and for all, any outstanding legal claims that tribes might have against the federal government. In practice, these tended to be claims for restoration of land illegally taken. Tribes who won suits still could not get their land back. The only remedy allowed was payment of compensation. Likewise, the amount of compensation would be limited to the value of the land at the time it was lost, even if that was a century or more before. No interest would be paid for the lost value of that land during the intervening decades or centuries. Any claims not filed in the next seven years would be barred forever.

Faced with this dilemma, the Board of Trustees authorized me to file two major suits against the United States. The first sought compensation for the destruction of Celilo fishery on the Columbia River due to the inundation of Celilo Falls by the reservoir created behind The Dalles Dam. The other suit (Docket No. 264) sought compensation for the 1859 taking of tribal lands for construction by the United States of irrigation dams on the lower Umatilla River, and for the erroneous survey of the boundaries of the Umatilla Indian Reservation.

Courtesy of the *Confederated Umatilla Journal*

Tribal member Joe Sheoships (far left) and CTUIR Chairwoman Maudie Antoine look on as tribal members Eli Quaempts (left at table) and Louis McFarland sign the Celilo Falls/Dalles Dam settlement with a representative of the U.S. Army Corps of Engineers.

Celilo Falls Silent

When the U.S. Corps of Engineers began constructing The Dalles Dam, which would cover the ancient and valuable Celilo fishery on the Columbia River, the Board of Trustees teamed up with the Warm Springs Tribes to try to negotiate a settlement. The Celilo Falls of the Columbia River, about twelve miles east of The Dalles, Oregon, was a beautiful and exciting place. In the fall of the year, when the flow of the Columbia was less

than in the spring, the mighty Columbia roared over a ten-to-twenty-foot drop, salmon leaping and wriggling up the torrent, a fine spray blowing off the falls, and dozens of wooden platforms jutting out from rocks below the falls, from which Indians fished with long poles. Two kinds of fishing gear were common, set nets and dip nets. The set nets were nets at the end of long poles, which the fishermen would place at locations close to the rocks where the salmon would rest before attempting to climb up the falls. The dip nets, likewise, were on the end of long poles, which the fishermen dipped in the current of the Columbia hoping to catch a salmon as it swam upstream. In the early fall, Celilo was a gathering place for Yakama, Warm Springs, Umatilla, and even some Nez Perce. Including the fishermen's families, five hundred or more Indians camped near the falls. It was a joyous ancient celebration.

Preparation of the Celilo Falls fishery claim required proof that Celilo was a "usual and accustomed station" protected by the Umatilla Tribes' Treaty of 1855. That in recent years 100 to 150 Umatilla fishermen — along with even larger numbers of Yakama, Warm Springs, and a few Nez Perce Indians — fished there for salmon every fall was not disputed. But what about 1855, the key date under the terms of the Treaty? Proof was complicated by the fact that Celilo Falls was about seventy-five miles west of the lands aboriginally occupied by the Walla Walla, Umatilla, and Cayuse. Proof was further complicated by the circumstance that within their own lands the Tribes had abundant salmon fisheries on the Columbia River and its tributaries, and there was no obvious reason to travel westward some seventy-five miles to catch fish they could easily catch at home. Then there was the assertion by the Yakama Tribe, whose aboriginal lands did include Celilo Falls, that they alone had the exclusive treaty right to fish Celilo. To overcome these difficulties of proof, I relied mainly on a comment in Governor

Isaac Stevens' report to Congress of his 1853 survey for a northern transcontinental railway route that "Wallah-Wallahs" had been observed at the Celilo Falls fishery. Of course, I also relied on the fact that the Umatilla Tribes presently had well-established fishing stations at the falls.

Assuming that the Tribes had a treaty right to fish at Celilo, what monetary damage would they suffer when the federal Dalles Dam destroyed that fishery? With the falls submerged, they could still catch salmon at different locations with different gear — for example, fish the main stream of the Columbia with gill nets, or use dip nets or set nets at Cascade Locks, where the salmon came through an old canal on their voyage upstream every year. Then there was the question: How many fish did the Umatilla Tribes catch each year at Celilo (questionnaires filled out by tribal fishermen reported an annual salmon catch at Celilo larger than all the salmon that were counted at downstream Bonneville Dam)? What was their market value? What expense, including labor, was incurred in making the catch? There were no records of their catch, and none of the Umatillas reported taxable income from the sale of fish. Oregon state game officials had estimated the total Indian catch at Celilo but had not attempted to estimate the separate catches of the members of each tribe. And if the Umatilla recovered damages for the destruction of Celilo fishery, should only the tribal members who fished share in the recovery? How could it be determined how many fish each fisher-

Courtesy of the *Confederated Umatilla Journal*

CTUIR Chairwoman Maudie C. Antoine looks over the 1950 Celilo Falls settlement with representatives of the Bonneville Power Administration.

man had caught or could be expected to catch?

To learn as much as possible about the Celilo fishery, I spent, all told, about four weeks at Celilo. On platforms with Joe Sheoships, Louis McFarland, and other Umatilla fisherman, I talked with them and observed their methods. The arrangements by which places for fishing platforms were allocated were hard to pin down. Custom and prior use seemed to be decisive. Each platform was used by a "company" of six, eight, or ten fishermen, usually but not always of the same tribe.

Their catch was sold to fish buyers and occasionally to tourists. Beautiful thirty-pound Chinook salmon fetched about twenty cents a pound. The proceeds of the sales apparently were evenly divided among the members of the company, but other than what records, if any, the fish buyers kept, there was no way to determine the actual catch of a given company or how proceeds from the sale of its catch were divided.

Clearly, the Celilo fishery case called for settlement. Litigation would have pitted tribe against tribe, and the problems of

The Nez Percians band, performing here in Joseph, Oregon, in 1947, included members of the CTUIR and Nez Perce tribes: (front, from left) Abe McCatty, Ralph Skannon, Titus White, and Arthur Motanic; (back, from left) Caleb Whitman, Bruce McKay, Jimmy Andrews, Pete McCormmack, and Benjamin Penny

proof of 1855 usage and 1955 damages would have consumed years of testimony and appeals. The Corps of Engineers, which was building The Dalles Dam, wanted to settle for all the reasons the Board of Trustees did, plus its concern about public sympathy for the Indians who fished at the falls and antipathy toward the Corps if the dam's reservoir covered Celilo Falls before the Tribes were assured compensation. Senator Guy Cordon of Oregon, a proponent of The Dalles Dam who was up for reelection in 1954, was, if anything, more eager than the Corps for a settlement.

To counter the Yakama's claims of exclusive treaty rights to fish Celilo and to strengthen the Umatilla Tribes' cause with Senator Cordon, the Umatilla and the Warm Springs tribes, the only Oregon tribes that fished Celilo, negotiated jointly with the Corps. They eventually agreed on a total annual value of the Indian catch at Celilo, capitalized that figure at the going rate of interest, divided the capitalized value by the number of enrolled members of the Yakama, Warm Springs, and Umatilla tribes, and allotted each tribe its share of the capitalized value according to its proportionate enrollment. This meant the Umatilla Tribes initially recovered $4 million. In the settlement contract, the Warm Springs lawyers and I insisted on an "equalization clause" to assure our clients that if the Corps settled with the Yakama for a higher per capita sum then the Corps would increase the tribes' settlement proportionally. This clause netted the Umatilla Tribes an additional $600,000, for a total of $4.6 million paid in compensation.

After the Confederated Tribes settled the Celilo fishery claim, I wanted to entertain the members of the Board of Trustees and their spouses to celebrate and sought to arrange a private room that the Elks Club had available for such parties in Walla Walla. I made the arrangements and then got a call from the Grand Exalted Ruler, the head of the Walla Walla Elks. He said that he had been told of the plan to hold a party with the Board of Trustees at the Elks Club and that this was not permitted by the By-Laws of the Elks Club. "Chuck," he said, "the Elks Club is a white man's club." I was shocked and embarrassed at this bigotry, but I did not wish to turn a joyous celebration into an ugly fight. I decided to entertain the Board of Trustees at my home in Walla Walla. That is what Mrs. Luce and I did, and a good time was had by all. There was, unfortunately, in the 1940s and 1950s still some lingering prejudice against Indians in the Pendleton and Walla Walla areas. Sam Kash Kash told me that certain Pendleton restaurants were reluctant, and several refused, to serve Indian customers. Oregon law at the time forbade the sale of liquor to Indians.

In terms of buying power, $4.6 million in 1953 was worth perhaps $40 million by today's standards. The Board of Trustees of the Confederated Tribes wanted to use a large part of the Celilo settlement as an annuity for tribal economic development and social programs. It was not to be so. Nonreservation tribal members who neither fished nor participated in tribal affairs as well as many reservation members began to attend General Council meetings to insist on a 100 percent payout of the settlement in the form of cash per capita payments. A Board of Trustees plan to offer nonresident tribal members an optional discounted payout was vetoed by the Bureau of Indian Affairs, which at that time favored the total liquidation of Indian reservations. Sadly, the Board was forced to dissipate almost the entire settlement as the nonreservation tribal members demanded.

The Confederated Tribes could not stop construction of The Dalles Dam, but they did successfully block construction of a dam near the headwaters of the Umatilla River. "Mission Dam," as it would have been called, was strenuously advocated by Ed Aldrich, editor of the *East Oregonian*, as a means of reducing floods of the Umatilla River. At a highly charged meeting on the reservation to which the Board of Trustees had invited the Corps of Engineers, Colonel F.S. Tandy, the Corps' district chief, announced "there will be no Mission Dam."

The Filing of Docket 264

The Umatilla Tribes' land claim included the taking of lands ceded by the Treaty of 1855 (Claim 1) plus lands lying south of the ceded area, principally in Grant, Malheur, and Baker counties (Claim 4). Like the Celilo Falls fish claim, they presented difficult problems of proof. Prior to 1855, the Umatilla, Walla Walla, and Cayuse Tribes had no system or concept of land titles. They moved about with the seasons and ranged as far east as Montana to hunt buffalo. Friendly neighboring Sahaptian-speaking tribes freely intermingled and intermarried with them, and they had no alphabet to record their history.

In the 1930s, Dr. Verne F. Ray, an anthropologist from the University of Washington, had studied and written about the culture of the Umatilla, Walla Walla, and Cayuse and other tribes of the northwestern Columbia Plateau. His writings were based largely on oral histories that he and other anthropologists took from older Indians. They described, among other things, village locations and hunting, fishing, and gathering areas. After meeting Dr. Ray, I retained him for the Tribes as a consultant and expert witness in support of their land claim.

Beginning with the Lewis and Clark exploration in 1804–1805, the lands of the Umatilla, Walla Walla, and Cayuse had been visited by a succession of traders, fur trappers, missionaries, explorers, government survey parties, and Oregon Trail wagon trains. In 1818, the North West Company founded Fort Walla Walla as a trading post at the confluence of the Walla Walla and Columbia Rivers. It was operated by that company and by Hudson's Bay Company continuously until 1855. I searched far and wide for any writing of these earlier visitors and employed a retired archivist formerly in charge of Indian materials at the National Archives to assist me. I even went to the archives of the Hudson's Bay Company in London, England, to examine the records of Fort Walla Walla, which was later renamed Fort Nez Perce when the Hudson's Bay Company acquired it.

In 1958, phase one of Claims 1 and 4 finally went to trial, the sole issue being the location of the lands to which the Tribes could properly claim aboriginal title. Four leading members of the Confed-

From Docket 264 of the Indian Claims Commission

The aboriginal religion was the guardian spirit religion, with a strong element of earth worship. The basic religion of the three tribes was the guardian spirit religion, and the religious practices of the three tribes were much the same. Closely related to religion was their attitude toward their lands. They regarded their land as sacred, not only because their ancestors were buried there, but because they had been placed upon the land to care for it, and the land, in turn, cared for them.

erated Tribes accompanied me to Washington, D.C., to be present at the trial — Gilbert Conner, Steve Hall, Elias Quaempts, and Bill Minthorn. In the two-week trial, the Umatilla Tribes offered over 600 exhibits, plus the expert testimony of Dr. Ray. More than two years later, on June 10, 1960, the Indian Claims Commission found that in 1859 the Umatilla Tribes had aboriginal title to 4,259,500 acres of land in northeastern Oregon and southeastern Washington — fewer acres than the Umatilla Tribes claimed but still a very large area.

Claims 2 and 3, though meritorious, never went to trial. Claim 2 involved one of the most egregious actions taken by the federal government in violation of its trust responsibility to the Confederated Tribes. In 1914, the Bureau of Reclamation built irrigation dams near the mouth of the Umatilla River without adequate fish-passage facilities. As a result, the salmon and the eel runs in the Umatilla River were destroyed. The Treaty had assured the Confederated Tribes the exclusive right to take fish from the Umatilla River and other streams running through or bordering the reservation, but the United States in 1914 made that exclusive right worthless.

Claim 2 also involved the failure of the United States to exercise its trust duties to protect the Confederated Tribes. In 1909, a State of Oregon proceeding adjudicated the waters of the Umatilla River for irrigation purposes to the point that the river was dried up at its lower reach in several of the summer months. A person could walk across the river near the city of Umatilla and never get his feet wet. The Confederated Tribes were not a party to that proceeding, and neither was the United States. There is a serious question of whether the adjudication limits the rights of the Umatilla Tribes to use the waters in the Umatilla River for whatever tribal purposes they now might wish. Tribal attorneys have thought it would be unwise of the Tribes to assert and use their water rights to the Umatilla River to the extent that that usage might damage well-established irrigation projects on the lower stretches of the river and that the public outcry would be very much against the Confederated Tribes.

In recent years, the Bonneville Power Administration, an agency of the federal government, has made it financially possible for salmon runs to be restored to the Umatilla River. This has been achieved by using an expensive pumping project to take waters from the Columbia River and substitute them for some of the diverted Umatilla River water, so that now 20,000 to 30,000 salmon enter the Umatilla River and swim to the reservation each year. So, there has been a partial righting of the wrong that was done to the Tribes back in 1909 and 1914. Nonetheless, that adjudication and dam construction were in flagrant violation of the rights of the Confederated Tribes at the time.

Claim 3 involved obvious errors in the government survey of the boundaries of the Umatilla Indian Reservation to the disadvantage of the Confederated Tribes.

Its misplacement of the source of Wild-horse Creek and the headwaters of Háwtmi (McKay) Creek excluded thousands of square miles that belonged in the reservation.

Percy Brigham, a well-known tribal member and a hunter and fisher, believed there was another mistake in the survey of the boundary of the reservation. He was convinced that a place called Lee's Encampment lay somewhat east of Meacham. When surveyors used Meacham as Lee's Encampment, they had cheated the Tribes out of some lands that should have been incorporated in the reservation. I was never able to find evidence that Lee's Encampment was other than Meacham. In fact, I was never able to find where Lee's Encampment was. Whether it was Meacham or someplace else, neither Percy nor anyone has found solid evidence of the true location.

When Claims 1 and 4 were finally settled for $2,450,000 in 1965, the Department of Justice required as part of the settlement that the Confederated Tribes surrender Claims 2 and 3. On November 24, 1965, the General Council accepted the settlement.

Fighting over the Settlement Money

As in the case of The Dalles Dam/Celilo Fishery settlement payment, a political struggle arose on the Umatilla Indian Reservation over how to spend the Docket 264 settlement money. Many Board of Trustees members were determined not to repeat what they saw as the "mistake" of the Cel-ilio distribution, in which all of the money was distributed to tribal members and none was retained for economic development or other tribal projects. Many individual tribal members, however, hoped to gain a financial windfall again. The problems were complicated by the fact that signing a settlement does not guarantee that the United States will pay the money; Congress has to pass a separate statute approving the payment.

By 1968, a bill had been entered in Congress (HR 3805, 90th Congress) that would have distributed a portion of the funds per capita to the members of the Tribe, with "the balance to be advanced to the tribe for such uses as authorized by the governing body of the Confederated Tribes and approved by the Secretary of the Interior."[1] Unfortunately, the Interior Department managed to confuse the situation by misunderstanding the intent of the Claims Commission when it entered into the settlement with the Confederated Tribes. Certain people in the Interior Department thought the settlement moneys had to be distributed to all descendants of the 1855 treaty signers rather than to all members of the Confederated Tribes. As various people benefited or lost due to these competing interpretations, a heated controversy arose around it. Meanwhile, a significant number of tribal members did not want any funds distributed to the tribal government but preferred instead that the entire settlement be distributed per capita.

On the reservation, these controversies came to a head when the voters recalled all Board members who supported retaining funds for use by the tribal government. A Board of Trustees that unanimously supported per capita distribution was elected to replace the recalled members. During subsequent congressional hearings on the settlement payment act, both the new Board members and some of the recalled Board members gave testimony. (The recalled Board members traveled at their own expense, and spoke on their own behalf rather than as tribal representatives.) The final legislation approving the payment of the settlement funds specified that the entire settlement was to be distributed per capita.

The Early Board of Trustees Establishes Tribal Institutions

The Board of Trustees began to play an active role in managing tribal assets. It sponsored a forestry program to prepare and supervise the competitive sale of selected marketable timber in the Johnson Creek area. It also took bids for successful construction of a new community hall on

1955 Looks Back to 1855

In 1955, the Confederated Tribes took the leadership in organizing a meeting of Yakamas, Nez Perce, and Umatilla/Cayuse/Walla Wallas at the site of the original Treaty grounds in Walla Walla. On a very warm day on June 9, 1955, they organized games, dances, and other ceremonies of their ancestors, followed by a Salmon Feast and a pageant in the evening at the fairgrounds. Before a packed stadium, they reenacted the treaty negotiations, using a script by Bill Gulick based on the original treaty minutes. In a series of tableaus, the Indian actors spoke in their native tongues with English translations.

At the Treaty Council reenactment, to his surprise, the evening ended with the Umatillas placing a war bonnet on Mr. Charles Luce's head and making him an honorary Umatilla chief by the name of White Eagle. The morning after the ceremony, Mr. Luce visited the Indian campsite, where older Indian women were taking down their teepees. Liza Bill, a dear friend and supporter of Mr. Luce in the General Council, looked at him sternly and said, "Mr. Luce, we're surprised at you!" He asked why? She explained, "Last night you let Governor Stevens make all those broken promises to us again."

Women as well as men were elected to the Board of Trustees. Anna Wannasay was a member of the Board, as was Viola Wocatsie. In 1954, Maudie Antoine and Louise Elk, in a hotly contested election, joined the Board and were instrumental in organizing the Treaty commemoration in Walla Walla.

The first Board of Trustees, photographed in 1951, included Arnold Lavadour and David "Steve" Hall (standing) and (seated, left to right), Elias Quaempts, Anna Wannassay, Edgar Forrest, Jr., Louis McFarland, David Liberty, and Richard Burke.

part of the July Grounds, replacing the old old barn where the General Council formerly met.

In August 23, 1951, the Board of Trustees started a credit program for tribal members by adopting a document entitled "Policies and Plans for Managing Credit Activities." This program was expanded in 1967. The Tribal Credit Program used a revolving fund to make low-interest loans to tribal members. The program is still in existence today governed by the tribal Credit Program Code.

In 1965, the Board of Trustees established the Tribal Farm Enterprise and adopted its plan of operations. The Tribal Farm Enterprise has steadily grown so that it now actively farms acres of tribal trust land on the Umatilla Indian Reservation.

On November 8, 1966, the Board of Trustees enacted Tribal Ordinance Number Eight, which created the Umatilla Reservation Housing Authority. The Housing Authority was empowered to act independently to seek and implement federal funding to establish improved housing on the reservation. The Housing Authority has proven to be an effective force on the reservation, having established numerous housing projects and serving as landlord to a large number of low-income tribal members. Tribal Ordinance Number Eight was repealed and replaced by the adoption of the Housing Code in 1994.

Tribal Scholarship Fund

On February 14, 1961, President Kennedy's newly elected administration appointed me head of the Bonneville Power Administration. With the Board's approval, I transferred responsibility for completing the trial of the land claim to the King, Miller, Anderson, Nash firm, which had represented the Warm Springs Tribes in a similar land claim. Mark C. McClanahan of that firm then took over as tribal attorney. Mr. McClanahan remained tribal attorney until 1972 and was responsible for the successful conclusion of the Claims Commission settlement.

At the time of my departure, I created the Nancy Oden Luce Trust to which I assigned my share of any attorney fee that might be awarded at the successful conclusion of the Tribes' land claim. The terms of the Nancy Oden Luce Trust (named in honor of my young daughter, who had been killed in a sledding accident) provided that the trustee would pay all the income to the Confederated Tribes to be used for scholarships to enable children of tribal members to attend college or trade school. When the claims case was later settled for $2.4 million, the Trust received $105,000. Invested conservatively, the Trust corpus has grown to $300,000 and has enabled many young tribal members to attend colleges and universities.

Part II: Sovereignty of the CTUIR

William Johnson

Tá'c haláχp 'íinim himyúume kaa láwti-waama. We'nikíse 'Iceyéeye Qeesqées. Wek'itke'wéet wées. Qe'ciyéw'yew' yóχ kem pí'nisem 'ée 'iníise núunim wiyáeleeheyn yóχ kaa núunim cúukwe wisíix kaa tamálwit. Wáaqo' sooyaapootímtki c'íiχce. Now in English. Greetings, my relations and friends. My name is Gray Coyote. I am the tribal judge. I am honored to provide the history of our sovereignty and our laws.

I have been the tribal judge since 1980 and a student of law since 1972, having served as tribal attorney, tribal chairman of the Board of Trustees and the General Council, and Chief Judge since 1988. I graduated from Pendleton High School, Oregon State University, and the University of Oregon School of Law. During my college years, I was a recipient of the Luce Scholarship, established by Mr. Luce in memory of his daughter. I was the first tribal member to graduate from law school and to pass the Oregon State Bar. I worked for the American Indian Policy Review Commission in 1975–1976 and have lived in the Waíiletpu (Cayuse) country all my life. I am very proud to have a family living and working on the Umatilla Indian Reservation.

Sovereignty is the ability of a government to exercise jurisdiction over a land base by making laws free from interference by other governments. Historically, the law that our people abided by was based on the cyclical aspects of the various plants and animals that our people depended on and needed to understand and respect in order to survive. Kinship relations and language were also integral parts of our sovereignty. In the contemporary sense, the exercise of our sovereignty depends on the Treaty of 1855 and the Constitution and By-Laws by which we govern ourselves. Sovereignty in this context means the ability to regulate hunting and fishing on tribal land, as well as to exercise civil and criminal jurisdiction, determine membership criteria, and collect taxes. In the next few pages, I will give a perspective on the impact of federal policy on our government and the exercise of sovereignty through our tribal law and justice system. Included in this perspective will be milestone events of our history and their impact on our government.

1850 — The Cayuse Five

Any discussion or perspective of our sovereignty must include the 1850 trial in the U.S. federal court for Oregon of our five tribal members known as the Cayuse Five, because their trial was the first gross violation of our inherent sovereignty. It has shaped our perspective on law enforcement ever since. The way in which the United States arrested the five Cayuse men, conducted an extremely biased trial, and summarily hanged the defendants certainly remains as an underlying factor in the Umatilla, Walla Walla, and Cayuse peoples' reluctance to trust law enforce-

ment and other officials in positions of authority.

In 1847, an outbreak of measles ravaged many Cayuse members, despite medicines they received at the mission established by Dr. Marcus Whitman and his wife Narcissa near present-day Walla Walla, Washington. At that time, Walla Walla was in Indian Country, completely outside United States jurisdiction (the U.S. did not create the Oregon Territory until August 1848). Dr. Whitman had been warned that tribal members were upset because his medicine did not work on them, though it did work on non-Indians. He was also warned that Indians killed doctors whose medicine does not work, yet he remained at his mission. On November 29, 1847, Cayuse Indians killed Dr. Whitman, his wife Narcissa, and twelve other non-Indians. Forty Cayuse people took part in the incident.[2]

In 1850, five Cayuse tribal members surrendered to Joseph Lane, the governor of the Oregon Territory, at a location near The Dalles. It is not clear whether the Five actually knew the reason for their surrender or what was about to occur. They were taken to Oregon City, where they were tried in U.S. District Court. The five Cayuses indicted for murder were Tiloukaikt, Tomahas, Clokomas, Isiaasheluckas, and Kiamasumkin. This is one of the earliest documented murder trials in the Oregon Territory.[3] The Tribes called the jail where the Five were held the "Skookum House."

Judge O.C. Pratt appointed attorneys to represent the defendants. The attorneys did not speak the tribal language, and the Five did not speak *suyápotimki* (English). The Cayuse Five's attorneys defended their clients by challenging the court's jurisdiction, because the crime occurred outside Oregon Territory and had occurred within Indian Territory (there was no treaty at the time that ceded tribal land to the United States). They also argued, and testimony established, that it was tribal custom or traditional practice to kill ineffective medicine men whose patients died. This was from testimony of Dr. John McLoughlin, the chief factor at Fort Vancouver, and Stickus, a Cayuse member. The testimony at the trial also supported the location of the crime as Waíiletpu (within the surrounding area of present-day Walla Walla), which was within the territory of the Cayuse and not in Oregon Territory.

The trial took four days, including indictment, arraignment, and appointment of legal defense council. On May 24, 1850, in the case of *U.S. v. Telokite, Tomahas (the murderer), Clokomas, Isiaasheluckas, and Kiamasumkin*, a jury of non-Indians found the Cayuse Five guilty as charged. They were publicly executed on June 3, 1850, and their remains were buried in an unmarked, unknown location. In modern times, it has been made known to tribal members that the graves were located in construction sites or building renovation sites near Oregon City. This is not substantiated, but the Tribe would undoubtedly seek repatriation if their location could be found.

After the verdict, the defense attorney for the Five filed a motion for a new trial based on erroneous rulings made by Judge Pratt. The principal challenge to the judge's ruling involved his instruction to the jury that the surrender of the Five by the Cayuse Nation was a good indication of guilt and should be considered by the jury as such. Under modern rules of evidence, the surrender would not be acceptable as proof of guilt, especially given that when they arrived in The Dalles the Five probably did not know they were going to be arrested and transported to Oregon City for trial. Another point of the appeal stated that the Whitman incident did not take place within U.S. territory, so the U.S. District Court–Oregon did not have jurisdiction to try and convict the five Cayuse men. Defense attorneys also could have argued that the prosecutors referred to Tomahas as "the murderer" throughout the trial and when addressing the jury, which could only have increased the jury's bias against the Cayuse defendants. The court denied the motion for new trial and the defense attorneys did not appeal, apparently because the Five had been executed. The bill of costs for the trial was $31.25. Obviously, judicial practices, costs, and defendants' rights have changed dramatically since this case.

The case of the Cayuse Five represents our first taste of *suyápo* 'white' justice and led to the end of hostilities between our Tribes and the U.S. government. More importantly, it negatively affects our perspective of law and judicial practice. It may be unconscious or subliminal, but we have a disposition to distrust laws and courts; and the outcome of this case, along many other events in history, surely contribute to that distrust. We are resolving that distrust through the exercise of our self-government authority, including the operation of tribal law enforcement and tribal court programs.

The Treaty of 1855 and the Allotment Act of 1885

The Treaty of 1855 between the United States and the Cayuse, Umatilla, and Walla Walla peoples is essential to the discussion of current tribal sovereignty, because it is the foundational document from which our inherent legal authority is recognized in the American legal system. The Treaty reserved for our people a land base that, although it has been carved up by faulty surveying and federal legislation, remains today a territory over which our people have authority. The Treaty also reserved our rights to hunt and fish subject to our own laws. In 1855, the *suyápo* society had not yet acculturated our people. Our relatives of that time represented the last vestige of our nation in its original form. Before the coming of the Europeans, our ancestors were free spirited, using the land and interacting with their neighbors without the restrictions of a foreign government. They were not enrolled as Indians in a tribe and probably did not want to be. At the time of the Treaty Council, they made brave and difficult decisions in the face of overwhelming odds, acted with responsi-

bility to their families and community, and preserved the right for future generations to govern themselves.

We are an old and a new government at the same time. Our traditional customs and laws are ancient and were the only form of "government" our ancestors needed to maintain order and the cycles of life for millennia. Under the *suyápo* standard of government, which is constitutional democracy, our government is young. It was formed in 1949. The policies and laws we adopt as a constitutional government establish the tribal institutions through which we exercise our sovereignty and affect federal policy. Federal law and policy from 1855 to the present have greatly affected how free or restricted we are to exercise our sovereignty under the Treaty and our Constitution and By-Laws.

The greatest limitation we have had placed on us is the concept of individual ownership of property or land. We once enjoyed the freedom to inhabit all lands. In March 1885, Congress passed the Slater Act, an allotment/homesteading act designed to assimilate our people by introducing them to the concept of individual property ownership while at the same time freeing up "surplus" reservation land, the land not allotted to individual tribal members, for non-Indian settlement. The Slater Act reduced our territory over which we now exercise sovereignty from approximately 245,699 acres to 158,000 acres. The theory behind this act was that individual ownership of property would teach us how to live like the white man, but what it

Courtesy of the *Confederated Umatilla Journal*

Umatilla Agency campus in about 1973

really did was divide our 1855 reservation for *suyápo* settlement. The concept of landownership with fee-simple absolute title was not part of our perspective. We still fight this concept under different guises, such as the right-of-way to private homes, church reverter clauses, and fractionalized heirship. The Indian Reorganization Act of 1934 stopped the practice of allotment of tribal lands.

1949 Constitution and By-Laws of the CTUIR

I recently had the pleasure of meeting our tribal attorney who helped draft our Constitution and By-Laws of 1949, Mr. Charles Luce. He arrived as tribal attorney amid the atmosphere created when the Tribes rejected adoption of a constitutional form of government under the Indian Reorganization Act. The apparent reason for this rejection was fear of the motives for adoption of such government. The Warm Springs Tribes adopted their constitutional government under the IRA in 1937, and it did not induce termination or other negative effects. In 1949, Mr. Luce provided a draft Constitution and By-Laws based on models suggested under the IRA and by the BIA, which was quite similar to the IRA-form Constitution and By-Laws adopted by the Warm Springs Tribes, but without the secretarial approval of tribal laws and ordinances by the U.S. government. That was quite a concern at the time, because it was offensive to our sovereignty.

When World War II began, the policy of self-government under the IRA waned. On November 4, 1949, the General Council of the Umatilla Tribes voted to establish a constitutional government, with a vote of 113 for and 104 against its adoption. It was quite an accomplishment, given that the Tribes had previously rejected a government under the IRA and that it established a government based on concepts foreign to us. It was not an unusual format for tribal government at the time, though.

Our Board of Trustees (BOT) and General Council (GC) are the focus of power under our Constitution and By-Laws. The Constitution and By-Laws mention neither a judicial branch nor an executive department. The BOT/GC has the exclusive authority to maintain executive, regulatory, judiciary, fire control, and police powers in our system of government. Those within the penumbra of these powers — including the tribal attorney, the BIA superintendent, the Indian Health Service director, and the executive director — have in the past implicitly exercised the powers of government and greatly influence the way the Tribes choose to go with their policies and laws. An example of this use of power in Indian Country occurs in the area of membership and disenrollment of tribal members, with disputes arising where tribes have constitutions and bylaws similar to ours.

In tribal governments like ours, the entity with decision-making power can initiate disenrollment because of erroneous blood quantums or ancestry. The individual whose membership is in question can appeal the decision to the tribal board of directors or to the tribal council. Where this happens, attorneys are paid by the tribe and, therefore, must advocate for their client's interest and, consequently, for disenrollment. Before we changed our enrollment and disenrollment procedures (membership laws), this scenario could have happened here.

Originally, under the tribal constitution, our tribal membership was in three classes. Original allottees were A members. To qualify as a B member, a person's parents must have been A members and have at least one-quarter blood Umatilla/Cayuse/Walla Walla. Persons not meeting the one-quarter blood quantum but who were descendants from A or B members were C members, who could not enjoy privileges of tribal membership except to hold tribal office and vote. We changed our enrollment criteria in 1990 to require one-quarter blood quantum from a Umatilla, Cayuse, or Walla Walla ancestor and/or another federally recognized tribe. This has eliminated "classes" of membership, but membership is still based on blood quantum. Now, by tribal law, there is also an appeal to the tribal court, although its decision could be affected by BOT/GC action.

This system worked for many years, but now change may be needed again. The judicial/law enforcement system is envisioned as providing fair and equal justice to anyone within its jurisdiction. There are, however, no checks and balances on how that might be influenced by the power and authority of the BOT/GC. The principle of checks and balances could most clearly be instituted by a constitutional amendment that established three branches of government, subject to the power delegated by the people to their government, but checks and balances do not need to be in the form of a constitutional provision. There can be laws made prohibiting interference with the judiciary and providing punishment if interference occurs. We have that now in our tribal criminal code.

1950 – 1953: Termination, Relocation, and Public Law 280

In the late 1940s and early 1950s, there was a turnaround of federal policies toward the termination of federal involvement in Indian affairs. The culmination of that policy was House Concurrent Resolution 108, introduced in Congress on June 9, 1953. That resolution basically established a federal policy of terminating the status of Indian tribes as federally recognized governments in order to free Indian people to integrate into the mainstream culture and get the U.S. government out of the Indian business. It was a policy designed to extinguish the status and rights of Indians, and it was done without Indian consent. The policy actually did very little to promote Indian freedom or eliminate discrimination against Indians. Termination resulted in more loss of land, services, lives, and, when it occurred to many tribes of Indians throughout Oregon and California, a com-

plete loss of political status as an Indian. After all that, we were still discriminated against because we were still Indian.

The termination policy also resulted in a relocation program, because the BIA, the primary federal agency responsible for Indian affairs, designed a plan that focused on relocation, which meant moving Indians into big cities to be trained and assimilated into *suyápo* society. Indians received training as welders, nurses, or whatever business people had. That policy of termination/relocation affected many things. Indian landownership was further eroded where land was sold, the proceeds were given to tribes, and the trust relationship between the U.S. and many Indian tribes — which said that the U.S. generally had a duty to protect and provide for tribes — ended. Special legislation was passed primarily aimed at terminating tribes in Oregon and California, though it also terminated other tribes throughout the U.S. in states such as Michigan and Minnesota. Once termination was accomplished the proceeds of the reservation property were appraised and sold, with the proceeds given to individual Indians whose tribes were terminated. The tribal members had no choice in the matter. Some tribal members would not accept the payments, such as the Klamath member Edison Chiloquin. Some of those tribes have been restored to full status as tribes, such as the Klamath, Grand Ronde, and Coquille.

The legislative history of House Concurrent Resolution 108 shows that it passed with little or no attention given to it. Individual Indians and tribes were opposed to it, but some tribes were too poor to comment on it. Some Indian supporters of the termination policy basically supported it under the supposition that they could liquidate their reservation property and the proceeds would be paid to individual members. In hindsight, the impact of termination was overwhelmingly horrible and has since been reversed in some cases.

Some laws or policies enacted during the termination era are still affecting us today. Some families who were relocated still live in San Francisco and Los Angeles and other big cities. The federal government transferred responsibility for education to the states, where the responsibility remains. The U.S. transferred community health responsibility from the BIA to the Indian Health Service. Congress never addressed economic development or law enforcement on the reservation. The most significant change brought on by the termination policy, however, was Public Law 280. Although termination brought freedom from federal government regulation, Public Law 280 extended state jurisdiction onto Indian lands.

Public Law 280, enacted in 1953, authorized certain states to exercise criminal and civil jurisdiction on Indian reservations, with some exceptions. Oregon was one such state, and the Warm Springs Tribes was one such exception. Our tribal attorney during this time period, Charles Luce, thought our tribe was probably not one of those that could afford to send people to testify for or against it in Washington, D.C. Mr. Luce explained that our tribe tended to be in favor of Public Law 280. No official tribal resolution or letter of support has ever surfaced showing such support. He explained that the Board of Trustees accepted it based on the fact that we had no law enforcement or court system on the reservation, and it did not seem to affect us because we did not have an abundant amount of crime.

We wanted access to courts to enforce child support on the reservation, and we thought we should do that. In retrospect, it matters little whether or not the Tribes supported it, because Public Law 280 would have become law anyway. It did not affect tribal court or police because we had no court or police, and at the time there were no appropriations corresponding to the enactment of that law. States that were responsible for law enforcement, including Oregon, did not extend services to reservations because they could not pay for it.

Public Law 280 contained limitations on civil jurisdiction transfer and did not terminate the trust status of reservation lands, meaning that the federal government maintained authority on tribally owned lands after the law passed. It did impose state laws in the areas of education and child adoption/foster care, alcohol and drugs, and judicial jurisdiction on our Tribes. Public Law 280 was the last vestige of termination, and it continues to affect us today in that our Tribes and Indian tribes in general continue to struggle to define their jurisdictional relationship with states.

Tribes did maintain concurrent tribal jurisdiction under Public Law 280; that is, tribes could operate their own law enforcement agencies on their land independently of the state government. The language of Public Law 280 and its legislative history show no attempt to exclude tribal concurrent jurisdiction. It appears that the intent was to fill a void in law enforcement where the federal government or the tribes did not have the capacity to conduct law enforcement. The Warm Springs Tribes had a functioning court and law enforcement system, and they were exempt from the impact of Public Law 280. CTUIR did not have a functioning court or police until the mid–1970s. In the late 1800s and early 1900s, there was a CFR Court established here with corresponding tribal police. CFR stands for Code of Federal Regulation, meaning that the court was established by BIA regulations, not by the constitution.

Public Law 280 did not allow states any authority over trust property or water rights, nor did it affect treaty agreements or statutes with respect to hunting, trapping, fishing, or licensing. Interestingly, 28 U.S.C. section 1360, subsection C, reads:

Any tribal ordinance or custom heretofore adopted by an Indian tribe, band, or community in exercise of any authority which it may possess shall, if not inconsistent with any applicable civil law of the State, be given full force and effect in determination of civil causes of action pursuant to this section.

This can be interpreted to mean that states must abide by tribal law if it is consistent with state law. The states must give full faith and credit to tribal laws under this analysis, without question. While this is only one interpretation, it would include the custom and tradition that tribes have for child rearing, hunting, fishing, probate, and land transfer under probate. If there is no federal preemption and tribes have the authority or jurisdiction, then the state has to abide and recognize tribal law.

The State of California illustrates the current problems arising under Public Law 280. In 2005, there were 109 tribes with various enrollment and land bases, ranging from ten acres to thousands of acres. In California, which is a Public Law 280 state, there has been and continues to be a clash between the state and the tribes. There are over three hundred thousand Indians and close to a hundred recognized tribes or rancherias. California tribes and the state are debating who should exercise jurisdiction on reservations and how that should be done. Some tribes desire better services and better coverage by law enforcement; they want to pay for it but also have dominion over it. There has been no solution reached at the time of this writing, but the state's governor, Arnold Schwarzenegger — who goes by the nickname of "The Terminator" — will not agree to tribal jurisdiction and hopes to get a share of casino money for the purposes of taxes.

Tribes in California do not agree and have had a difficult time securing better law enforcement services on their lands. Some have turned down state money offered in casino agreements in order to protect their sovereignty.

1953 – 1957: Wayám (Celilo Falls)

One of the greatest natural beauties of Indian Country was Wayám (Celilo Falls) and the area around it. If it were visible today and the Corps of Engineers wanted to dam the Columbia and flood it, there would be enormous opposition and outcry — and not just by Indians.

My personal remembrance of it dates to 1953 at a time when my father Leslie Johnson and my uncle Del LaCourse would take me there. Usually, it involved an old pickup or a car with no backseat, traveling at night to get there and fishing the next day. We were the "Rez Indians" and obeyed the elders at the site. Cable cars, pulled by hand, crossed above the falls to islands in the middle of the river. My father would take me about halfway across on one of the cable-car boxes and start swinging it side to side just so he could see me hang on for all I could — while he would laugh and yip. One time while we were there, I found a ten dollar bill stuck to the rock as we walked, and right then I thought this is a place where money comes from. When we would get all the *nusux* 'salmon' we could haul home, we would fill the backseat area with ice and *nusux* (and me) and go home.

On March 10, 1957, the gates of the Dalles Dam were closed, and Wayám was under water. The tribes who frequented the area were compensated for the flooding of their ancient fishing sites, but it was an irreplaceable way of life and ended one of the great marketplaces of Indian Country. Much has been written and recorded about this time and place. Suffice it to say now that its existence demonstrated the economic viability of Indian commercial marketplaces and that Indians can "get with the program," even without market studies and all the trappings of modern-day business. We were free and independent, and we exercised our sovereignty the same way. We could provide for ourselves. We have regained that now with a different economy, which still includes the Wayám values.

1967 – 1970: Indian Claims Commission Docket Number 264 – Per Capita versus Investment

Mr. Luce and the Tribes' governing body provided great effort and expertise in protecting tribal land rights in Indian Claims Commission (ICC) case No. 264. It seemed at the time like a hundred-year-old wrong was mitigated by money judgment.

In 1967, I was a senior at Pendleton High School, and I remember tribal members arguing over full per capita distribution (of the money from all ICC judgments to be dispersed among tribal members) versus economic investment. It was a very political argument, which came down to individual choice versus the general economic benefit of all. Individual choice meant distribution of most of the judgment funds to individuals (per capita) and some to an education fund for future use. Investment meant most of the funds would be controlled by the Tribes for economic development (e.g., housing, recreation, farming, land purchase) and some money would be available for individual withdrawal.

In 1968–1969, the BIA funded a study by Ernst & Ernst, a Washington, D.C., management firm that prepared a report recommending using the funds for development of a hotel/golf course resort area, an industrial park, and community buildings on the Umatilla Indian Reservation. The Tribes would have had to take out loans to complete the projects.

The political turmoil started after the Tribes secured the Indian Claims Judgment in 1966 as payment for lands lost by the Tribes over one hundred years before. On September 9, 1967, the Tribes held a vote concerning full distribution versus investment, in which newspaper reports indicate the vote was 154 to 1 for full distribution of all funds. The November 1967, 1968, and 1969 tribal elections held pursuant to the Tribes' Constitution and By-Laws resulted in a change of majority on the General Council and the Board of Trustees to people who favored the distribution of funds. According to the December 1, 1969, *East Oregonian*, Roy McIntyre was elected Board chairman in the tribal election. Lillian Kanine Hoptowit, Kathleen Gordon, and Alphonse Halfmoon

elected as Board of Trustee members; Cecil I. Thompson was elected alternate. General Council chairman-elect was Raymond T. Burke. Marvin Picard was re-elected vice chair, Barbara Chalakee was re-elected secretary of General Council, and Eliza Bill was elected interpreter. Bill Minthorn was also on the Board of Trustees. He is the father of Antone Minthorn, present-day chairman of the BOT.

The vote to fully distribute the claims judgment money was by a three-to-one margin. According to the *East Oregonian*, 888 tribal members voted, with 514 for full per capita distribution and 173 for investment. Most of the people voting lived off the reservation. Even the majority for distribution prevailed for those residing on the reservation. In retrospect, we clearly exercised our sovereignty under the system established by our 1949 Constitution and By-Laws. The political activity of those who voted for full distribution (called the Progressive Association) demonstrated a full corporate takeover of the governing board of the Tribes to accomplish their goal — "give me the money."

Moneys were set aside for education, and the rest was distributed by sometime in 1970. Approximately $1,800 went to each member over the one-year period in three installments. In the 1970s, we did not invest in ourselves with enterprises and government structure. It was not until the 1990s, through investment from casino earnings, that we began the process of self-investment that we enjoy today.

1954 – 1970: Protection of Hunting and Fishing Rights

When our people agreed to the Treaty on June 9, 1855, we ceded or relinquished vast tracts of land (estimated at 2,900 square miles) to the United States in return for the obligation of the United States to protect and preserve the tribal people, the reservation (estimated at about 800 square miles), and reserved rights to fish, hunt, gather roots and berries, and pasture livestock. This included the right to hunt and fish off reservation. Article 1 of the Treaty provides:

that the exclusive right of taking fish in the streams running through and bordering said reservation is hereby secured to said Indians, and at all other usual and accustomed stations in common with citizens of the United States, and of erecting suitable buildings for curing the same; the privilege of hunting, gathering roots and berries and pasturing their stock on unclaimed lands in common with citizens, is also secured to them.

Throughout the Treaty negotiations, which occurred over a fourteen-day period in May–June 1855, assurances were given at different times to each tribe negotiating that they could continue to fish, hunt, and gather roots and berries as they always had, even to places as far away as Montana. The Tribes were very concerned that they could continue to practice their rights at locations on and off the reservation according to custom, tradition, and kinship and for subsistence purposes. When we agreed to the Treaty, our way of life as we knew it was ending. We had always traveled and hunted and fished free from all regulation except custom, tradition, and knowledge of the resources. If we had not, we would not have survived. We have always been especially leery of state regulation or intrusion into these ways and rights.

This was very much so in the early 1970s, when we formed the Fish and Wildlife Committee and the Law and Order Committee. We were concerned with preserving and protecting the practice of these rights; and all agreements, negotiations, or written laws we developed were done with this in mind. At one group Fish and Wildlife meeting held in Portland with the other treaty tribes — Nez Perce, Warm Springs, and Yakama — a *National Geographic* photographer took our picture and published it nationally. I was sitting next to Mose Dick, and Percy Brigham was also there. This is a time before the creation of the Columbia River Inter-Tribal Fish Commission. We were negotiating the settlement of the *U.S. v. Oregon* fishing rights case, which involved all the Columbia River tribes.

In the 1950s and 1960s, the state regulation of our hunting and fishing became a serious concern. In 1954, the State of Oregon attempted to regulate on-reservation hunting because of Public Law 280. In 1958, the state attempted to regulate off-reservation fishing by our tribal members, specifically the use of gaff hooks in salmon fishing at Catherine Creek, near La Grande. In 1964, the state attempted to regulate off-reservation hunting by our members who had not purchased state hunting tags. Through these years, the Tribes challenged these attempts and each time won in federal court protecting these rights from state regulation.[4]

The Indian Civil Rights Act of 1968 — Application of Due Process and Equal Protection

Our people have become much more sophisticated about their legal rights than when the United States executed the Cayuse Five in 1850. Concepts such as due process of law, equal rights under the law, the right to an attorney, the right to remain silent, just compensation, and conflict of interest are terms made familiar through mass media and contact with other governments or court systems. Many Indians and non-Indians alike would be shocked to learn that the U.S. Constitution and its Bill of Rights do not apply to tribal governments and that principles of due process and equal protection are defined under tribal law. While this is the case, it is not the whole story.

In 1896, in *Talton v. Mayes* (163 U.S. 376), the U.S. Supreme Court decided that the Cherokee Nation possessed sovereign powers that predated the adoption of the U.S. Constitution and that these inherent sovereign powers of the tribe could not be subject to the U.S. Constitution. This strong affirmation of tribal sovereignty eventually led to limitations imposed on tribal governments.

Tribal governments, including the Confederated Tribes, were free to interpret and apply civil rights without limitations, taking into account cultural factors as they saw fit, under the U.S. Constitution and tribal constitutions until 1968, when the U.S. Congress imposed the Indian Civil Rights Act (ICRA). It had come to the attention of the U.S. Congress, and specifically to Senator Sam Ervin from South Carolina, that tribal governments, including their courts and police, were not subject to the same constitutional limitations as state and federal governments. The U.S. Congress conducted hearings to explore the situation in Indian Country. Congress heard individual horror stories about the lack of due process or fair treatment, the lack of right to counsel, or the lack of a jury trial. The United States government did not consult with Indian Tribes on a government-to-government basis prior to enacting the new law (25 U.S.C Sections 1301-1303).

The ICRA applied many of the provisions of the U.S. Bill of Rights to tribes and their governments. Selected provisions and concepts were imposed on tribes, which protected individuals, including non-Indians, from tribal government action and included such rights as the right against unreasonable search and seizure, self-incrimination, and cruel and unusual punishment and the right to a jury trial, due process and equal treatment under the law, and bail. Noticeably absent from these rights is the right to counsel, the right to bear arms, and the separation of church and state. Federal enforcement of the ICRA is through the application for a writ of *habeas corpus*, which requires a tribe to explain the basis for its detention of an individual. The ICRA also limits the sentencing authority of tribal courts to basic misdemeanor crimes (now one year in jail and a $5,000 fine).

Ten years after the act's enactment in 1978, the U.S. Supreme Court interpreted the ICRA in the landmark case out of New Mexico, *Santa Clara Pueblo v. Martinez* (436 U.S. 49). The case involved tribal enrollment procedures, which allowed male members of the Santa Clara Pueblo to marry outside the tribe/pueblo and still enroll their children in the tribe/pueblo. Female pueblo members who married outside the tribe could not enroll their children, and Julia Martinez had married a Navajo tribal member. In the Southwest, under tribal custom/tradition and law, children were usually enrolled in the pueblo or tribe of the father.

The Supreme Court did not address these facts or the actual merits of the case. The Court basically held that because of inherent sovereignty and because tribal forums were the best place to resolve issues of tradition and custom, even under the ICRA, the federal courts lacked jurisdiction to hear these matters. This does not mean that the ICRA will not be enforced in federal forums or tribal forums. The writ of *habeas corpus* is still available and allows a federal court to determine the validity of a person's detention by a tribal court. Federal policy or law can be changed to allow federal jurisdiction, even involving matters such as enrollment and tribal membership. In considering tribal

custom and tradition, tribal governments can enforce the ICRA in their own way. They can allow *habeus corpus* in tribal forums. If the perception of how tribal governments administer justice is that they lack due process or fundamental fairness, however, new laws or policies that reduce sovereign powers could occur. Most tribes consider this problem or perception when enacting laws and procedures, especially for their judicial systems. They act responsibly and with consideration for the ICRA, as well as for their traditions and customs, in treatment of individuals. Tribes that do not honor due process or fundamental fairness concerns will put tribal sovereignty in peril of further limitations or restrictions.

1970 – 1981: Retrocession of Exclusive Criminal Jurisdiction under Public Law 280

The politics of retrocession began with the ICRA, which contains the authority to allow retrocession (25 USC 1323(a) 1970). Retrocession means the relinquishment of jurisdiction, in this case by a state to the federal government under Public Law 280, with the federal government ultimately returning jurisdiction to the tribal government. The state initiates retrocession, and the final decision is with the U.S. government as delegated to the secretary of the Interior. The state consults with the U.S. attorney general, but the law does not require tribal consultation. Tribes usually have requested retrocession and prepared plans of operation, codes, and laws, if necessary, for tribal law enforcement and judicial services.

In reality, jurisdiction was never absent from the Umatilla Indian Reservation. We have always possessed inherent sovereignty and jurisdiction and concurrent jurisdiction under Public Law 280. The main problem with providing services under Public Law 280 was that there was no commitment of funding or taxing ability allowed in the states in which it occurred. Consequently, states did not extend services to reservations when Public Law 280 authorized state law enforcement on reservation lands.

Our drive toward exclusive criminal jurisdiction actually began in the early 1970s with our planning department and our lawyers. Based on a comprehensive plan for the Umatilla Indian Reservation, an assessment was made by the Tribal Development Office of our people, resources, and land base and the best way to maintain our sovereignty, culture, and way of life. An important component of that plan was the ability to enforce the laws we enacted on our reservation. Another was enlarging or reclaiming the land base of our reservation. We also wanted better services provided to our community, including zoning, law enforcement, health, and fire protection. The most important thing we wanted was self-government, self-determination, and the ability and authority to do it ourselves.

In the early to mid–1970s, we sought legislation through the U.S. Congress that would allow us to abide by the rule of law, enforcing our laws, contracts, and regulations. We also wanted to be able to mortgage our land like any other person and to protect our land from further fractionation. The legislation introduced through Senator Mark Hatfield's office was in three parts: (1) retrocession of exclusive criminal and civil jurisdiction from Public Law 280; (2) land consolidation of tribal lands, allowing us to mortgage trust tribal lands to fund the purchase of other lands or for business purposes; and (3) inheritance act to prevent further fractionalized heirship of trust property so that ostensibly it is useless for business.

In reviewing the *East Oregonian* about this proposed legislation there was fear about Indian jurisdiction and the rights of non-Indians on the Umatilla Indian Reservation. One of the biggest fears was that the Tribes would confiscate real property and force people to move from the reservation. There was also the fear of taxes without representation and the loss of land values. Another concern was that all tribal members did not agree on the proposed bill and opposed jurisdiction. These so-called controversial measures were discussed at various public hearings from 1975 to 1977 on the reservation and in Pendleton.

Looking back and considering the economic development the Tribes have accomplished with cooperation from federal, state, and local authorities, these fears were groundless. The Tribes are restricted by the ICRA and would not take property unless it was for a public cause and with just compensation and due process of the law. Besides, if the Tribes had the money to exclude non-Indian landowners, it probably would have done so well before 1975. The majority of tribal people on the reservation supported the jurisdiction and land-base proposals, although not all thought we had capability to do so. That could be said of any government.

The proposals met defeat, and we took another course. It actually took five to eight years to secure the return of criminal jurisdiction to the Tribes through Public Law 280 but took only a few months to implement it. Land consolidation and fractionalized heirship (multiple owners of one piece of land through inheritance) are still problems, but national legislation is attempting to address them.[5] The behind-the-scenes work involved our planners, our community, our leaders, our lawyers, legislators in Oregon and in Washington, D.C., local law enforcement, local district attorneys, local judges, and the BIA. The period involved planning and assessment for better services and communication for all concerned. It embodied self-governance and determination. We had the competence and intelligence to succeed, and we documented our goals and objectives.

One very important person who listened to Indians and his constituents was Victor Atiyeh. He first became familiar with the CTUIR as a member of the state-created Commission on Indian Services in Salem. He was a legislator then, and he listened to our Tribes as well as to other tribes about the difficulties we faced and the plans for the future. The Burns–Paiute Tribe, Umatilla Tribes, Warm Springs Tribes, Klamath Tribes, Siletz Tribes, and Grand Ronde Tribes were represented on

More on Traditional Law

There were laws here before the immigration of Europeans, Americans, Spanish, and others to this part of the country. Our own laws were rooted deep in the culture. When the headmen made decisions, they would follow the guidance of law that goes way back. There are many facets of our Indian law. Not only is there religious law, there is civil law, laws which governed the day-to-day living in the community. People knew what was community property and what was private property. Laws were in existence that governed the children; the whipman was a prime example of one of those laws. The whipman would keep order and discipline the children when it was called for.

— Thomas Morning Owl

this unique commission. Its aim was to provide better services to the Indians of Oregon. Atiyeh became governor of Oregon in 1979.

We continued our efforts toward retrocession by establishing a fish and game court, and we began the operations of our court system. Raymond T. Burke was named chief judge and Matthew Farrow, Sr., was named associate judge to that court. Dave Gallaher was also named associate judge. The other tribes in Oregon supported us in our efforts, as well as local law enforcement personnel and judges. We had done our homework, our objectives and assessments were sound, and we requested retrocession under the amendments to the 1968 ICRA from Governor Vic Atiyeh.

In May 1980, Executive Order 80-8 offered to retrocede to the United States all criminal jurisdiction exercised by the State of Oregon over the Umatilla Indian Reservation under Public Law 280. In the *Federal Register*, the U.S. accepted retrocession effective on January 2, 1981. The court operations were immediately expanded and the exercise of our sovereignty continues in the tribal court to this day.

When we sought retrocession, we wanted to govern ourselves and our tribal lands. We wanted better law and order services and the authority to be able to enforce our laws. We had a focused effort — a belief or vision that we could do it — but it was not easy. Things may appear closer than they actually are.

1970 — Indian Self-Determination

The Indian Self-Determination and Education Assistance Act, passed in 1975, authorized tribes to contract or take over operations of federal programs from the Bureau of Indian Affairs and the Indian Health Service, whichever was authorized for operation of services on reservations. That was one reason we wanted to retrocede; we wanted to garner authority and have a basis for requesting the funding that the federal agencies got. We had not yet decided about all of the other tribal programs, but we knew we wanted better police, fire, and court protection or court services on the reservation.

In 1970, President Nixon announced the Indian self-determination policy in a speech. Interestingly, it was the time of the Cold War and negotiations with the USSR. It was a time when the USSR asked the United States government: "Why do you treat Native Americans the way you do?" I think that was a kernel of thought for the government about Indian self-determination, which was high on the agenda for the Nixon administration. Also, Nixon was no doubt influenced by the Red Power and Civil Rights movements, which were in full swing during the termination era.

We continue to contract and take authority for operations of the BIA, including our superintendent services on our reservation. Reservations across the United States continue to seek self-determination contracts and funding under the authority of the Indian Self-Determination Act.

Conclusion

From our perspective, modern sovereignty began in 1855 with the signing of the Treaty that made the Umatilla Indian Reservation our homeland. The Bureau of Indian Affairs, however, was the de facto government until the Cayuse, Umatilla, and Walla Walla people voted to adopt a modern constitutional form of government in 1949, when we became the Confederated Tribes of the Umatilla Indian Reservation. The Board of Trustees then made the decision to contract 1960s War on Poverty programs, Housing and Urban Development homes, and Indian Health Service programs. These programs became the basis of the CTUIR's capacity to manage its own business affairs. The opportunity for the CTUIR to strengthen its sovereignty came with the 1975 Self-Determination Act, which allowed the BOT to contract and manage BIA programs.[6] This act removed incompetent BIA management. Thus began the CTUIR renaissance. We cannot preserve CTUIR culture without sovereignty. Our tribal economy relies on the total community to survive.

The Treaty of 1855 illustrates the vision and foresight our peoples had for future generations. The flame of sovereignty continues to burn through oral traditions given to us throughout time. This is our true law — our language, tradition, and custom. As a group, we do not have the mastery of our language anymore, simply because of all the cultural influences that have been added to our world. But we exist, and we continue to view ourselves as a distinct group of people because of our ancestors' actions and their foresight in seeking to preserve our rights through treaty.

We must, as our ancestors did, maintain the vision of our sovereignty, represented by our old ways, and we must do so while adapting to new predicaments. Our vision of sovereignty is much the same as it was before the coming of the Europeans — we want to preserve and protect our families, hunt and fish as we always have, and live in an environment that is relatively safe for all. We independently and collectively work for the community to preserve our ways in the future. The key is that we want to do it ourselves.

Notes

1. Brief on Meaning, Validity and Effect of the Commission's Interlocutory Decision of September 28, 1964, Regarding Eligibility to Share in Judgment Funds, *In the Matter of the Judgment Funds of the Confederated Tribes of the Umatilla Indian Reservation,* Mark, C. McClanahan, Attorney for Tribe (April 29, 1969).

2. See Ronald B. Lansing, Ronald B., *Juggernaut: The Whitman Massacre Trial, 1850* (Pasadena, Calif: Ninth Judicial Circuit Historical Society, 1993).

3. Ibid.

4. See *CTUIR v. Maison,* National Archives, Seattle, Washington. Also cited but not complete report of findings, conclusions, and judgment as *CTUIR v. Maison* Civil Action 8004 (March 13, 1956) US District Court, *CTUIR v. Maison,* 186 F.Supp 519 (D. Ore 1960), *CTUIR v. Maison* 262 F.Supp 871 (D Ore 1966).

5. See Indian Land Consolidation Act, 25 USC §2201 *et seq.* (2000); American Indian Probate Reform Act of 2004, PL 108-374 (2004).

6. In 1969, Alvin M. Josephy, Jr., prepared a study and recommendation on the state of Indian affairs to help form Indian policy at the request of the Nixon administration. Among his major recommendations were to reassure Indians that the termination policy was dead and that the administration supported instead Indian self-determination and self-government, that the BIA be elevated in the Interior Department, and that Indians hold top policy-making jobs. While not enacted until 1975, it would eventually come to pass, as a foothold was created by the Josephy study before the Indian civil rights protests of Alcatraz and Wounded Knee erupted.

Indians Then and Now

On this 100th anniversary of our Treaty, as we commemorate the acts of our ancestors, we implore the people of America to examine the records, based upon the most begrudging and limited opportunities under which the only true Americans in America have been subject. During these 100 years, Indians' pleas in Washington have gone unheeded, so we must turn to the people of this nation as Just and God-thinking Americans for corrections and fulfillment of our Treaties.

Today we should be ready to accept withdrawal of the government of responsibility, but facts here related prove this cannot be done. These are not dictations of fiction, but true facts — not of a dead past — and by experience we know them to be true. They exist at the very core of a nation that proclaims loudly to the world its greatness and strength that we as a people with every patriotic and American citizen have contributed to and built, a nation that advocates with determination to restore other conquered peoples to the dignity of human beings, with freedom from want, freedom of religion, freedom of speech, and freedom from fear. What consideration has the Indian received in these freedoms? We cannot uphold decency, honor, or respect by honorably discharging any person who has failed to honestly fulfill his obligations and responsibilities toward a people of a nation. Yet the U.S. government wants to terminate its Trusteeship of the Indian as having done its job. Before this government can demand total respect of others, it most certainly should act respectfully toward its own citizens, with fulfillment of all its obligations and responsibilities, not only to Indians, but to every American. Peoples of every race in America have sacrificed and contributed to her greatness, yet do not receive as much consideration as peoples of other nations. Nations around the world have been hallowed by the graves of your sons, many of whose families are destitute. We can properly define equality, justice, and freedom in our own acts through the understanding that our fellow men will bring greater enrichment to our own knowledge. In these days of struggle and strife all around us, our hearts ought not be set against one another, but set with one another, that we may be able to work more strongly against evil. We live in a world full of misery and ignorance, and the sacred duty of each is to try and make the little corner he can influence somewhat less miserable and less ignorant. We want equality of opportunity and political and social freedom. We are not asking to be relieved of responsibility, but the right to consideration and a part in building a healthy and progressive community to which we are willing to contribute. I can claim many distinctions for my people, the greatest of these is that America began with us and we have shared all of it with you.

Maudie C. Antoine, Chairwoman, Board of Trustees, Confederated Tribes of the Umatilla Indian Reservation. These remarks were made at the 1855 Treaty Centennial observance in Walla Walla, Washington, June 11, 1955.

Self-Determination and Recovery

John David Tovey, Jr., and friends of the late Michael J. Farrow

As tribal members point to their own families and tribal histories rich in living off the land, tribal elders often recall the local effects of the Great Depression. Many will say that because our people lived on and close to the land, tribal members weathered the widespread hunger most of the country experienced. "There was no Depression on the Umatilla Reservation" is often said. The railroad was the transportation corridor for work-desperate wanderers, and many found generosity and sustenance from tribal families. Whole camps of "hobos" would be fed and sometimes clothed in exchange for menial work or hunting. The last four decades demonstrate the resilience of that generation of tribal members, who were very much in transition between worlds, as well as the remarkable set of living skills they had that allowed them to subsist on the available resources.

These values provided the foundation for the Tribes' work and business ethic from the early days of its organizational history. Many tribal programs were sparsely staffed, and many enterprises were managed directly by various committees, such as Credit, Farm, and Forestry/Range. While committee management had its drawbacks, these forums became learning circles, where the values of the Depression generation were conveyed to the next generations.

Mike Farrow used to speak of the teachings of his mentors — Sam Kash Kash, Joe Sheoships, Philip Guyer, Bill Minthorn, Elzie Farrow, and others. Through their guidance, he was taught that no matter what we might think of our adversaries, we will gain more by treating them as neighbors than by taking them head-on as enemies. Several of those values continue in the Tribes' philosophy today, such as diligence, selfless service, fiscal conservatism, avoidance of debt financing, honorable business relations, and sharing of the fruits with all tribal members.

Reflections on Tribal Development in the 1970s

History is like a foggy morning. Hard work is involved in remembering, researching, and fact-checking. Reflection, on the other hand, seems a whole lot more enjoyable. This effort is an attempt in both history and reflection.

By 1973, the War on Poverty campaign of social and economic development that Lyndon Johnson launched in the 1960s made its way to the Umatilla Reservation. At the time, just a few had started the Tribal Development Office (TDO). Michael Farrow, a young man who had just returned from two tours as a medic in the Vietnam conflict, was hired as an assistant planner, along with fellow tribal members Amelia Enick and Susan Sams as secretary-bookkeepers. The TDO was funded by an Economic Development Administration (EDA) planning assistance grant and a Housing and Urban Development (HUD) 701 planning grant. A planning firm from Portland was just completing the first comprehensive planning study, and the Tribes were negotiating to adopt the first-ever joint zoning ordinance with Umatilla County.

The Community Health Representatives Program funded Woody Patawa, Tessie Williams, and Elizabeth Jones. The Indian Health Service was planning the Mission sewer line. The BIA was transitioning from the superintendency of Harold Duck to what would be a series of activist superintendents. Tribal Treasurer Leslie Minthorn had just returned to the

Courtesy of the Farrow family

Michael "Jughead" Farrow at Tasmástslikt Cultural Institute in about 2002.

reservation to build his house up on McKay Creek, on the first allotment on the reservation. The Relocation Program took him to Portland for several years. Louie Dick, Jr., had recently been elected to the Board, along with some elders — Sam Kash Kash, Joe Sheoships, Bill Minthorn, and others. The Board of Trustees was poised to recover from the battle of the land claims settlement and make some real and positive changes. There was no place to go but up.

Many things were stirring in various corners of the organizational universe that was the CTUIR. These forces, like small breezes, swirled around the campus of the BIA and the traditional July Grounds — where veterans' ceremonies took place in lieu of Independence Day celebrations — and they began to mix and come together. They did not come together in any neat or systematic way. Many times, things spun off and were not seen again or disappeared for many years. These little clusters of activity, as they combined and grew, became the dust devils of the renaissance. The next five years were a whirlwind.

Plans and Planners

Sam Kash Kash was the Chairman of the Tribes for many of the years during this period. Elders such as he were members of the buffer generations — those who bridged the world of the Treaty signers and this place we call the "modern world." We received our guidance from the Planning Committee. Everyone had to take his or her turn at General Council and take one's tongue-lashing, deserved or not. "It is good for you," it was said, like a trip to the woodshed of humility.

The first Overall Economic Development Plan (OEDP) was finished in July 1974. The themes that were struck in that document remain the themes that underscore our work in economic development today. To quote the elder Philip Guyer: "My idea of comprehensive planning is to see how we can cut out what makes us poor...to see if we can get rid of the load

that we carry which makes us lose our energy to help ourselves."[1]

The plan was as much a statement of vision as it was a road map. It represented what was in the hearts and minds of those who continued to do the work of laying the foundation for the renaissance. The OEDP is also a document that expresses the dreams and visions of its authors, Mike Farrow and Tom Hampson. Hampson was a young planner who came to the Tribes via the U.S. Forest Service (USFS) on the advice of tribal member Louie Dick, his USFS supervisor in the late 1960s. Planning was directed as much, if not more, to the land and water, as the ideas grew about how these resources might benefit the people. A not-so-young graduate student getting his masters of urban planning at the University of Oregon (and today's tribal chairman), Antone Minthorn, came to intern in the TDO and stayed. Andy Dumont was the first zoning inspector, who still works in a related capacity today. This was the era of land-use planning environmentalism in Oregon. There were more ideas and opportunities than hours in the day or qualified people to follow them through.

Within the first year, the seven tribal staff had morphed into more than one hundred. The federal gravy train was running right through the reservation; and, unlike the Union Pacific, it was stopping at Mission. We wrote grants that staffed the education department and the employment office. We created a three-reservation Manpower Consortium with the Burns–Paiute and Warm Springs Tribes.

Religious leader Armand Minthorn in the tribal longhouse.

We acquired grants for the ballfields, Cay-Uma-Wa (which houses the Tribes' language program and early education Head Start), and the expanded Yellowhawk Clinic. We designed the tribal longhouse with the Celebration committee and the Portland-area office of the BIA. Because we were still under Public Law 280, we had to comply with Oregon state health regulations, and they would not allow a dirt floor in the longhouse, which the Wáashat religion calls for, in the same building as a kitchen. We compromised by having a removable floor in the center of the longhouse.

Les Minthorn pursued the re-establishment of tribal law enforcement with

tribal attorney Doug Nash. Once we wrote the initial grant, each cluster of activists — like planners Dale Magers and Deborah Whitely, who ran the employment and training program; and education specialists Woesha Hampson and Louella Farrow, who ran the education department — took it from there and built their centers under the guidance of their own committees. The TDO was simply the greenhouse.

We assumed Alphonse "Frenchy" Halfmoon's position in the Halfmoon Market and were able to acquire the property. The Small Business Administration let us zero out Frenchy's loan. We got a grant to rebuild it and manpower money to staff it. We started the initial planning for the rural fire district. We got the grant for the campground at Indian Lake, and we watched as the well-digger hit water in the drizzling sleet of November.

Building the Foundation

We hired some good hearts but some ineffective managers in those days, some absolutely superb people, and some well-meaning charlatans. The Tribal Construction Enterprise started and collapsed. The Forestry and Range Enterprises started and sputtered. The Farm Committee — under the guidance of Sam and Joe Sheoships, and later under Mike Farrow — continued a slow and cautious program of land acquisition and stewardship of the remnants of tribal agricultural land, which used to be the source of true wealth for the Tribes before the coming of the non-Indians.

The Manpower Consortium developed the first set of tribal personnel policies, and we began to centralize the administration of the various committees (except health and housing.) Dale Baldwin, a retired BIA area director, was the first business manager. Tribal member Taz Conner was his assistant. That was the beginning of the tribal central administration.

We all walked tortuous paths in developing the next phase of the tribal government. We were attempting to centralize program functions for administrative efficiencies, while avoiding stepping too deeply into the well-protected turf of the program managers and their committees.

The legacy of that tension between centralizing and decentralizing forces is the current maze of programs, committees, commissions, and chartered enterprises that is the CTUIR.

Gathering up the Horses

The work of building the foundation for the renaissance was all done within the context of what was, by any standard, a hostile environment. The local power structure within and outside Umatilla County saw the emergence of the Confederated Tribes as a threat. Always happy to see the Indians at Round-Up, they cringed to have them at the negotiating table on issues of water rights, land consolidation, inheritance, and retrocession of Public Law 280. The Inheritance Act and the Land Consolidation Act were bills that Sam Kash Kash and company had worked for decades to get through Congress. Those bills would simply allow the Tribes and their members to acquire and to pass on their lands in an orderly and economically beneficial manner, but they were stymied by local agricultural interests and their puppet politicians. Even good political friends of the Tribes could not see their way clear to overcome local resistance to this legislation. Little did they know, they were simply delaying tactics in what would be an unstoppable re-emergence of the original landowner in the region.

Throughout the 1970s, the economic and community development activities gained momentum, attracting more and more soldiers — technicians and political leaders. The reassertion of sovereignty took hold under the guidance of tribal leaders who refused to be intimidated and who, most importantly, refused to lower themselves to the bigotry that characterized their neighbors.

The groundwork for the Umatilla Basin Project, the fisheries program, the casino and resort — every program that is now an integral part of the landscape of the reservation — was laid during this period. It was not the doing of the Tribal Development Office. We were simply one of the vehicles for the expression and implementation of the vision of those people that made up the Planning Committee. It was a vision and a hope for a people that persisted in the face of negativity, despair, doubt, and jealousy. Given the period we had just lived through, in which our own people proved to be adversarial, we had no reasonable expectation to believe that it could happen. We ignored the evidence to the contrary and plowed on with determination. The Tribal Development Office was simply one of the horses we road.

Mike Farrow carried a newly established tradition into the management of the Department of Natural Resources (DNR), in that the best way to serve the interests of the enrollees of the Confederated Tribes was to hire the best people, native and non-native. Our other commitment was that we needed to create, as best we could with the resources available, a training slot for enrolled tribal members for every management position and a commitment of every non-enrolled manager to train his or her replacement.

Another tradition that was established was that plans and their implementing ordinances were critical to establishing a legal and a moral authority to be managers and stewards of the lands and all the creatures. As irritating as the rule of law can be — especially because the rule had to be applied to all, enrollees, Indians, and non-Indians, and after all that was done that was so unfair, all that had been done to erase the footprints of the Indians — it was the rule of law and the principles that the Tribes adhered to in our application — to seek equity, to be fair, to be good neighbors. It was the rule of law and these principles that gave the Tribes the rightful place we now own in the region.

It is a position we have worked incredibly hard for. It is a place we deserve. It is a place that many have died to keep — veterans of wars, foreign, domestic, and tribal. It is a place that has always been ours but will take constant vigilance and continued hard and creative work to sustain. It is an honor to play a very small part in the keeping of that place that Mike Farrow called "the center of the earth."

Laying the Groundwork

In the mid-1980s, there was a focus to bring the economic development planning documents up to date and to accelerate economic development results. These efforts provided extensive dialogue with tribal members and leaders in various forums to shape the Tribes' ambitions and expecta-

Courtesy of the *Confederated Umatilla Journal*

Ike Blackwolf, Jesse Jones, and Douglas Minthorn pose in traditional regalia.

tions. These took the form of annual updates for the Overall Economic Development Program, an analysis by the Council of Energy Resource Tribes (CERT), a "strategic" planning process, a partnership with the First Nations Financial Project, a Land Project Policy Statement, and a capital improvements planning effort.

Generally, these planning processes demonstrated that additional administrative and professional staff was necessary to carry out the priorities and that a separate business corporation was necessary to "separate the business from the politics." Over the years, the Board of Trustees struggled with the concept of a business corporation. Each time a new structure was proposed, anxieties arose when the Board realized that daily business decisions would be made by the corporate hierarchy rather than by tribal government. Although there were few business operations to have such power over, the Board was consistently reluctant to surrender such control.

The seminal point from several tribal leaders' standpoints was a General Council meeting in the late 1980s where the result of one of the planning efforts was being reported. A tribal member took the floor and demanded to know why yet another plan was being developed. His point was essentially: "We have to do something. We have to take some risks if we're going to do business." Although such rebukes can be difficult to endure, leaders saw that people were now ready to support action.

Throughout these planning days in the late 1980s and early 1990s, any number of external business interests approached the Tribes with ideas ranging from coffin assembly to plastic bullet manufacturing to offers to acquire hot springs resorts in the area. Typically, these deals were merely "good ideas" that required the Tribes to fully finance the project with their own resources of cash, debt financing, and grant sources in exchange for 51 percent of

the business and the complete surrender of operational management and oversight. This was the typical "joint venture" model in much of Indian Country. Although the potential business partners assumed otherwise, the Tribes held trust fund accounts, mostly in educational scholarships, in the neighborhood of only a million dollars. Tribal leadership had long held the position that this core nest egg was not to be touched. Most of the deals withdrew when this fact came to light, and when the Tribes' leadership asked for reasonable levels of due diligence.

Early on, we relied on the expertise of the Council for Energy Resource Tribes, which was already a major outside contractor with the Tribes through funding from the Department of Energy for the Tribes' participation in oversight of the proposed nuclear repository at Hanford. After performing an internal analysis of the Tribes' preparedness for business activity, CERT recommended that we submit a proposal to the Administration for Native Americans (ANA) to fund those activities, which we would relate to Hanford oversight. After the first effort failed, in part affected by the phase down of Hanford work, the Tribes' staff accepted the challenge to fund our own projects when it became apparent CERT technical assistance was not forthcoming.

The Tribes were successful in a subsequent effort with a project that detailed an accountant, a financial planner, and an attorney. It should be noted that this was consistent with a direction set earlier by the

Courtesy of the *Confederated Umatilla Journal*

Andrew Dumont, Rod Cowapoo, Sr., Eliza Bill, Carl Sampson, and Kathleen Gordon at a Housing Authority meeting on the Umatilla Indian Reservation in about 1973.

Tribes' Department of Natural Resources of hiring staff positions rather than relying on consultants to manage projects and programs. While the Tribes had done numerous studies and had fielded wide-ranging business ideas, it was felt that on-reservation professional staff were needed to fully understand the complexities of doing business in Indian Country and, specifically, on the Umatilla Reservation.

Activities accelerated as the new staff began efforts to research and analyze not only opportunities but also the rules. Existing enterprises were bolstered with

It Began with a Grain Elevator

In 1985, the development of the tribal grain elevator in conjunction with Pendleton Flour Mills (PFM) was a big success in terms of return, benefit to Indian landowners, and convenience for reservation farmers. It was a clear institutional success for the CTUIR. The germ of the idea could be traced to public expressions by PFM leadership of their search for a new rail-shipping facility. This project served to expose some of the internal organizational decision gaps that existed. After the Tribes had approved the project, there was some scrambling to fully secure the trust allotment into tribal ownership, requiring additional intensive negotiations and cross-country travel to secure all the necessary owners' approval. Further, in the midst of an important continuous pour of concrete for the grain towers, a dispute with the Tribal Employment Rights Office (set up to get tribal employment contracts of federally funded projects) caused a project shutdown, potentially compromising the integrity of the structure. Nonetheless, the Tribes, the Mills, and the contractors persevered, and the project was successfully completed in the summer of 1985.

Several lessons can be pointed to with the PFM elevator project. First, it highlighted the role tribal government can play in a major joint venture with a corporate partner. The company provided the management, existing market, and project guidance, while the Tribes could use its governmental protections, low-cost financing, and property availability. Second, the project and its successful completion conveyed a "success mentality" in the Tribes' leadership, offsetting the natural bureaucratic tendency to study an opportunity until it expires. The project was cited in later years when business decisions were made. Lastly, the project provided discretionary governmental revenue on an annual basis, which the Tribe used to leverage into other projects and initiatives.

better administrative policies and tighter oversight on leasehold arrangements. These new staff were quickly used in other projects and programs. Two of them are currently tribal department directors.

During the late 1980s, a related event transpired that was very telling of the relationship the Tribes' leadership had with the trustee, the Bureau of Indian Affairs. With minimal discretionary revenue, the tribal government relied heavily on external sources to operate tribal programs and services, primarily BIA and Indian Health Service. Tribal leadership was found almost daily in the offices of the Agency asking advice and counsel. When the new staff attorney began to research the legal basis of various authorities to oversee land tenure issues, the local Agency began to raise the specter of an obscure law that requires BIA approval of all attorneys that work for any tribe. Even though the new position was funded with a non-BIA source and many tribes no longer provided such certifications, the local Agency was insistent that the new attorney sign an onerous contract to continue his employment with the Tribes. The terms of the BIA-driven agreement were unacceptable. Although hoping for some Board backing, it became clear that the Tribes' leadership was too afraid of veiled threats by the BIA and presented an ultimatum that the attorney would sign or resign. This law has since been overturned, in part due to testimony presented by the then director of Enterprise Administration but mainly because so many tribes considered it a relic of BIA paternalism. This was a seminal event in advancing the notion that tribal solutions are to be found within the tribes themselves.

Another key event was the Tribes' application to the First Nations Financial Project, a national Indian organization based near Washington, D.C. First Nations approved the Umatilla Tribes as a project site and assigned their field staff to begin working with the Tribes. The staff of the Enterprise Administration have suggested that although not many tangible projects resulted, the First Nations visits helped focus the Tribes' efforts in several arenas and helped advance more national movements in key issues. Most of the early Enterprise Administration staff were eager and hard working, but their collective experience in Indian Country was limited. The First Nations connection provided some needed context to the work. This relationship over time has blossomed into the Indian Land Consolidation Conferences, the Indian Land Working Group, and the Indian Land Tenure Foundation.

Still, much of this work tended to be oriented toward building capacity and improving existing plans rather than actual projects. Still found to be reacting to external ideas, the Enterprise Administration commenced a capital improvements planning process, similar to that used by municipalities to set longer-term visions for community infrastructure and buildings. After canvassing the various programs and committees, the Community Development Commission approved a list of ten projects in 1988 that served as the Tribes' priorities for much of the 1990s. Six of these projects were components of what would become the Wildhorse Resort and Casino complex.

The Capital Improvements List

There used to be an adage for what was known as Enterprise Administration: "If we had a nickel for every good idea that came in the door for the Tribe to make money, we'd have so stinking much money, we wouldn't know what to do with it all." While such a statement was mainly for figurative effect, concepts for tribal businesses were constantly hitting the small staff from internal and external sources. Given the level of research and due diligence required, such ideas were increasingly viewed as distractions to the ultimate desire of the Tribe setting its own economic vision.

Given this backdrop, Enterprise Administration invited its oversight commission, the Community Development Commission, to begin a capital improvements planning process similar to that employed by most municipal jurisdictions. Although part of the process for the annual Overall Economic Development Plan update (by way of the annual planning grant from the U.S. Economic Development Administration) was to produce long lists of potential projects, there was no direct tribal connection for organizing staff time and budgets. Staff felt strongly that if they could get a list of projects that

they could focus their time, energy, and effort on, the Tribes might start seeing the result of its own direction.

Long hours were spent by dedicated volunteers, sitting through hours of discussion, usually in the evenings, to provide perspective and guidance to the staff and the Board.[2] An invitation was sent to all tribal programs, boards, and commissions to submit what they saw as their major projects. A list of over seventy projects was assembled, and the Community Development Commission set a list of the ten priorities, which tended to focus on business and economic development concerns.

Still, with no development resources — except the small nest egg in the Education Trust account that would not be available — and the limited staffing dollars, the challenge of Enterprise Administration became to build the capacity to take on the list of projects. It was very much like the situation faced by fledgling nonprofit organizations, where each staff works two jobs — one for the purpose of the organization and the other for raising the resources to continue the work. Luckily, boundless energy and optimism made up for such obstacles.

Indian Gaming

This set the stage for the active monitoring of the growing Indian gaming industry. With the passage of the Indian Gaming Regulatory Act (IGRA) in 1988, the Tribes were generally secure in the notion that we would venture into the business at some point, but it seemed bigger and more complex than anything done previously. So, monitoring the industry became the task of young bingo manager, John Barkley. While the small program toyed with additional evenings for the bingo program, it was clear that the existing market could only sustain a once-a-week program. As John's job was increased to full-time, however, clearly more than necessary given the operation, he was further assigned the role of observing and infiltrating the growing Indian gaming arena. John began to attend conventions, build a network, and track legislation and publicity.

Several key findings were established by John's investigations. First, some of the best negotiated agreements between states and tribes were those where the tribes of a particular state unified and negotiated as a collective group. Second, it was increasingly clear that the laws and courts were supporting the rationale that when a state approves video poker or any similar mechanized gambling, it opens the door under IGRA to the tribes of that state to get slot machines. Lastly, the industry was in tremendous flux early on with the negotiations and legal wranglings occurring across the nation.

While these events were being played on the national scene, the staff of Enterprise Administration turned their attention to the opportunity at hand. With no video poker authorized in Oregon as yet, there was an effort to pull together a project to construct a new bingo hall on the site approximately where the RV park is

today. The plans were very conservative and austere — basically a large Quonset hut with a small kitchen and offices. The cost was in the neighborhood of $250,000, and the plan was to use existing staff to manage the program.

John Barkley began to line up meetings with the local banks to talk about the project. Unbelievably — even at that rather humble point in time — he could not get so much as a sit-down visit with local bankers. Hindsight would suggest that this reaction was for two basic viewpoints: gambling was not considered a legitimate business and the Tribes with our Enterprise Administration had little external credibility. It was clear that more preparation was necessary.

The Big Meeting

In 1989, at the suggestion of General Council Chairman Antone Minthorn, the staff organized an internal economic summit that was held at the large meeting room upstairs at the Tapadera Inn in downtown Pendleton. Presentations were scheduled from TERO, the BIA, various enterprises, and partners. The event was intended to pull together the people working on various components of economic and business development to disclose and coordinate those efforts and to start securing buy-in toward a collective vision. Several soon-to-be major initiatives were highlighted at the summit, with political intrigue galore.

The meeting launched the idea to host the first annual Indian Land Consolidation Conference in Pendleton, which itself spurred the creation of the Indian Land Working Group and eventually the Indian Land Tenure Foundation. The other major presentation involved the pre-planning for the Oregon Trail 150th anniversary celebration in 1992. The group organizing the plans suggested that four major interpretive centers be constructed across Oregon that would highlight various perspectives of the Oregon Trail migration. It was a sweeping vision. One would be at Baker City to highlight the pioneers' overland trek, one at The Dalles to feature the Columbia Gorge and the pioneers' choice between a rough ride on the river or a difficult journey over the mountain, one at Oregon City to commemorate the official end of the Oregon

Courtesy of CTUIR GIS Program

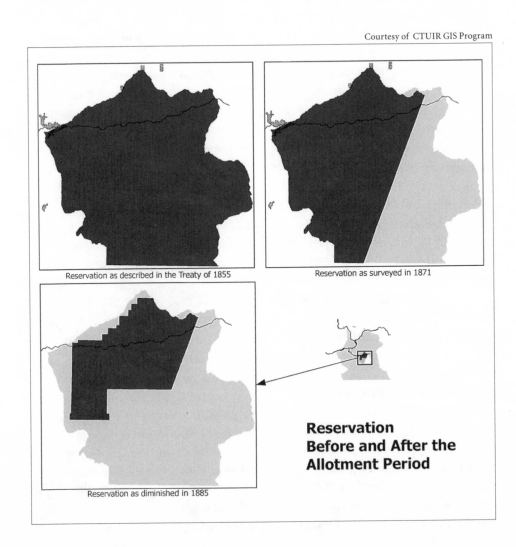

Reservation as described in the Treaty of 1855

Reservation as surveyed in 1871

Reservation as diminished in 1885

Reservation Before and After the Allotment Period

Trail, and one on the Umatilla Reservation. That center — which is now the renowned Tamástslikt Cultural Institute — would examine the Tribes' view of the migration.

The reaction was mixed. Several prominent tribal leaders provided the immediate, reasonable reaction: "Why would we want to celebrate an event that nearly led to our extinction?" Others had questions of who would tell our story and who would "own" it. Still others, mostly staff, saw the unique opportunity. Could this idea be shaped and made tribal and accomplish a long-standing goal of the Tribes to have a cultural museum facility?[3] A series of work sessions were scheduled with the Board of Trustees. In only two weeks after the economic summit, the Umatilla Tribes officially agreed to participate in the facility planning, contingent on the project being planned, developed, owned, and operated by the Tribes. The Oregon Trail Advisory Council readily agreed.

Fund-Raising

In 1989, the Enterprise Administration faced its first conventional fundraising task, raising $80,000 for the "master plan" for the Oregon Trail interpretive project. The Board of Trustees authorized a "soft donation" of $10,000 contingent upon the successful raising of the other $70,000. As this project was the first time the Tribes had tried to raise external resources in this manner, it is fair to suggest that several Board members believed they would not have to deliver on the commitment. Introductory meetings with the major Portland foundations were organized. The small team put on wonderful presentations and conveyed tremendous project excitement, but all had extreme difficulty in "making the ask." Although the entire tribal organization was small in resources and staff, the Tribes were unaccustomed to asking anyone for help.

After a lengthy review and selective processes, a committee of the planning group selected a multi-disciplinary consulting team to conduct the Master Plan. After considerable and often heated discussions between tribal participants and the consultants—mostly regarding the location of the proposed gaming facility—a site plan nearly identical to the existing mix of development was completed. The balance of the Master Plan was mainly design suggestions and considerations in a format intended to make the entire document a marketing tool for further fund-raising. Time was then spent lining up meetings with local, state, and federal officials along with regional foundations.

The Casino

At about the same time, the Tribes began to endorse more formal plans to pursue the gaming opportunities. With our continuing monitoring of the industry, the opportunity became more substantial when the Oregon State Lottery Commission authorized video poker in taverns.

Dallas D. Dick, photographer, courtesy of Tamástslikt Cultural Institute

Wildhorse Casino and Resort.

Precedent had clearly been established elsewhere that when any state had opted for video poker or any similar electronic gambling device, the tribes of that state had been successful in negotiating for video slots. Slots were known to make up the vast majority of income in conventional casinos.

The Board of Trustees formed a broad-based Gaming Task Force to provide some oversight and coordination on the effort to move into this industry. It was an unusually large committee, but thankfully Woody Patawa, a skilled meeting manager and the tribal chairman, was an active participant. At one point, when the task force was falling into the "paralysis by analysis" syndrome, the tribal chairman instructed General Manager Gary George to instruct Enterprise Administration to follow the Nike motto and "just do it." The staff then had a mandate to push through the decisions and keep the project moving.

Several pivotal events occurred during this period: a survey of Pendleton and tribal members, an effort by the Umatilla Tribes to unite the Oregon tribes, and the selection of British American Bingo, later known as Capital Gaming, to manage the casino for the first five years. While making a presentation on the project to a local group, the director of Enterprise Administration was interviewed by the regional reporter for the *Oregonian*. At the assertion that there appeared to be solid local support for a casino, the reporter pressed the point on how that was known. React-

ing to the question, the director said that the Tribes were planning to do a survey of the tribal membership and Pendleton residents. After the interview, frantic efforts were made to scope out and secure Board support to conduct such a survey. Working with Eastern Oregon University's technical assistance arm, a survey instrument was designed and sent to the best available tribal member mailing list — from the Yellowhawk Clinic — and a random sampling of the Pendleton community. Thankfully, the results were nearly identical with what the chairman suggested, with just over two-thirds of each group very supportive of the Tribes' plan to develop a casino. This provided the tribal leadership with the sense of powerful local support and a mandate to move forward.

The Tribes were being increasingly courted by gaming management firms. One of these, the Berry Group of Wendover, Nevada, began working to help the tribes of Oregon unite, while using the opportunity to market their services. A meeting was convened at Kah-Nee-Tah Resort on the Warm Springs Reservation. The Umatilla Tribes, with the support of the management firm, were acting on information gathered by John Barkley that the most favorable compacts were those where a state's tribes joined together to negotiate a collective compact, with the most successful being the Minnesota tribes. All Oregon tribes were represented at the meeting, but only the Umatilla and Cow Creek Band were actively working to develop a casino. All the other Tribes had not yet made the policy decision to move forward, and several suggested that they might never go into the business. As such, each tribe — sometimes to the collective expense of the other tribes—began to negotiate their own compacts with the State of Oregon.

A meeting was arranged with Governor Barbara Roberts to commence compact negotiations. The tribal negotiating team was led by Chairman Patawa, General Manager Gary George, DECD Director Dave Tovey, and Tribal Attorney Dan Hester. Over the next several months, an aggressive schedule of generally cordial meetings transpired. When hosting the state negotiating team on the reservation, however, a briefing package intended for supportive Pendleton officials was given to the governor's lead staff negotiators. They took offense to statements in the briefing summary that suggested that if the governor would not provide the terms necessary for a successful project, then the Tribes and Pendleton leadership should hold her politically accountable. The infuriated lead negotiator stated that he did not think it appropriate to make this a political matter, but the tribal team responded that the state should know that the Tribes were free and right to build political alliances with its neighbors.

Later that same day, a luncheon was held at Raphael's restaurant in downtown Pendleton, and the two teams met with a Pendleton delegation comprised of Mayor Joe McLaughlin, City Council President

Craig McNaught, and two prominent citizens Mike Kilkenney and Larry O'Rourke. When asked about a potential for increased crime, the delegation noted that gambling was very much part of Pendleton's history and they welcomed the opportunity for new jobs. The negotiating team came back to the table after lunch and offered to add horse racing to the existing mix of slots and keno, set by precedent in the Cow Creek compact.

Negotiations concluded in a generally congenial manner, and a compact was set for approval in late November 1992. At the same time as the state compact was presented for action, the Tribes conducted its regular elections. A new election procedure had been adopted. Instead of electing Board representatives who, in turn, selected their own officers, each position was open to challenge. Long-time Chairman Patawa was successfully challenged by tribal fish biologist Donald Sampson. This leadership change resulted in numerous changes; but fortunately, the new young and energetic chairman enthusiastically supported the existing economic development plans.

During the planning and design phases of the project, it became increasingly apparent that the construction period would last longer than expected and hoped, at least until the spring of 1995. The decision was made to place one hundred slots in a modified modular building near the planned entrance. The results were impressive. Although only about a quarter million dollars was realized after costs for the short period, the project served to accomplish significant human resource objectives. First, roughly one hundred workers were employed, 98 percent of whom were tribal members. With this initial experience, those employees became middle and upper managers when the full facility opened. Second, the fledgling Tribal Gaming Commission was able to establish and refine their licensing system with a smaller group and less pressure.

In March 1995, the Wildhorse Casino and Resort opened for business with a series of events and functions, including local visits by state luminaries such as the Oregon governor. The Capital Gaming officials remarked that the Wildhorse opening was the smoothest and best organized they had been involved with. The tribal community actively attended, maintaining a watchful vigil in stuffed chairs in the horse-racing lounge. A spectacular fireworks and laser show capped the festivities.

The project feasibility, designed for conservative outcomes, anticipated first year earnings of about $1.5 million. Over $5 million was realized. At least equally important was the influx of jobs for tribal members, other local Native Americans, and citizens from surrounding communities. The wages were nearly at "family wage" levels, but the superb benefits package was cited as one of the best in the region. A substantial majority of the workforce was tribal member or members of other tribes. Any number of tribal members expressed that this was the first job they felt they could think of as a career.

The most telling result occurred several years into the operation of Wildhorse, when there was the coincidental mass exodus of key middle and upper managers, mostly non-Indian, including the controller, maintenance director, and food and beverage manager. Each area had been grooming potential leaders as seconds-in-command, but it was widely felt that it may be too soon and too much to ask young tribal members to assume management roles. But they accepted the challenge and performed wonderfully without any external disruption or perceived change. As such, almost 90 percent of today's core department heads and managers are tribal members, most of whom have been with the enterprise from its earliest times.

The implications of the Tribes owning a casino have caused political complications that extend to the present day. The casino indelibly changed that landscape. Early on, the press conveyed the positive messages of young tribal members who were moving back to the Reservation for good careers, but gradually news articles shifted to detail on the expanding influence and purported wealth being generated by the Tribes. Formerly supportive funding partners — both agency and philanthropic — began to turn their interest away with the perception that resources were no longer required. The frustration was best expressed at a foundation meeting, where one of the tribal team stated:

"After almost 150 years of bad luck, it seems we're being punished for having one good one."

Local and State Relations

During the times of Woody Patawa as Board chair and Antone Minthorn as General Council chair, they crafted an approach to follow up on the Tribes' recent successes and to start building relations with the Pendleton leadership. The interaction between the city and the Umatilla Tribes was strained at best and mostly took the form of mutual avoidance.

One sunny day in the late 1980s, however, the two chairmen showed up for a trip into Pendleton for purposes not quite known. Certain organizations were on the agenda, including the Chamber of Commerce, the Small Business Center, the Round-Up City Development Corporation, and the Greater Eastern Oregon Development Corporation (GEODC). We were instructed to attend those organization's gatherings. In particular, it was made clear that we were expected to "show them our plans" in the hopes that the Tribes' intentions were understood and hopefully supported. "We'll need their help someday," was stated. That help would be called upon in the Gaming Compact negotiations, fund-raising for the Tamástslikt Cultural Institute, and other initiatives.

As the tribal organization had such reliance on federal support to pursue its goals, the tribal leadership has tried to build and maintain effective working relationships with the Oregon congressional delegation. Over much of the modern history of the tribal organization, the Tribes were extremely fortunate to have inspired leadership from Senator Mark O. Hatfield, who had a long record of public service to Oregon at all levels of government. Senator Hatfield was a stalwart supporter of tribal governments and worked to obtain recognition for most of the newer Oregon tribes.

In the early days of building support for the Tamástslikt Cultural Institute, Senator Hatfield agreed to a rare visit to examine the Tribes' plan and ambitions and to speak at a hosted dinner at the tribal longhouse. As the open invitation to hear Senator Hatfield speak resulted in a rather "hoity-toity" social gathering of Pendleton elite, the senator proceeded to give an animated and pointed lecture of the power of the Tribes' Treaty, their sovereignty, and the congressional mandate to uphold the "law of the land."

Casino Politics

The Tribes, along with the other Oregon tribes, have forged a tremendously positive working relationship with all levels of state government. Tribal leaders have pointed to a continuous succession of Oregon governors that have maintained supportive positions back to Governor Vic Atiyeh. As the positive relationship evolved, increasingly the level of detail of state/tribal issues required more focused attention. The idea of cluster groups around key subject areas — cultural resources, economic development, education, natural resources, and public safety — came about shortly after the signing of an executive order by Governor John Kitzhaber. State agencies were mandated to participate in their respective clusters and report annually on their accomplishments for that year. This practice was later formalized further with the passage of legislative action. The process continues to be an excellent tool for not only state/tribal collaboration, but also a means for intertribal coordination within these subject areas.

Another key piece of the state relations picture is the Oregon Commission on Indian Services. The commission has existed for roughly twenty years, generally with active participation by the tribal chairmen along with selected leadership from the Oregon House and Senate. Balancing the line between education and advocacy, the commission has become a tremendous resource for confused or anxious state officials and agencies. It has also bolstered the Tribes' understanding of key issues that may have impact on tribal interests.

Friendly Competition

In about 1989, the Tribes had begun their effort to secure the resources to plan and develop the Tamástslikt Cultural Institute. Wildhorse was not yet an idea to be included on the overall project Master Plan — at $80,000 it was already a daunting enough figure. A contingency of Pendleton leadership arranged a meeting with the Board of Trustees leaders. The basic message from the Pendleton contingent was "how can we help?" Long-time tribal observers noted that in many ways this was the first time the local community had extended such an offer. The gathering was considered "historic." Pendleton relied on the Round-Up City Development Corporation to spearhead events, which included an advertising appeal for donations, a mail campaign, and eventually a community meeting on the proposed casino. It should be noted that the resources contributed by individual Pendleton residents as a result of this support provided a broad indication of support to other partners, but the inspiration from receiving the very small, sincere contributions of children and elderly women was sustaining and reinvigorating to the project team.

Over the years, the Tribes collaborated with such enlightened Pendleton leaders, as they confided that the tribal projects would revitalize the local economy. Given the near exclusive nature of economic leakage from tribal enterprises and the vast payroll generated, the retail sector has grown. Still, one could sense the local anxiety of the Tribes' growing organizational and political power. Carefully cultivated confidants would detail disturbing conversations and attitudes. Fortunately, many civic leaders turned such feelings toward positive outcomes.

Prior to the 1990s, Pendleton was in the midst of economic transition. In addition to the reductions in farming, ranching, and mining, the stalwart employer

Tamástslikt* — Connecting with History and Cultural Pride

"Tamástslikt Cultural Institute will become the foremost trusted source of knowledge on the culture and history of the Confederated Tribes of the Umatilla Indian Reservation. [The Institute] will conduct work in a responsible and respectful manner using the highest degree of integrity, objectivity, thoroughness, and skill. The Institute welcomes diverse perspectives, values inquiry, and encourages active exploration and appreciation of knowledge."

— Vision and Values Statement, Report to the Board of Trustees, 2005

Balloons over Tamástslikt Cultural Institute (top)

Roberta "Bobbie" Conner tours students in Tamástslikt Cultural Institute's permanent exhibit (left).

*Tamástslikt translates as "to interpret, turn over, or turn around" in the Walla Walla dialect.

Harris Pine Mills closed just before Christmas. These events plagued the local government, with a citizenry clearly adverse to any new tax initiatives, which were consistently defeated in the 1980s. But it seemed that after the enthusiasm that Wildhorse brought, valuable civic endeavors advanced, including a river walk, an art museum, the refurbishing of the county courthouse facilities, the recruiting of Continental Mills, and a number of operating levies for city government and schools. Again, there was little or no evidence of such, but the clear sense from interested observers was that Pendleton would not let itself be so "upstaged" by the Tribes; and as the improvements served the entire community, it only served to strengthen the city/Tribes partnership.[4]

Steady as She Goes: The Development of Natural Resource Protection

Telling the story of tribal economic development and the parallel story of natural resource recovery and salmon return is essential to this chapter. They serve as evidence of cooperation on a local, regional, and grander scale, elements that are swiftly becoming the legacy for the Confederated Tribes. At the time of his death in 2004, Michael "Jughead" Farrow was the most tenured CTUIR employee, and he had seen many changes in his twenty-four-year career on the Umatilla Reservation. Farrow went to work for the Tribes in 1974, two years after he was discharged from the army, where he served as a medic

in Vietnam. He was famous for telling it like it was. And when he had something to say, people would do well to listen. Here are some of his words:

There was a time when tribal government operated on guts because there wasn't any money. When I was hired as an assistant economic planner, the Confederated Tribes were pulling themselves up by the bootstraps. I was one of twelve employees working with approximately $150,000 in small federal contracts. My motto was, 'You can force the hand or be invited.' The CTUIR is not part of the corporate world. Brown-nosing and backstabbing may work out in the rest of the world, but it doesn't work on the Rez. Patronage is not valued here. It is despised. If you want to make it, you've got to be tolerant, patient, and get some mileage. If you are an overbearing know-it-all, you gain no respect. One must observe and learn and be willing to be counseled or disciplined. My mother, Emma Sheoships Farrow, served on the Board of Trustees but didn't offer me any advice. Rather, she offered me no slack. She was tougher on me than any other Board member.

Farrow's experiences included good as well as bad memories. He first became aware of tribal government in the early 1950s, a few years after the 1949 Constitution and By-Laws were adopted. It was the first stab at self-determination, setting in place the document by which the Tribes operate successfully today. That Constitution came at a time when Indians were still considered second-class citizens. Even in Pendleton, Indians were not allowed in certain restaurants and were unwelcome in many businesses. When Farrow left college to take a summer job as an assistant planner for the Tribes, relations with other governments, particularly with the state, were considered hostile. The biggest debate was over fish harvests. Northwest tribes took the states to court and ended up with the now-famous Belloni decision, which reserved 50 percent of the harvest for Indians.

After World War II, many men and women — the first generation to go off-reservation and experience the non-Indian world in numbers — came back educated and motivated. The termination act — House Concurrent Resolution 108 — which sought to destroy tribal cultures, was one of their first challenges. Fearful tribal members converted thousands of acres to fee and sold their land to non-Indians. The Indian Claims Commission docket was finally settled in 1969, and tribal members chose per capita payments, a decision that still lingers as a mistake to many.

During the 1970s, the Tribes were in a planning and development mode. In 1975, with Les Minthorn as Board of Trustees chairman, law and order was re-established on the reservation through Public Law 280. The Comprehensive Plan was developed after heavy debate and rejection more than once by the General Council and the Board of Trustees. That plan helped centralize government, putting in

place general operating policies and procedures that had been sorely lacking. It outlined economic, governance, natural resources, and administrative tasks. Myriad committees were replaced by a half-dozen commissions.

Protecting Our Way of Life

In 1974, a land zoning ordinance was adopted jointly by the county and the Tribes. The Tribal Development Office (TDO) was given the responsibility of administering it. In 1981, in response to the Supreme Court case, *Colville Confederated Tribes v. Walton*, the CTUIR believed that the state had no jurisdiction over water.[5] The water code written and passed in 1981 took over water management and the allocation of all water resources on the Umatilla Indian Reservation, as well as the permitting and directing of ground and surface water by the Tribes. This event marked the transition from the TDO to the Department of Natural Resources, established in 1983. The Tribal Stream Zone Alteration Regulation of 1984 allowed the Tribes to begin managing their own natural resources.

In 1983, the Tribes adopted the land development code, which expanded the 1974 zoning code and created the big game winter grazing zone. This was important for the Tribes in that it helped preserve the hunting lifestyle. The Tribes also had exclusive farming land use. There are now commercial, industrial, agricultural, residential, public use, forest, and big game zones. Things happened one permit

Michael Farrow (left), Les Minthorn (third from left), and housing director Tommy Holmes (standing) at a meeting of the Tribal Development Office, Umatilla Indian Reservation, in about 1973.

request at a time through the BIA; but little by little, officials warmed up to the idea that we were going to have to fix the water and the salmon problem. Due process was vital. We established the policies, procedures, and standards and applied them fairly and across the board. People wanted to avoid a procedure; but when you cut corners and do not follow the process, it comes back on you. Mike Farrow, who spearheaded these efforts, was a "sovereignist." He believed in the capability of the Tribes, but he was also a regulator. Mike believed tribes had the right to manage their own affairs. He advocated responsibly creating a government so it

could act as a sovereign and protect its interests.

Tribal Fisheries

In 1982, the Tribes started a fisheries program and hired one fisheries biologist. The next program was Environmental Planning and Rights Protection. The Wildlife Program and Cultural Resources Protection Program (CRPP) followed. Outside legislation such as the Archeological Resources Protection Act of 1979 (ARPA) and the Native American Graves Protection and Repatriation Act of 1990 (NAGPRA) created much of the impetus for the work carried out by the CRPP. The territory expanded, too. Initially, in the 1970s and 1980s, the focus was on the reservation land base only, except for the Columbia River Inter-Tribal Fish Commission, which oversaw fishing rights for the four Columbia River tribes. With the fisheries and rights protection programs in place, the Tribes started expanding into the Umatilla River Basin, then to the ceded homelands and the Columbia River Basin, where our concerns with fishing, hunting, gathering, and grazing were addressed, as well as our tribal rights on federal land.

The Tribes began to develop a relationship with the U.S. Forest Service, the U.S. Department of Fish and Wildlife, and the U.S. Army Corps of Engineers, crossing two states (Washington and Oregon), several cities, counties, and national forests. Some projects would not have happened twenty to thirty years ago without the incredible acceptance of the Tribes' chances to succeed. Government officials in Oregon — namely, Governor Vic Atiyeh, Senator Mark Hatfield, and Oregon Attorney General Dave Frohnmayer — were proponents of tribal rights and sovereignty early on.

In Defense of our Sacred Salmon

In 1855, the Treaty was signed with the understanding the CTUIR would be able to fish in all our usual and accustomed areas. This also applied to hunting and gathering of our traditional foods. The Tribes went to federal court to reaffirm the fishing right to prevent private landowners from cutting off access to fishing areas.

Dams were constructed on the Columbia River during the Depression era, creating jobs for non-Indians and promising to provide cheap electricity. Promises were made to the Columbia River tribes that the concrete walls across the Columbia River would not have a negative impact on the salmon and, if they did, that hatcheries would be built to mitigate for those impacts. The Mitchell Act was passed in 1938 to build hatcheries for that mitigation. The BIA was put in charge of determining where the hatcheries would be built. The BIA, however, did not have any salmon management experience, so they agreed to let the states determine where these hatcheries would be built. The states determined that most of the fish would be lost at the dams and decided to build all but one of the Mitchell Act hatcheries below the Bonneville Dam. The salmon returned upriver but only to the point of their origin, which was the hatcheries.

One of the dams built was The Dalles Dam in 1957. This dam covered Celilo Falls, a prominent and ancient fishing and gathering area for many of the tribes in the Pacific Northwest. Celilo Falls was a usual and accustomed fishing area for the CTUIR and other river tribes. Four of the Columbia River tribes received compensation for the loss of the site. After the falls were covered, many of our tribal members quit fishing on the Columbia River. One tribal member said he went to war for the United States and came back to see the U.S. government cover a very important

Fish technicians Gene Shippentower (center) and
Daryl Thompson (right) work in the Walla Walla River.

tribal fishing site. After Celilo Falls was covered, many of our Tribal fishers had to find another area to fish. One tribal fisherman, Percy Brigham, went to Cascade Locks in the late 1950s, where the old navigation locks were no longer used by the barges. This was a good place to put a scaffold. Percy's sons and his grandchild and great grandchild still fish this area.[6]

The tribal fishers' catch went down to 13 percent after Celilo Falls was covered. In 1966, fourteen tribal fishermen filed against Oregon in federal court that the state had no right to restrict tribal fishing. The four Columbia River tribes —

CTUIR, Nez Perce, Warm Springs, and Yakama tribes joined the case. Judge Robert C. Belloni required that the four tribes keep the fourteen tribal fishermen informed. The case became know as *U.S. v. Oregon*. In 1969, Judge Belloni reaffirmed that the four Columbia River tribes had a right to harvest fish in all their usual and accustomed areas, a right to harvest a fair share of the available harvest, and that the state could only regulate the tribes for salmon conservation.

For the next ten years, the Tribes were in federal court challenging state management and winning. The four Columbia

Swindell Survey of accustomed fishing sites at the dry Umatilla River near present-day Hermiston in about 1940.

River tribes continued to receive technical assistance from the U.S. Fish and Wildlife Service. During many of these meetings, the states of Oregon and Washington would hand the Tribes a proposal on how the tribal fishery would be set, and yet they still continued to manage the non-Indian fishery as they had in the past. Non-Indian seasons were set according to political pressure as opposed to fish or tribal needs.

In 1974, in Washington State, U.S. District Court Judge George Boldt again reaffirmed our rights and went on to say that tribes have a right to harvest 50 percent of the available harvest. It took the CTUIR years before we reached 50 percent of the available harvest. Twenty of the twenty-four Washington tribes were involved in the *U.S. v. Washington* case, which went on to identify which tribes had authority and shared use areas to fish. In the *U.S. v. Oregon* case, this was not done. Therefore, the CTUIR have tribal fishers all along the Columbia River.

During this time, many non-Indians were demonstrating against the federal court decisions. One of the meetings was held at the U.S. Forest Service building in Portland, where tribal representatives from the four Columbia River tribes were greatly outnumbered by the non-Indians. The non-Indians were picketing the meetings with signs saying "Down with Treaties," "Treaties are Old," "Save a Salmon, Can an Indian," and many others. The meeting was held to set a non-Indian season on the Columbia River.[7] At this meeting, local and state politicians seeking non-Indian support for their positions testified, objecting to a federal court decision and telling state managers to set a good season for the non-Indians. Once the seasons were set, the tribal attorneys would go to the federal court and file documents letting the judge know that action was taken that would not protect the salmon or allow a tribal season. The federal judge would then order the states to make changes to their season. This was the usual process that we went through from 1970 through 1976.

Then, in 1976, Judge Belloni ordered the parties in the *U.S. v. Oregon* case to develop a Columbia River Fish Management Plan. A five-year plan was developed and adopted by the federal court in 1977. In 1976, the CTUIR Fish and Wildlife Committee (FWC) closed the Grande Ronde tributary to fishing because the Spring Chinook was not meeting escapement levels. This action upset a number of tribal members who fished in this area. The committee even took a tour of the area with a few of the tribal fishermen who were challenging the FWC actions. They did not find the salmon.

In the fall of 1976 , the Bonneville Power Administration contacted the four Columbia River tribes, inviting them to a meeting to discuss a proposal. The proposal was to provide funding to the four Columbia River tribes for fishery projects.

This also got the tribes a seat at the salmon management table. BPA representatives thought that tribes had a vested interest in the salmon resources. Sam Kash Kash, chairman for the FWC, Kenneth Bill, and Kathryn Brigham were the CTUIR representatives who attended these meetings. The CTUIR was prepared and willing to put a proposal on the table for possible funding; but in order for the Columbia River Tribes to receive the funds, a central location was needed. A Memorandum of Understanding (MOU) was developed and signed with the four Columbia River tribes and Bonneville Power Administration.

Many meetings were held to form the tribal organization. BIA staff worked with the four Columbia River tribes in developing the Columbia River Inter-Tribal Fish Commission (CRITFC) bylaws. Sam Kash Kash traveled many miles to fish committee meetings in Portland. He oversaw a particularly important confab on one such trip, spending over a week with representatives of the four Colombia River tribes and helping them write the charter for CRITFC. CTUIR sent down our planners — Antone Minthorn, Mike Farrow, and Tom Hampson — to assist in the development of CRITFC, which was established in February 1977. CRITFC became a valuable means for organized intertribal representation to ensure and protect treaty reserved fishing rights and our sacred salmon heritage on the Columbia River and its tributaries.

With the organization of the Columbia River Inter-Tribal Fish Commission,

Courtesy of Tom Gralish, photographer, *Philadelphia Inquirer*

Linda Jones and Loretta "Lonnie" Alexander prepare a meal in the longhouse.

not only were we able to receive funds for the four tribes but we were also able to hire technical staff to review state and federal projects and make comments from the four tribes' points of view. When the hiring of tribal staff at CRITFC was discussed, there was a huge discussion on who should be hired. In the next few years, tribes would be in federal court defending our positions with the states of Oregon and Washington. It was decided that we needed qualified staff to prepare information that would hold up in federal court, and it was recognized that the goal of each of the member tribes was to hire tribal members at CRITFC. It has taken the tribes a few years, but we now have staff who are equal to or better technical staff than those in the state and federal agencies.

The Bonneville Power Administration provided approximately $100,000 for salmon projects under the original memorandum of understanding. This marked the beginning of tribes, states, and federal agencies working together on joint proposals to rebuild salmon on the Columbia River.

The Northwest Power Act, approved in 1980, was the first salmon act mandating that all fish management actions required working with the tribes. The act also said that the Northwest Power Planning Council had a responsibility to rebuild naturally spawning salmon habitat above Bonneville Dam. The act also required that a plan be developed to balance power and fish.

In the late 1980s, tribal committees and staff began to discuss an approach for getting water back into the Umatilla River for restoring salmon. After much discussion, a decision was made to negotiate rather than go to federal court. The first meeting was a real test. Many statements were made, not only asking why CTUIR wanted water and fish in the Umatilla River but also objecting to the request to work together to accomplish the task. The irrigation districts did not want to put water back into the Umatilla River because they did not want to give up any water for fish. When we approached the irrigation districts asking for water for fish, we were told: "You have no fish, why do you need water?" And when we approached Oregon Department of Fish and Wildlife (ODFW) asking for fish, we were told: "You have no water, why do you want fish?"

It took a while for the irrigation districts and ODFW to accept CTUIR's goal to restore salmon in the Umatilla River, but it happened. When the first salmon returned to the Umatilla River in 1988, we had a huge dinner at our longhouse to celebrate our success. After the first chinook returned, we started seeing a steady increase. In 1984, CTUIR hired our first full-time tribal biologist, Gary James. Our next tribal biologist was tribal member Donald Sampson. We were finally able to have tribal staff review and prepare comments that reflected CTUIR's views.

In 1985, the Pacific Salmon Treaty was signed with Canada. The treaty recognized tribes as co-managers and gave each US party a veto. This was the first time the Tribes had a veto over the state and federal agencies. Not only were the twenty-four Pacific Northwest tribes given a veto vote, but they also were given a seat at the different levels of the Pacific Salmon Treaty. After the federal legislation passed, federal agencies started to develop a tribal policy that recognized their trust responsibility to the tribes.

Today, the Columbia River tribes are recognized as co-managers. CTUIR and other tribes now have their own technical and legal staff to assist in management decisions. It has taken us years but we are finally sitting at the table as real co-managers of our natural resources. We can plan for the next seven generations to protect, restore, and enhance our natural resources.

Stones, Bones, Hearts, and Minds: Culture Committee and Cultural Resources Protection Program

Under the leadership of the late Mike Farrow, the Department of Natural Resources (DNR) grew in leaps and bounds. Because of the program, the Confederated Tribes have come to the forefront in working with water, salmon, eel, other wildlife, traditional foods, and cultural resources. Our system for protecting resources works. Our DNR has gained attention nationally, from the state, and from other tribes. It is

On *Tamánwit*

There is so much to this word or to this way, this *tamánwit*. It's how we live. It's our lifestyle. There is so much that we as Indian people are governed by, through our traditions, our culture, our religion, and most of all, by this land that we live on. We know through our oral histories, our religion, and our traditions how time began. We know the order of the food, when this world was created, and when those foods were created for us. We know of a time when the animals and foods could speak. Each of those foods spoke a promise. They spoke a law — how they would take care of the Indian people and the time of the year that they would come. All of those foods got themselves ready for us — our Indian people who lived by the land. It was the land that made our lifestyle. The foods first directed our life. Today, we all have these traditions and customs that recognize our food: our first kill, first fish, first digging, the first picking of berries. All of those things are dictated to us because it was shown and it directed our ancestors before us.

The songs we sing with our religion are derived from how we live on this land. Our cultural way of life and the land cannot be separated. Even though we recognize that our life is short, it all goes back to that promise that was made when this land was created for us as Indian people, the promise that this land would take care of us from the day we are born until the day that we die.

When we recognize our foods, we recognize our ancestors, we recognize the language. It's all within the same context and teachings that we live day by day. The promise that this land made and the promise that we made as Indian people to take care of this land, to take care of the resources, and to live by those teachings is the grander principle of the bigger law that was put down on this land when this world was created. This is the law that we recognize on Sundays, that we recognize when we lose a family member, and that we recognize when the seasons change. When we can live by those traditions and customs, then we're fulfilling that law, we're living by that law.

These few thoughts I try and bring out to do a little bit of justice for this big word, this big way, this *tamánwit*.

— Armand Minthorn

at the forefront due to the combination of traditional education and knowing the system and how it works.

Returning our Ancestors

The Cultural Resources Protection Program (CRPP), within the Department of Natural Resources, has the goal of protecting culturally sensitive areas within the ceded homelands and tribal joint-use areas. The Cultural Resources Committee, formed within the last couple of years, has a similar philosophy and serves as their oversight committee. The committee has some regulatory responsibility and can use the program to leverage actions of repatriation or to encourage us as a Tribe to protect cultural resources.

In 1993 and 1994, a number of discoveries of human remains were made on the reservation and ceded lands. At that time, the Board of Trustees wanted an entity to address and handle inadvertent discoveries, so an ad hoc committee was formed. Within one week, there were three inadvertent discoveries back-to-back — one in Union, another in La Grande, and another in Richland, Washington. The CRPP was initially intended to monitor construction sites and protect existing areas against looting of village and grave sites. The committee worked specifically on these inadvertent discoveries. We did not have to go to court for the original three inadvertent unearthings; we just handled it in house. The Board and committee did not have experience with inadvertent discoveries, and we depended on our elders to guide us.

The CRPP is now guided by several Board resolutions and by the original philosophy from the late director of the Department of Natural Resources, Michael Farrow. The program has grown significantly since that time and has been able to refocus its efforts on the repatriation (or return) of human remains, funerary objects, and objects of cultural patrimony. Because of that refocus, we are now able to expand the scope of cultural resources to include Treaty resources. That expansion of scope is a result of the growth of the Tribe and the increased support for repatriation and cultural resources protection.

The Tribes' position is to rebury any returned human remains or funerary objects. We have re-substantiated that in our policy through our experience with ARPA and, later, NAGPRA. Initially, there was little experience with handling inadvertent discoveries, and mistakes were made by everyone. We learned from those mistakes, and now we have been able to create our own policy. The intent has always remained clear — to return the remains back in the ground where they belong. We do not condone any testing, and we do not condone the intentional excavation of ancestral remains. Even though NAGPRA was signed in 1990, it took eight yearsbefore we had our own policy.

Since the inadvertent unearthing of the Ancient One in 1996 in Richland (the so-called Kennewick Man), all of the effort, time, meetings, and traveling to reclaim and repatriate him has been worth it. None of that work was for naught, because every tribe involved was guided by the same principle. We were all going in the same direction in our efforts to get the remains back. Due to that experience, we have all been able to focus our efforts on the importance of ancestral remains. Since 1996, we have made several joint repatriations with the Army Corps of Engineers, the Department of Energy, and the Smith-

Repatriation Success on the Umatilla Indian Reservation

• Since 1998, there have been eleven comprehensive repatriations from museums, institutions, and private collections containing human remains, associated and unassociated funerary objects, as well as objects of cultural patrimony and sacred items.

• Approximately 217 to 457 human remains have been returned and reburied. This estimate of human remains is broad due to the fragmentary nature of the remains.

• Approximately 8,000 associated funerary objects (items that were excavated with a burial) have been repatriated.

• Approximately seventy-seven unassociated funerary objects (items found nearby but not part of a burial) have been repatriated.

• Umatilla, Walla Walla, and Cayuse remains and objects have been listed in 140 inventories and summaries of museums, institutions, and federal agencies in the United States, Canada, and New Zealand.

• The Cultural Resources Protection Program has developed a donation policy, whereby the CTUIR will not purchase back any burial items or looted excavated material.

• The CTUIR are now working cooperatively with other Columbia River tribes on joint repatriations.

• Planned for the summer of 2006 is the largest reburial ever done by the CTUIR and neighboring tribes, the Palouse cemetery repatriation. Burials at the Palouse Cemetery were excavated for the construction of the Lower Monument Dam in 1968 on the Snake River (in CTUIR ceded and joint use territory) and never relocated. The Tribes will rebury a minimum of 143 individuals and over 37,000 funerary items.

sonian, and we are going to continue with more repatriations.

Building Relations

Our treaty rights and the exercising of those rights depend on abundant, healthy resources. We are dependent on our resources for our lifestyle, and, in turn, our lifestyle is dependent on the traditions that go with those resources. To survive as Indian people, we cannot afford to not be educated, on occasion, by the non-Indian, but we must have our traditional education happening in tandem. Today, the Umatilla Tribes have been recognized nationally for our program to protect culturally sensitive resources.

The Tribes are very aggressive in maintaining our institutional policy on reburial. When new appointees (whether in the military or at state and federal levels) enter their positions every two years or so, this policy is already there, to be implemented by the new managers and staff. It is always ongoing. On the day that a new colonel begins his two-year post on the Army Corps of Engineers, we meet him and remind him of what the former colonel did. We then say: "We expect no less from you." We do the same with new generals. We cannot afford to hesitate and wait for the new colonels or generals to learn. We just push forward, and the people within the Corps that have the longer memories help us do that. It is a nice twist on acculturation — bringing them around to this way. That is a change.

Government-to-government relations are so important. They allow us to sit down with policy people and have policy discussions. Some think that government-to-government means sending a letter or making a phone call. But we say that it is truly when we can sit down and have discussions, to make policy recommendations and decisions together. That is our "government-to-government," and we constantly remind our non-Indian friends what that means to us.

Laying the Foundation

The Tribes' history suggests that the unique qualities of the three Tribes combined for a mix of humor, internal fortitude, verbal adeptness, hospitality, style, quiet confidence, and class. These attributes are part of successful negotiations and high-level diplomacy. It may be easily asserted that the seminal events of the Tribes' history — securing the additional Umatilla Reservation at the Treaty negotiations, active partnership in the formation of the Pendleton Round-Up, and the Umatilla Basin Project, among others — were products of such diplomacy.

The modern tribal organization has had a consistent focus on the principles of planning to guide its organizational, business, and policy-making. The discipline lends itself to thoughtful preparation and the conscious sequencing of events and assignments toward a given desired end — in other words, lining things up. These are effective principles for managing a project, developing legislation, preparing for a lawsuit, or establishing a positive interpersonal relationship.

This same approach was employed in the forging of political alliances. Allies and enemies were fairly well-known, and the occasional open confrontations served to provide further insights into the character of both friend and foe. But the tribal leadership exhibited a patient and forgiving eye toward the Tribes' neighbors and governments. While frustration and anxiety may be shown toward an affront of some kind, it was clear that the Tribes' relationship and relative need for positive dealings overshadowed any heightening reaction. Tribal leadership maintained a clear intention to why any given government or political figure was necessary as an ally or, more importantly, worthy of the Tribes' regard.

River of Hope

The Confederated Tribes of the Umatilla Indian Reservation was honored in 2002 by the Harvard University Honoring Nations program for our successful salmon restoration efforts in the Umatilla River. Two years later, the University invited Indian Nations to showcase some of the best examples of governance in Indian Country. Ours was one of the fea-

Indian Pride on the Umatilla Reservation

Those of us growing up in the late 1960s and early 1970s were attached to Indian pride and a sense of justice, but the indignities and racial slurs that we grew up with were still plentiful. To many growing up on the reservation and the neighboring town of Pendleton, all politics was local. The first Indian club, Nanuma Natitite, at Pendleton High School started in 1972 with Indian and non-Indian members.

The American Indian Movement, or AIM, was occurring at this time, and those garnering attention with Red Power, our own form of the Civil Rights movement, were taking stands across America. The empowerment for this tribal community came during the War on Poverty. Community Action Program projects were started that galvanized people. Pi-Em-Nat Enterprises, a youth silk-screening business, started in 1971 and was run out of a building at St. Andrews Mission. This was an example of a War on Poverty program.

Our impacts here were more community-based than national in scope. When the Board of Trustees commissioned the Ernst and Ernst economic development study in the 1960s, this had substantially more impact on us than AIM did. We didn't need outsiders to teach us to be Indian.

— Roberta "Bobbie" Conner

tured projects. The following is adapted from a speech given at that conference by Chairman Antone Minthorn, Board of Trustees, on September 10, 2004.

The Umatilla River Basin Salmon Recovery Project exemplifies how treaty rights can benefit non-Indians, too. The Confederated Tribes view leadership and cooperation in natural resource management as standard operating procedure. It is a concept that we have turned into reality, a concept that has proven successful for us and for our non-Indian neighbors. The Tribes' philosophy of cooperation has specifically aided our successful efforts in restoring salmon to the Umatilla River.

We accomplished this through cooperation, creativity, commitment, leadership, and the Supreme Law of the Land.[8] Those were the key ingredients for success in the Umatilla River Basin in northeastern Oregon, where we have achieved a marvelous feat — we have restored stream flows and salmon in a river where they were absent for seventy years. If that is not miraculous enough, we did it without harming the area's irrigated agriculture economy, an economy that had been built using the precious river water that once served as the salmon's home.

One must understand tribal culture and the close ties we have with water, the rivers, the land, and the salmon to understand our drive and will toward natural resource recovery. Our people are river people. We are part of the native cultures of the Columbia Plateau. We have a close connection with the Big River — Nch'i-Wána — or as most people know it, the Columbia. We also have close relationships with many of its tributaries, including the Snake, Walla Walla, Grande Ronde, Imnaha, and Umatilla. The Umatilla is the river that runs through our Reservation and the river in which we successfully returned salmon. Without the rivers and the salmon and the land, we are not Cayuse or Umatilla or Walla Walla people. Without the rivers and salmon, we become a different people. Salmon, the rivers, the land, and all things related are so central to our culture that we honor and pay respect to these things each year in age-old ceremonies.

These things were so central to the lifestyle of our ancestors that they reserved specific rights related to them when they signed our Treaty with the federal government in 1855. When our ancestors put their mark at the bottom of the Treaty papers, they said, "This place and lifestyle is for our children — forever." As a modern tribal government, we have a huge responsibility to uphold that Treaty and protect the rights that our ancestors reserved — fishing rights, hunting rights, livestock pasturing rights, and rights to gather traditional foods and medicines within our historical homeland. This responsibility was the driving force behind our efforts to restore salmon in the Umatilla River. But not only did the Treaty of 1855 represent a great responsibility, it also represented a powerful tool for salmon restoration.

While the Treaty of 1855 served as a legal tool in the successful restoration of

Gaffing on the Granite River are (from left) Van Sohappy, Dominique Sohappy, and Law Enick.

salmon in the Umatilla River, there are other ingredients that have to do with the attitudes and personalities of the people involved. Cooperation was the foundation on which discussions with the local farmers and irrigators were built. Our Tribe had no intention of talking with these folks through our attorneys or through correspondence. Instead, we had the intention of getting to know them as people and working together to find solutions that would fit everyone's needs. We did not want to wreck their livelihood or force them to give up their irrigation water without getting something in return. We understood that it was, in fact, the federal government that got us all into the predicament of too little water for too many needs.

The federal government knew that it had treaty right responsibilities to our Tribe, but it ignored that obligation when it allocated all of the water in the Umatilla River to irrigators in the early part of the twentieth century. It was this Umatilla River water that built the thriving agricultural economy of the area, and it was also this Umatilla River water that once served as a home for huge salmon populations. This water that connected us as Indian people to the land, to the salmon, and ultimately to the promises made in the Treaty. When the irrigation water was taken from the river without any consideration for salmon populations, the river dried up and salmon were extinguished from the Umatilla.

Secure in the conclusion that the Tribes' objectives were environmentally, morally, and legally correct, the tribal leadership chose a rather unique approach to maintain a cooperative tenor to the negotiations. The Tribes could just as well have been aggressive, knowing that such an approach would have generated a similar reaction from the agencies and downriver farming interests. Legal advisors were secure that the Tribes' Treaty guaranteed the right to fish. But the time, costs, and risks of pursuing a legal outcome were not desired. The phrase "cooperation over confrontation" was repeated internally and in the press coverage of the negotiations. The Tribes' team sat through hundreds of hours of negotiations, always offering solutions that protected all interests. Antone Minthorn has noted that a watershed event occurred when the convening official of the negotiations told the local farming interests that it was time "to let the Indians win one." The phrase "cooperation over confrontation" became a core principle of many tribal operations. Staff was empowered with the notion that

they were encouraged to collaborate within and outside the tribal community to work toward solutions that had broad benefits but that still accomplished key long-range goals of the Tribe.

While the overall tone of our success in the Umatilla Basin has been cooperation, we did use the Supreme Law of the Land to our advantage as one of the key ingredients in the success we have achieved in the Umatilla Basin. The farmers and irrigators always knew that we had a powerful legal tool backing us up. They knew that we would use our legal options if we had to. But they also knew that our Tribe's guiding philosophy was "cooperation before litigation," and, as our neighbors, they agreed with that philosophy.

We wanted to work cooperatively with our neighbors to hold the federal government accountable for its actions and to make the federal government help us figure out a solution to this predicament. This is where creativity played a key role. We needed innovative solutions that would keep water in the Umatilla during critical times for salmon migration and yet maintain water supplies for irrigation. We found those solutions in a creative water swap — a bucket-for-bucket exchange whereby the irrigators would not receive their water from the Umatilla River but instead would receive it from the nearby Columbia River. This would provide much-needed water to remain in the Umatilla to again provide habitat and migration paths for salmon. So the engineers and biologists went to work to make this concept happen on the ground. The irrigation piping part of this effort is officially known as the Umatilla Basin Project. It was congressionally authorized and funded, thanks to the direct involvement of Senator Mark O. Hatfield, who believed in what we were doing and continually encouraged us. To date, we have completed Phases I and II, which provide water to most of the irrigation districts. We hope to someday get Phase III congressionally authorized and funded so that the Umatilla will have water year-round. Even with Phases I and II there are still certain periods during the year where the river is too low for salmon migration.

While the Umatilla Basin Project was being built, we began other fish restoration projects that would include the use of hatcheries, fish acclimation facilities, habitat improvement, and in-river planting of salmon. These projects also required a lot of creativity, because we did not want to simply use hatcheries with the goal of just producing food. We are using hatcheries as a supplementation tool to jump-start salmon runs that we hope will eventually be self-sustaining.

We do not just take hatchery fish and dump them in the river with the hopes of them returning to the Umatilla River someday. We have built several acclimation facilities, where the young fish taken from the hatchery are held for a period of three to five weeks. They are acclimated to that portion of the Basin with river water running through the acclimation pond. When they are released to go to the ocean, they are imprinted on the Umatilla River waters and are more likely to return to the Umatilla River as adults a few years later to spawn. This has produced meaningful, real results. In the Umatilla Basin, a father can now teach his son or daughter to fish for salmon in their own backyard. In the Umatilla Basin, non-Indian sports fishermen can land twenty-pound spring chinook in downtown Pendleton. In the Umatilla Basin, our tribal members are using traditional gaffing and dip netting to catch salmon the way their ancestors did.

The next key ingredient was commitment. All the parties were committed to finding innovative, beneficial solutions. Why were we all so committed? Simply put, the Tribes are not going anywhere and neither are our non-Indian neighbors. This place in northeastern Oregon — where we raise our children, earn our livelihood, carry on long-held traditions, and bury our dead — is called home, a home now shared by all of us. Not many people these days have an intimate tie to the land and a place on this earth that they truly call home, but we do. The non-Indian farming community in our area does, too. When people have strong traditions and close ties with the land, they also tend to have a strong commitment to preserving those things.

The final and perhaps the most vital ingredient in this successful mix was leadership, not just common, assumed-by-title leadership, but extraordinary, visionary leadership. We worked with some non-

Courtesy of Tom Gralish, photographer, *Philadelphia Inquirer*

Mike McCloud tends the fish hatchery.

Indian community leaders in the early days of this immense project. They were people who grew up in the area. They were people that we had attended school with or knew through playing sports. These individuals, most importantly, were recognized business, civic, and political leaders in our communities. They were people who had the qualities of great leaders, ones that lead by example and are true to their word. This project came to fruition, in the end, because of the people who were setting the tone, making the commitment, and demonstrating forward-thinking leadership. This can be said not only about the non-Indian community leaders but about our tribal leaders as well.

The Umatilla Basin Project serves as a model for how people can resolve water and salmon conflicts peacefully and without spending time and money in the courtroom. It provides a tried-and-true method for resolving conflicts that are the result of historic practices that failed to recognize the Treaty-reserved rights of the Cayuse, Umatilla, and Walla Walla people. Instead of years of divisive litigation, the Umatilla Basin approach has been to devote the parties' efforts and resources to creating a solution that works for all interests.

For nine of the last twelve years, enough adult spring chinook have returned to the Umatilla River to provide a spring chinook fishing season for both Indian and non-Indian fishers. In 2001, a record number of coho salmon returned to the river — including three thousand in just one day. Salmon are beginning to naturally reproduce in the river. Although hatchery supplementation remains a primary tool for restoration, fishery managers will become less and less reliant on that tool and more reliant on natural reproduction. This is a project where the results are benefiting everyone in the region. The problem was created by the federal government, but the solution had to be initiated and crafted by the area's citizens.

Tribal leaders, local irrigators, and community leaders worked together to develop the ideas for solutions, then put the responsibility back on the federal government to help make those solutions real. Other state and federal agencies became involved in the funding and implementation of the project, including the U.S. Bureau of Reclamation, Bonneville Power Administration, Oregon Water Resources Department, and Oregon Department of Fish and Wildlife. Former Oregon Senator Mark O. Hatfield played an important role in helping the parties negotiate the solutions and in 1988 introduced legislation to authorize the fish restoration and water-exchange project. Additional funding from the Bonneville Power Administration and other sources followed, which helped with fish-passage improvements, stream habitat enhancement, hatchery use, and research to measure success.

Spring chinook, fall chinook, and coho salmon are once again living and thriving in the Umatilla River, yet the local irrigated agriculture economy remains intact. Salmon and agriculture can co-exist. People of the Basin take pride in the fact that this remarkable achievement was crafted and implemented by local citizens. Indian and non-Indian residents are now able to take their children fishing for salmon in the Umatilla – an opportunity that had not been available for seventy years. We as tribal people are able to preserve, practice, and teach ancient tribal traditions. Schoolchildren are able to learn about salmon and other fish and wildlife and learn how the ecosystem is interconnected and interdependent. A two-week Salmon Expedition for Students is held each spring, and public events happen throughout the year to help educate the general public about salmon restoration and other natural resource issues.

The Confederated Tribes of the Umatilla Indian Reservation took the initiative to begin the salmon restoration process. It was not the federal or state government, but rather Tribal leaders who made the decision that they needed to take action themselves if salmon were ever to live in the Umatilla again. This is self-determination at work. This contribution to the region has promoted effective governance by showing that tribes can shape their own solutions by choosing the way they deal with their neighbors, including local government entities, community leaders, farmers, and other citizens. The CTUIR's cooperative philosophy has carried over to other projects and relationships in the local area. The Tribe is recognized by many of the local governments and organizations as a progressive, open-minded

government that is willing to work with its neighbors, not against them.

As a result of this philosophy and way of conducting business, the CTUIR has enhanced its level of self-determination. Because local governments and organizations know the CTUIR and its reputation, they recognize and respect the CTUIR's decisions, laws, and regulations. The CTUIR has exceptional relationships with Umatilla County government and the City of Pendleton. The project has been so successful because our tribal philosophy has been to negotiate rather than litigate. If we have to, we will litigate to protect our Treaty-reserved rights, but we have seen that we can create solutions that meet everyone's needs by sitting down with our neighbors, listening to each other, and developing our own solutions. We want to apply what we have learned locally to help revive threatened salmon populations in the region. We believe that the cooperative process between neighbors can be used as a model for success in the region and beyond.

This philosophy and guiding approach is now being implemented in the Walla Walla River Basin, where the CTUIR is working with citizens to restore salmon and retain the irrigation needs of the local farmers. The CTUIR is showing the citizens of that basin the successful results achieved in the Umatilla Basin and working to achieve those same results in the Walla Walla. The CTUIR is also implementing this philosophy by initiating a citizens group that is working to address salmon and economic conflicts in the Columbia and Snake River basins. The small group of selected individuals, who have been working together since February 2001, has not shared its existence or discussions with the public, but someday it hopes to influence decision-makers in resolving conflicts between threatened salmon populations and competing river and habitat uses.

Conclusion

The last three decades have seen many of the Tribes' successes, including restoration of salmon to the Umatilla River, development of a modern reservation economy, and re-acquisition of tribal land. We are dedicated to inter-tribal coalitions and cooperative enterprises, and we can take pride in being a confederation of tribes known for its cooperative and innovative approach to issues.

In the 1980s, the formally educated generation of the 1950s took over. We had established sovereignty and a reputation for quality. All the work of the previous forty years prepared the CTUIR for the 1990s, which was the green light for development. Since then, the Tribes have seen the rise of an economy with Wildhorse Resort, preservation of tradition with the Tamástslikt Cultural Institute, more and better housing, and a strong tribal government that holds it all together. In addition, we can take pride in the day that a land-use watchdog organization, 1000 Friends of Oregon, told the Tribes that 99 percent of its decisions were proper. We have always

had a component here that would not stand for anything but quality. As long as we are moral, legal, and logical in decision-making, we will be okay. Once we start making decisions with any one of those components missing, we will be in a bind.

The development of tribal government is a central core of the Tribes' move toward sophisticated self-governance and peer relationships with local, state, and national government organizations and private-sector partners. The thirty-year period of health, housing, and education on the reservation go hand-in-hand with the story of economic development. The grain silo was the beginning of a turn upward for the Confederated Tribes. We do not get restoration of the river, restoration of land, the Wildhorse Resort, or Tamástslikt without that tribal government. That is the trunk of the tree. We do not get a reduction of unemployment from 40 percent to 20 percent without that government. Indian gaming and the casino have shifted employment, have led to contributions to the community and the capital investment into housing and the foundation. Tribes that were strong and well-positioned have done well with casinos, while tribes with geographic disadvantages have not benefited so greatly. Casinos donate to outside charities and are hiring Indians as well as non-Indians in the local community.

We cannot shy away from hard things. The status of health and wellness is still a major issue for our people. We are still laden with a high rate of diabetes among our tribal members. Addiction to drugs and alcohol still plagues some in our community, and we are devising new ways to face and handle this terrible social crisis. We are not without cultural, economic, physical, and social challenges, and we face them as a Tribe collectively and as individual tribal members.

Our Constitution's Article II says we are to "attain a maximum degree of self-government in all tribal affairs." This is the goal, and a goal cannot always be achieved in one's lifetime. Therefore, we must keep moving forward, rapidly or slowly, but always accomplishing our objectives and adapting as we go. The CTUIR will remain strong as long as the people behind the government stand firm. The words of our elder, Philip Guyer, ring true. He said, "I'd like to cut out whatever it is that makes us lose the energy to help ourselves. When you take care of the land, it will teach you to take care of yourself." This is what we must remember in strengthening our organization. Let us at least keep this in our minds for another fifty years.

Notes

1. Philip Guyer, Planning Committee January 29, 1974, OEDP, p. 165.

2. At the risk of missing someone, the commissioners of the Community Development Commission and its later successor the Economic and Community Development Commission over the past twenty years were tribal members Michelle Thompson, Hilda Alexander, Judy Scott, Arnold Lavadour, Sandy Sampson, Pat Walters, Brian Conner, Gerald Reed, and others.

3. A staff member of the Enterprise Administration, John Chess, was the first to see the opportunity and asked to take the project on.

4. One indication of reluctant acknowledgement was the 2004 award from the Pendleton Chamber of Commerce to Wildhorse for the prestigious business of the year. Despite multiple nominations for this award or similar recognitions, it took all of a full decade to obtain this appreciation. Indeed, as some related discussion occurred with Chamber leaders in 2003, one of the supportive Chamber board members remarked, "If aliens from outer space came down and created over 500 jobs in this community, we would be falling all over ourselves to honor them. But, because it's been the Tribes, we don't."

5. 47 F.2d 12, 52 (9th Cir.) Cert. denied 454 us 1092 (1981).

6. Other Indian families also moved their traditional fishing sites. Virgil Hunt, Sr., went below The Dalles Dam to an area called Lone Pine. The Totus's went below McNary dam. The Alexanders went to Cooks Landing. The McClouds went to the John Day area. The Hoptowits went to the Blalock Island area.

7. The non-Indian commercial area is from the mouth of the Columbia River to Bonneville Dam called Zones 1-5. The Tribal commercial area is from Bonneville to McNary Dam called Zone 6. The non-Indian sport season is all of the Columbia River and its tributaries. The Tribal area in the tributaries is based on the Tribal usual and accustomed (U&A) areas by the 1855 Treaty.

8. The Treaty has been proclaimed by U.S. Courts as the "Supreme Law of the Land," a proclamation that we continually have to remind the federal government about. We continually have to remind today's federal bureaucrats that not only did our ancestors sign the Treaty, their ancestors did as well. It was their federal government that made promises to our people. And it is the federal government today which is legally bound to uphold their end of the deal.

Other Important Events in Contemporary Tribal History

1964: The Economic Opportunity Act programs were opened to Indians. Under President Lyndon Johnson, the Confederated Tribes received funding for a variety of programs under the War on Poverty. The tribal government began social and economic services under Upward Bound, Head Start, and Vista, Community Health Program, and Community Action Program.

1966: The U.S. District Court in *Confederated Tribes of Umatilla Indian Reservation v. Maison* upheld treaty rights to hunt on unclaimed land in the Umatilla and Wallowa-Whitman national forests without restriction by the Oregon Game Commission.

1968: The historic fishing rights suit, *US v. Oregon,* was filed in U.S. District Court in Portland. The suit sought both a judgment and an injunction to enforce off-reservation fishing rights in the Columbia River watershed for the Umatilla, Warm Springs, Yakama, and Nez Perce tribes.

1976: The Sahaptin Language Consortium was formed by Umatilla, Yakama, Warm Springs, Nez Perce, and Colville representatives for the creation of a printed alphabet system for all tribes sharing the larger Sahaptin language.

1976: The U.S. Supreme Court ruled that enrolled members of the Umatilla Reservation and other Indians living and working on reservations were exempt from the powers of the State of Oregon to tax individual Indian incomes. The high court ordered refunds for the unauthorized tax withholdings.

1976: The bones and artifacts of an old Indian gravesite were discovered at Old Umatilla Town on the south side of the Columbia River by the U.S. Army Corps of Engineers. The burial site was estimated at

1,500 years old. Some of the artifacts were identified as knives, arrowheads, fishing harpoons, net weights, needles, and elk teeth. In a special ceremony at Old Agency Cemetery at Mission, the remains from the ancestral graves were reburied with the artifacts found along with the remains. The reburial was accompanied by special Wáashat services.

1977: A federal judgment prevented dam construction on Catherine Creek, located in the ceded ancestral homelands of the CTUIR, which would have infringed on treaty fishing rights. Judge Belloni issued his opinion and declaratory judgement in *Confederated Tribes of the Umatilla Indian Reservation v. Alexander*: "The evidence is clear in this case," wrote Belloni, "that the primary method of Indian fishing on Catherine Creek before 1855 was by spear and gaff. The fishermen would locate a hole, usually 30 or 40 feet long, in which salmon were likely to be found. Those wielding spears or gaffs would be stationed at one or both ends of such a hole while the others in the fishing party beat the banks so as to drive the salmon toward the shallow ends of the hole where they would be speared or gaffed. The Indians camped at various sites along Catherine Creek and ranged up and down its length, fishing wherever they found holes which were likely to harbor salmon or steelhead."

1978: Congress enacted the Umatilla Inheritance Act of 1978, which preserved the trust status of inherited allotments.

1981: The Board of Trustees adopted its Comprehensive Water Management Plan and put the interim water code into effect across the reservation. The water code frightened non-Indian water users in the area.

1986: President Reagan signed the Columbia River Gorge Act, which contained a treaty rights disclaimer to ensure that it did not alter or repeal treaty rights of tribes in the Gorge area.

1992: Wanaket (Water in Trees) Wildlife Area is managed by the Confederated Tribes of the Umatilla Indian Reservation (CTUIR) to provide wildlife habitat protection, enhancement, and mitigation. The Bonneville Power Administration (BPA), working with the Northwest Power Planning Council, purchased the property in 1992 as partial mitigation for the impacts associated with the construction of McNary Dam and the inundation of wildlife habitats by Lake Wallula. The area includes over 2,700 acres of upland, wetland, and aquatic habitats, including many important natural and cultural resources.

1993: In the late summer, a contingent of tribal members welcomed a re-crossing of emigrants commemorating the anniversary of the Oregon Trail and challenged them to assist the Umatilla, Cayuse, and Walla Walla people to meet their own goals.

1994: The *Confederated Umatilla Journal*, began publishing monthly, tabloid-sized

Dallas D. Dick, photographer, courtesy of Tamástslikt Cultural Institute

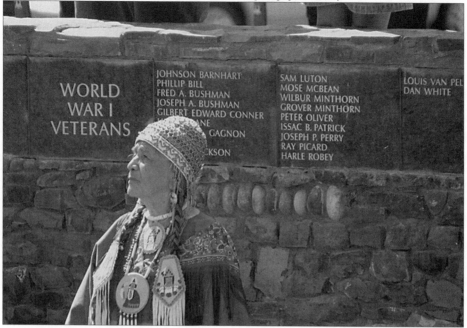

WORLD WAR I VETERANS

JOHNSON BARNHART
PHILLIP BILL
FRED A. BUSHMAN
JOSEPH A. BUSHMAN
GILBERT EDWARD CONNER
...NE
...GAGNON
...CKSON

SAM LUTON
MOSE MCBEAN
WILBUR MINTHORN
GROVER MINTHORN
PETER OLIVER
ISSAC B. PATRICK
JOSEPH P. PERRY
RAY PICARD
HARLE ROBEY

LOUIS VAN PEL
DAN WHITE

Lillian Spino at Veterans' Memorial July Fourth Celebration

pages. On the first Thursday of each month, 6,000 to 7,000 copies are printed and distributed by various methods. The *CUJ* is the award-winning monthly newspaper of the Confederated Tribes of the Umatilla Indian Reservation, winning General Excellence awards in 2000, 2001, 2002, 2003, 2004, and 2005 from the Native American Journalists Association.

1995: The first per capita distribution checks of $400 relating to the Wildhorse Casino profits were disbursed to enrolled tribal members on the eve of the Christmas holidays.

1996: As a sovereign nation, the Confederated Tribes had the power to tax commercial activities on the reservation. The Board of Trustees adopted by resolution a new Tribal Tax Code, deciding to tax the utility rights of way and easements that cross the reservation, such as railroad lines, gas lines, telephone lines, cable lines, cellular phone relays, oil lines, electric transmission lines. All will have to pay a three percent tax on the value of their easements running across the reservation.

1996: Interior Secretary Bruce Babbitt visited the Umatilla Basin, including stops at McNary Dam, Three Mile Dam, the Umatilla River, a tour of tribal salmon supplementation and acclimation facilities, and, finally, a salmon dinner at the Umatilla

Longhouse, where he announced to the Tribes: "You have done a magnificent job of seizing control of your destiny."

1996: The Warrior's Memorial and Wallula Stone, an obsidian and basalt semi-sub-teranean memorial, lists the names of all tribal members who served in the Armed Forces of the United States during war and peacetime. It includes the names of the 1855 Treaty signers. Traditional warrior ceremonies honoring veterans are held in the memorial every July Fourth. Protected inside the memorial is a petroglyph-cov-ered basalt boulder known as the Walulla Stone. The sacred artifact sat near Port-land City Hall for eighty-six years after railroad construction forced its removal from the banks of the Columbia River near Wallula Gap. It was repatriated back to the Confederated Tribes by the City of Portland and Mayor Vera Katz. The sym-bolic carvings are believed to have been made 15,000 years ago.

2000, 2001, 2002: Tamástslikt Cultural Institute hosts three annual convocations of elders, students, and scholars, which convened on tribal history and culture, tribal perspectives on the the Treaty of 1855, and Sahaptian native place names of the ancestral CTUIR homeland.

2004: Our new low-power 100-watt FM radio station went on the air with the call letters, KCUW. This non-commercial radio station broadcasting from the Uma-tilla Indian Reservation is owned by the Confederated Tribes, operated by commu-nity volunteers, and features national Native American news, music, and origi-nal programming.

2005: Treaty of 1855 Sesquicentennial Com-memoration. Several events were held in late May and early June in Walla Walla, Washington, where the Treaty Council was held 150 years ago. The organizers had four major goals for the Treaty Sesquicen-tennial: to honor the ancestors who nego-tiated the Treaties, to teach tribal youth the historical and cultural significance of the Treaties, to educate the public about how Tribes are rebuilding their nations following post-Treaty oppression, and to use the opportunity to strengthen rela-tionships and plan for the future of the Tribes.

2005, 2006: Lewis and Clark Bicentennial Commemoration. Events and program-ming to commemorate and coincide with the arrival of the Corps of Discovery to the CTUIR homeland in October 2005 and on their return trip in May 2006 were held at Tamástslikt Cultural Institute and else-where in the region. The Tribes' purpose for involvement was foremost to highlight the message that native cultures were thriving on the Columbia River Plateau when Lewis and Clark arrived, which began the detrimental process that lasted for nearly 200 years.

Source: Through 1996, from Richard V. La Course, "Days of Nicht-Yow-Way: A Political History" (unpublished manuscript, 1997).

Epilogue
Asserting Sovereignty into the Future

Donald Sampson

The path to our future and the journey for the Natíitayt — our Indian people — will be guided by the footsteps, heart, and vision of our children. Will they be influenced by the spiritual beliefs and morals of our ancestors seven generations ago or practice what remains of those beliefs from our current generation? Will our members practice our tribal Wáashat religion, speak our native languages fluently, gather and eat our traditional foods and medicines, participate in our traditional ceremonies and social events? Will they find a balance between the Indian way and the white man's way?

I remember one of my elders, Rose Sohappy, testified in our longhouse that she worried about our children and the path they will follow. She explained that if we teach our children by example about *tamánwit* 'the Creators laws' and our Indian foods, language, and lifestyle, then we will make a clear path for them to follow. They see and learn. It will be a path

that leads them to a good life. It will also lead them to Hawláak Tiichám 'the spirit land'. Rose went on to say that we can find comfort in knowing that our children will join us in the promised land. I still think of these words spoken by such a humble and quiet woman and heard by only a few. That is why I repeat them now. That is the promise of *tamánwit* and what we work for while we live this life. This belief is part of the religious doctrine that the prophet Smohalla espoused to our people in the mid-nineteenth century.

Today's generation is responsible for ensuring that the path is well-beaten and used over and over again so it will be easy for our children to follow. It will then be their obligation to do the same. If fewer and fewer travel that path, however, it will grow dim and they will become lost. For hundreds of generations we have tried to follow this belief. The legends and songs of our people remind us that we have strayed away from *tamánwit* and have suffered the consequence. We know that the world has been destroyed before and transformed anew. When we consider the thousands of years our people have lived and the many tribulations we have survived, the last two hundred years seem like a horrible nightmare. Relating the Confederated Tribes of the Umatilla Indian Reservation's history to termination, to Indian Freedom of Religion, to Red Power, and even to current Lewis and Clark events, places our own tribal history in a larger context.

Up until two hundred years ago, our people were healthy and happy, our economy was thriving, and our natural resources were managed sustainably. The bonds in our families were strong; our languages, arts, and culture were magnificent; and our tribal society was probably the most civil and democratic in the world. We lived in a balanced relationship with our natural environment. It was like heaven on earth.

Is it possible that we can reclaim some of this legacy? Can we improve the health and happiness of our people? Can we re-create our economy and restore the natural environment? I believe we can and we will. Louie Dick, a traditional tribal leader has said many times, "We are creative, unique people." We are like Coyote; we adapt and survive.

Just a brief 150 years ago our people faced the great challenge in our history. We had welcomed a trail of poor, hungry immigrants to pass through our homeland. Little did we know that they were here to stay — forever? The mass migra-

tion flooded our lands and decimated our natural resources, and the emerging United States of America almost exterminated us from the earth. Epidemic disease eliminated half our population, war and encroaching settlement dispossessed us of our lands, religious persecution and boarding schools stripped us of our dignity, language, and religion. We endured 150 years of systemic policies, the majority of which were genocidal. We survived. As a people and as a confederation of Tribes, we are now poised for the future. We have successfully taken on the management of our natural resources, and our health and social challenges are the next frontier.

What has kept us here? What will keep us into the future? It is our belief in us and our spiritual perseverance. Our elder Edith McCloud reminds us in our Walla Walla language *Chawna muun naampta* 'we will never fade'. We have seen many examples of our perseverance and our creativity. Many tribal members left the reservation and gained purchase in the larger world and returned to work with and for the Tribes. The number of tribal members who are coming home and using their education to benefit this community is growing steadily. But the future is not without challenges we must face. People coming home leads to positive tribal growth, yet this creates new pressures in the form of growing pains. We must face the changing dynamics of our membership qualifications. Homes for tribal members must grow with the growing tribal population and enrollment. Concurrently,

Mission Falls on the Umatilla River

health care on our reservation must grow to meet the needs of our growing community. Our dynamic workplace creates the need for increased preparedness to exercise self-governance.

We also have an environmental responsibility to act locally. Underground plumes at Hanford are a direct concern to the health of the rivers, to the salmon, and to people. The eastern boundary of our reservation is still an unresolved issue, with miles of acres still in public management. We will undoubtedly continue to face challenges in protecting cultural resources on and off the reservation. We must stay vigilant in the protection and enhancement of social and natural resources for wildlife, as well as cultural resources.

For years, salmon returned to the Umatilla River in the thousands to provide us spiritual and physical sustenance. The Umatilla Tribes negotiated a treaty with the United States government that obligated them to protect and preserve salmon runs in the Umatilla River. In the early 1900s, irrigated agricultural development and logging in the river basin dewatered the river, destroyed the habitat, and salmon runs went extinct. The non-

Digital flashcamp youth pose in traditional clothing. In front (from left) are Travis Bumgarner, Isaiah Simonson, Kari Edmiston, Anna Harris, Keri Kordatzsky, and Marisa Dick. In back (from left) are Sadie Mildenberger, Mary Harris, and Jeremiah Farrow.

Indians' development and exploitation of the natural resources were guided by Manifest Destiny — the doctrine of human dominion over the land and exploitation of its resources.

In the late 1970s, however, the Tribes began a concerted effort to restore salmon and their treaty fishing rights in the Umatilla River. Our doctrine of restoration was *tamánwit*. Protect the natural resources, restore the natural environment, and put the salmon and water in the river where they belong. The Tribes were armed with the Treaty law and newly formed tribal capacity with technical experts in law, fisheries science, and political strategy. The Tribes worked collaboratively with our non-Indian neighbors to restore the habitat, put water in the river, and reintroduce salmon to the Umatilla River. After nearly twenty years of political leadership and perseverance, today as many as twenty to thirty thousand salmon return each year. Since the beginning of time, *tamánwit* had taken care of the salmon and guided us in preserving them. Manifest Destiny has not prevailed. The Umatilla Basin Project, our river of hope, is central to contemporary history because it not only addresses the water but also the fish and the food. It embraces the controversy. It embraces our stakeholders when they are in disagreement, and it embraces inter-governmental relations. It is a manifestation of our Indian law.

The Umatilla Tribes are now using the same model of salmon restoration in other river basins, including the Walla Walla River. Eventually this model and these principles will be applied throughout the entire Columbia River Basin and will be the driving force behind saving salmon for future generations. It is this same determination that will also save our tribal culture.

Religion still has strong influences on our reservation. Ties to the Catholic and Presbyterian churches are still strong, but many families have returned to the traditional longhouse ways or practice traditional religion in their own homes. Still others have found a way to blend the two, participating in current religious practices at the longhouse and elements of the old missionary activity.

For decades our tribal elders were sent to public and Catholic boarding schools on and off the reservation. Boarding schools were established to do two things — strip native children of their identity and culture and educate them in the white man's ways. For the benefits reaped — including occupational skills, spouses, and lifelong friends — there were enormous costs. Young children were taken from their families, their hair was cut, and their native clothes taken away. They were beaten for speaking our native languages and disciplined by military protocol. My grandmother — Carrie Sampson — told me of the time at St.

Andrews Catholic school when she was chained outside during the winter because she refused to give up her language. Many of the Catholic nuns were mean to the children. Subsequently, she did not want my father to go through the same torture — she did not teach him fluency in our language. He also went to Chemawa boarding school, over two hundred miles from the reservation, and more of our language and culture was lost. At least three generations of our people went through this experience, but we never gave up. Many of our native language speakers have gone, yet a handful are working to document and restore Walla Walla, Umatilla, and Nez Perce language.

Today, we are turning the tables. In 1994, we began our tribal language restoration program — led by a few younger speakers and our elders. In 2004, we began our own Nixyáawii Community High School on the Umatilla Indian Reservation. It is the only such school in the state of Oregon. The students, most of them native, are learning our tribal languages and history. I remember when we dedicated the grand opening of the school, many of our elders — especially those who had been through the boarding school experience — cried with joy for our young children. Never again would the children have to face the humility and pain they endured. In fact, many of these elders are now their language teachers.

The students also go to the old St. Andrews Catholic school, which closed in the 1960s. It is not a boarding school anymore. In 1995, it was transformed by tribal

New and Proposed Projects

Walla Walla River Basin Project. The Confederated Tribes of the Umatilla Indian Reservation, in conjunction with the US Army Corps of Engineers, completed a feasibility study in 2006 focusing on the restoration and management of a viable ecosystem within the Walla Walla River Basin. As in the neighboring Umatilla Basin, the Walla Walla River lost its once-plentiful salmon runs early in the 20th Century but actions are underway to reestablish this valuable resource. Early in the 20th century, major impacts occurred to salmon habitat due to water diversion structures, reduction of flows, stream channelization and various developments adjacent to streams. Until recently, very little was being done to address improvements for the rebuilding of fisheries resources in the Walla Walla Basin. A comprehensive program is being implemented which includes removal or laddering of diversion structures, screening of irrigation canals, irrigation ditch consolidation and conservation, instream flow enhancement, stream habitat enhancement and hatchery actions. The program will benefit spring chinook salmon, and ESA-listed summer steelhead and bull trout.

Freshwater Mussel Project. The Freshwater Mussel Project is restoring freshwater mussels to the Umatilla River as part ongoing efforts to rebuild ecosystem diversity, function, and traditional cultural opportunities in the Basin. Historically freshwater mussels were vital components of intact salmonid ecosystems, but have been affected directly and indirectly by dams, habitat deterioration, and declines in salmon populations. Changes in habitat from dams, channel modification, agriculture and forestry are major reasons for decline of freshwater mussels throughout North America.

Proposed Coyote Business Park. CTUIR proposes to develop, build and manage a light industrial and commercial business park known as the Coyote Business Park. The proposed Coyote Business Park would be located on a 520-acre site south of Interstate 84, approximately seven miles east of Pendleton, Oregon on the Umatilla Indian Reservation.

Community Wellness. CTUIR has been successful in planting and tending a community garden for two seasons and is distributing a wide array of fresh vegetables to community members. The Annual Yellowhawk Fun Run is alive and well with healthy competition in every age group. The Rez Watch Community member and artist Jim Lavadour into the Crow's Shadow Institute of the Arts. Now our children learn state-of-the-art techniques in printmaking and computer graphics as well as traditional arts.

Our community swells with pride when we hear our children speak our language, when we watch our students excel academically, and when we watch our Nixyáawii Golden Eagles play sports and represent us. In 2004, six native students — our first graduating class — made history during the graduation ceremony. Instead of the usual pomp and circumstance, tribal chiefs, followed by elders and students, danced to the honor song and the drum. The graduates donned eagle feathers, and the packed community center wept in honor of these young people and in memory of our ancestors. It was only the beginning of a long journey.

Eventually, the school will expand to include junior high and grade schools. A new school will be built. The boarding schools of the past will be a part of our history that we endured. Our students will excel academically, athletically, and culturally. We look forward to increased graduation success across all education and training levels. And, most importantly, a new generation — the seventh generation — will lead the path for our tribal nation. Our nation will strengthen and grow.

Drug Curtailment Project is in the beginning stages of providing a safe and secure, drug-free community. A proposed Wellness Center will enhance and inform nutritional and social health practices on the reservation.

Energy. The Confederated Tribes have long sought to be leaders in developing and promoting alternative sources of energy, thereby lessening the dependence on hydro-power, which is so detrimental to salmon. A new tribal venture called Timine (meaning heart or core) Development Corporation is being organized to develop various energy projects. The preliminary projects involve energy marketing and power generation primarily through renewable resources such as wind.

Natural Resources. Slated for 2007, the Tribes' Department of Natural Resources will take over the functions of the Bureau of Indian Affairs, primarily in the area of forestry and range. As the BIA had done, DNR will continue to manage timber on reservation lands, but with new responsibilities consistent with tribal goals and cultural values. Protection of and access to hunting, digging, and gathering of traditional first foods is of paramount concern.

Young Chief's stand at winning the land for the Umatilla Reservation and Walla Walla Chief PeoPeoMoxMox's ability to negotiate at the Treaty Council are our legacy. We endured thirty years of warfare. One hundred years ago, people were still moving onto the reservation from the outlying ancestral homeland. What we stood for then, as we do now, is freedom. When the allotment acts led to our assets being taken away, we were plunged into poverty. Our remarkable turnaround, which is gaining momentum, is our legacy. We are recovering from past repression. That recovery is a legacy in and of itself. The new living culture village at Tamástslikt Cultural Institute is proof of our survival, and every year we restore more of our traditional knowledge. The Umatilla Basin Project leaves a legacy for the future. It exemplifies the medicinal power of water.

These are but a few examples of the perseverance and creativity of our people. We have been guided by *tamánwit* and strengthened by our spiritual beliefs. We have survived, and we will survive far into the future. I remember what one Northwest tribal leader, Billy Frank, Jr., said: "We've been here for thousands of years, and we'll be here for thousands more. We ain't goin anywhere." As we have seen in the past, the new generations will step up and excel. They will lead the greatest renaissance of a nation of people in the history of the world. And it will be the Umatilla, Walla Walla, and Cayuse people — along with our indigenous brothers and sisters — who will change the world for the better.

Index

Act of Congress (1882), 103, 105

Administration for Native Americans (ANA), 200

agriculture, 40, 44, 92, 110, 229, 247, 250

Alaska, 33

Aldrich, Ed, 165

Alexander, Loretta, 222

Algonquin Indians, 44, 46, 53

Allen, Andrew, 133, 35

Allen, Kenny, 135

allotment period, 97

Alpowa, 29

American Board of Commissioners of Foreign Missions (ABCFM), 49, 63

American Indian Movement (AIM), 228

Ancient One. *See* Kennewick Man

Anderson, Rupert, 155

Antoine, Maudie (Maudie Craig), 21, 86, 125, 161, 163, 169

Archeological Resources Protection Act (ARPA), 217, 225

Arikara villages, 42

assimilation, 111, 119, 121, 134, 136, 140, 141, 174, 177

Astor, John Jacob, 41–43

Atiyeh, Victor, 186, 187, 212, 218

Babbitt, Bruce, 241

Babcock, O.L., 155

Badroads, Jim, 112

Baker City, Oregon, 206

Baldwin, Dale, 197

Bannock Indians, 32, 33, 81, 120

Barkley, John, 205, 209

Barnhart, Alice, 123

beadwork, 53

Belloni, Judge Robert C., 219, 221, 240

Berry Group, 209

Bill, Eliza (Liza), 169, 181, 201

Bill, Kenneth, 221

Billy, Jim, 112

Birch Creek, 27

Bitterroot Mountains, 28, 32, 38

Black Elk, 80

Blackfeet Indians, 32

Blackhawk, Chief, 134

Blackwolf, Ike, 199

Blanchet, Fr. Francois Norbet, 50

blood quantum, 106, 115, 116, 176, 246

Blue Mountains, 26, 28, 32, 42, 50–53, 61, 63, 64, 81, 84, 85, 94, 105, 113, 119, 122, 123, 128, 131, 132, 135, 141

Board of Trustees (BOT), 86, 156, 157, 160, 165, 168–71, 176, 178, 181, 188, 194, 200, 203, 204, 207, 209, 213, 215, 216, 225, 228, 240, 241

boarding school, 95, 106, 111, 119, 124, 246, 247, 251

Boiling Point, 118, 132

Boldt decision, 216

Boldt, Judge George, 220

Bonneville Dam, 162, 218, 225

Bonneville Power Administration (BPA), 154, 163, 167, 171, 221, 222, 234, 240

Bowman, Frank, 132

Brigham, Kathryn, 221

Brigham, Percy, 168, 182, 219

British American Bingo, 211

Broughton, Lt. William, 34

Brown, John, xiii

Buckaroo Canyon, 118

buckskin, 49, 129, 158

buffalo, 28, 35, 48–50, 62, 68, 166

bull trout, 250

Bureau of Indian Affairs (BIA), 52, 73, 86, 92, 106, 107, 111, 115, 117, 119, 137, 139, 142, 147, 151, 152, 154–6, 165, 175, 177, 179, 186–8, 194–7, 203, 205, 217, 218, 251

Bureau of Reclamation, 167, 234

Burke, Clarence, 112, 118, 136

Burke, Marvin, 87

Burke, Chief Raymond T. "Popcorn," 112, 181, 187

Burke, Richard 153–5, 170

Burns–Paiute Tribe, 186, 195

Burnt River, 27
Business Committee, 138, 153–6
Butter Creek, 27
Byers, W.S., 103

camas, 29, 48, 49, 79
camp crier, 61, 95, 106, 141, 133, 134-5, 136, 140, 141
Canada, 41, 42, 51, 84, 96, 226
Canyon City, Oregon, 28
Cascade Locks, 162, 219
Cascade Mountains, 28
Catherine Creek, 26, 158, 159, 182, 239
Cathlamet Indians, 34
Cay-Uma-Wa, 196
Cayuse Five, 64, 65, 68, 75, 81, 82, 83, 172, 173
Cayuse horse, 31
Cayuse Indians, 5, 17, 26-28, 30-1, 33-6, 40-42, 44-
    51, 53, 54, 60-65, 66-69, 71, 73, 74-76, 78-79, 81-
    88, 93-95, 97, 99, 103, 111, 112, 113-15, 117, 118, 123,
    125, 128, 132, 136-7, 141, 169, 171-4, 176, 183, 188,
    214, 229, 234, 240, 252
Cayuse War. See wars, warfare
Celebration Committee, 196
Celebration Grounds. See July Grounds
Celilo Falls, 29, 34, 35, 47, 122, 128, 149, 160–4, 166,
    168, 180, 218, 219
ceremony, 30, 68, 78, 79, 83, 86, 89, 195, 245
Chalakee, Barbara, 181
Charbonneau, Jean-Baptiste, 37
Chelan Indians, 29
Chemawa Indian Boarding School, 249
Cherokee Nation, 183
Cheyenne Indians, 40
chiefs. See headmen
Chiloquin, Edison, 177
Chinook Indians, 33, 34, 42, 47, 53
Chinook jargon, 69
Chinook (Wind) Dance, 123
Christianity, 44, 49–51, 60, 62, 64, 72, 73, 88, 95,
    130, 249
circle of life, 89
Citizen for Veterans Act, 106
Civil Rights movement, 187, 228
Clark, John, 52
Clatsop Indians, 33
Clearwater River, 29, 37, 39, 49, 61, 74, 83
Clokomas, 64, 172
Code of Federal Regulations (CFR), 154, 179

Coeur D'Alene Tribe, 82
Collier, John, 139
Columbia Plateau (Columbia River Indians),
    68, 77, 78, 84, 88, 94, 229, 240
Columbia River, 27–29, 34, 36, 40, 41, 43, 45, 48,
    53, 61, 62, 66, 73, 74, 82, 93, 111, 113, 161, 162, 167,
    218, 220–2, 229, 226, 236, 239, 242, 249
Columbia River Fish Management Plan, 221
Columbia River Gorge, 42, 82, 206
Columbia River Gorge Act, 240
Columbia River Inter–Tribal Fish Commission
    (CRITFC), 182, 218, 221, 222
Columbia River Tribes, 218–21
Colville Confederated Tribes v. Walton, 216
Colville Reservation, 82, 84, 101, 124, 239
Commission on Indian Services, 186
Community Action Program, 228, 239
Community Development Commission, 203,
    204
Community Health Representatives Program,
    194, 239
Comprehensive Plan, 185
Comprehensive Water Management Plan, 240
Confederated Tribes of the Umatilla Indian
    Reservation (CTUIR), 81, 98, 136, 151, 156,
    159, 163, 164, 186, 188, 195, 197, 202, 215, 216,
    218–20, 226, 227–30, 235-7, 245, 247, 249–50
Confederated Tribes of the Umatilla Indian
    Reservation v. Alexander, 240
Confederated Tribes of the Umatilla Indian
    Reservation v. Maison, 239
Confederated Umatilla Journal, 240, 239
Conner, Cecil, 126
Conner, Duane, 126
Conner, Gilbert, 26, 159, 167
Conner, Earl E. "Taz," 197
Conner, James, 50
Conner, Roberta "Bobbie," 214, 232
Constitution and By-Laws (1949), 86, 113, 138, 141,
    156, 157, 172, 174, 175, 176, 181, 215, 237
Continental Mills, 215
Cook, James, 34
Coquille Tribe, 177
Cordon, Guy, 164
Council of Energy Resource Tribes (CERT),
    199, 200
Cowapoo, Chief Luke, 112, 137
Cowapoo, Rod Sr., 201

Cowapoo, Sistine Craig, 125
Cow Creek Band, 209, 210
Cowlitz, 29, 33, 34
coyote, 8, 10, 15, 23, 26, 122, 246
Coyote Business Park, 250
Craig, Col. William, 124
Craig, Fermore, Sr., 8, 88
Craig, Johnny, 125
Craig, Joseph, 124, 125
Crane, Winnie Kanine Crane Burke, 154
Creator, 18, 23, 26, 53, 77, 78, 79, 137, 140, 142, 245,
    247
Credit Committee, 193
Crickie, 50
Crow Indians, 24
Crow's Shadow Institute of the Arts, 250
Cultural Resources Committee, 225
Cultural Resources Protection Program
    (CRPP), 217, 225, 226
cúukwen'in, 14

Dawes Act (1887), 96, 105, 109, 110, 113, 115, 116, 117
Dawes, Sen. Henry L., 105, 116
Demers, Fr. Modeste, 50
Department of Energy, 200, 226
Department of Natural Resources (DNR), 198,
    201, 216, 223, 225, 251
Deschutes River, 33, 43
de Tocqueville, Alexis, 54
Dick, Louie, Jr., 118-20, 194, 195, 246, 248
Dick, Mose, 182
digging (roots), 32, 33, 251
dip net, 161-2, 232, 280
disease, 26, 30, 52, 53, 63, 64, 85, 91, 96, 246
Docket No. 264, 160, 166, 168, 180
Douglas, David, 47
Dreamer religion, 60, 72, 73, 75, 76, 88, 124, 166,
    247
Duck, Harold, 194
Dumont, Andy, 195, 201

Earth Blanket, 81
Earth-Mother, 122, 136
East Oregonian, 113, 165, 181, 185
Eastern Oregon University, 209
Economic Development Administration (EDA)
    Planning Assistant Grant, 194
Economic Opportunity Act, 239

eels, 167, 223
Egan, Chief, 81, 83, 84
Elephant Rock, 8
Elgin, Oregon, 27
Elk, Louise, 169
Emigrant Springs, 81, 132
Enick, Amelia, 194
Enick, Law, 230
Enlightenment, 36
enrollment. See blood quantum
Enterprise Administration, 203–5, 207, 209
Environmental Planning and Rights
    Protection, 217
Ernst & Ernst, 181, 228
Ervin, Sam, 183
Executive Order 80, 8

fall chinook, 122, 234
farewell ceremony, 81
Farm Committee, 193, 197
Farnham, Thomas J., 31, 50
Farrow, Elzie, 193
Farrow, Emma Sheoships, 215
Farrow, Louella, 196
Farrow, Matthew Farrow, Sr., 187
Farrow, Michael "Jughead," 193–5, 197, 198, 215–
    17, 221, 223, 225
feasts, 123, 124, 126, 128, 130, 132, 169, 179-80, 182
Federal Register, 187
First Americans, 95
first foods, 15, 23, 79, 124, 128, 224, 245, 251
First Nations Financial Project, 199, 203
Fish and Wildlife Committee, 182, 221
fisheries program, 198, 217
fishing, 34, 67, 78, 110, 147, 152, 157, 158-63, 161, 166,
    172, 174, 179, 182, 188, 218-19, 221, 229, 234, 239,
    240, 241, 248, 250
Fletcher, George, 118
Forest Service, 195, 218, 220
Forrest, Edgar, Jr., 156, 170
Forestry and Range Enterprises, 193, 197
Fort Astoria, 42, 44
Fort Colville, 50
Fort George. See Fort Astoria
Fort Hall, 48
Fort Nez Perces, 44–46, 48–50, 62, 66, 83, 166
Fort Sutter, 52
Fort Vancouver, 46, 48–50, 85

Fort Walla Walla. *See* Fort Nez Perces
fractionalized heirship, 185, 186
Frank, Billy, Jr., 252
Franklin, Arlen, 118
French, Isabelle Craig, 124, 125
Frenchtown, 83, 85
Freshwater Mussel Project, 250
Frohnmeyer, David, 218
fur trade, 41–48, 50, 51, 62

gaffing, 158, 230, 232, 240
Gallaher, Dave, 187
games and gambling (traditional), 30
Gaming Task Force, 209
Gass, Patrick, 41
gathering, 29, 32, 33, 66, 67, 78, 96, 119, 122, 123, 130, 131, 132, 141, 147, 162, 166, 182, 197, 212, 213, 218, 251
General Council (GC), 115, 121, 152, 153, 154, 156-7, 165, 168, 169, 170, 171, 176, 181, 194, 195, 200, 205, 212, 216
General Land Allotment Act of 1887. *See* Dawes Act
George, Gary, 209, 210
Gibbon, Oregon, 132
gill net, 162, 218-19, 221, 239-40
give-away, 140
gold mining, 101
Golden Eagles Protection Act, 107
Gordon, Kathleen, 181, 201
government-to-government relations, 226, 227
grain elevator, 202
Grand Ronde Tribe, 177, 186
Grande Ronde River and Valley, 26, 28, 29, 33, 75, 76, 119, 131, 137, 158, 159, 160, 221, 225
Granite River, 230
Gray, Robert, 34
Great Basin, 33
Great Britain, 44, 46, 48, 53, 62
Great Chain of Being, 36
Great Sioux Uprising, 136
Greater Eastern Oregon Development Corporation (GEODC), 212
Gulick, Bill, 169
Guyer, Philip, 155, 193, 195, 237

Hair Knotted in Front. *See* Old Chief Joseph
Halfmoon, Alphonse "Frenchy," 181, 196

Halfmoon, Hilda, 80
Halfmoon Market, 196
Halfmoon, Mary, 125
Halfmoon, Otis, 137, 138
Hall, David "Steve," 153–5, 159, 167, 170
Hampson, Tom, 195, 221
Hampson, Woesha, 196
Hanford Nuclear Reservation, 200, 247
Happy Canyon Pageant, 124, 133
Harris Pine Mills, 215
Hatfield, Mark O., 185, 212, 218, 232, 234
Hawláak Tiichám, 245
Háwtmi Creek, 123, 168
hayaytám, 87
Hays, Molly Penny, 125
Heading, Elijah, 52
headmen, 24, 36, 39–41, 43, 47, 49, 62, 64–68, 73–78, 87, 94, 99, 111, 112, 114, 115, 119, 133, 134, 137, 138, 141
Head Start, 196, 239
Hermiston, Oregon, 220
Hester, Dan, 210
Hill, Fred, 6, 17, 87
himyúume, 24
Hinmatóowyalahtq'it. *See* Chief Joseph
hiwah, 86
Holm, Tom, 138
Holmes, Tommy, 217
Homli, Chief, 111, 112, 114, 137
Hoptowit, Lilian Kanine, 181
Horse Heaven Hills, 27
horses, 30–32, 43, 46, 62, 85, 87
House Concurrent Resolution 108, 177, 178, 216
House Resolution 3805, 168
Housing and Urban Development, 188, 194
Howard, Gen. O.O., 76, 83
Hudson's Bay Company, 33, 46–50, 62, 82, 86, 85, 166
Hunt, William Price, 42
hunting, 66, 147, 152, 157, 174, 179, 182, 188, 193, 216, 218, 239, 251
Hurricane Creek, 33

'iceyéeye (NP). *See* coyote
'Ichishkíin, 5, 6, 9, 11, 17
Imatalamthláma, 5, 17
Imnaha River, 160, 225
Indian Bureau. *See* Bureau of Indian Affairs

Indian Citizenship Act, 106, 107, 139, 148, 148
Indian Civil Rights Act (ICRA), 183, 185, 187
Indian Claims Commission (ICC), 107, 159, 160, 166–68, 171, 180, 216
Indian Country, 61, 65, 75, 81, 82, 101, 109, 172, 200, 201, 203
Indian Freedom of Religion, 246
Indian Gaming Regulatory Act (IGRA), 1988, 204, 205
Indian Health Service (IHS), 176, 178, 187, 188, 194, 203
Indian Lake, 110, 197
Indian Land Consolidation Conferences, 203, 205
Indian Land Tenure Foundation, 203, 206
Indian Land Working Group, 203, 206
Indian Reorganization Act, 107, 110, 121, 139, 156, 175, 176
Indian Self-Determination and Education Assistance Act, 187, 188
Indian Village, Round-Up, 133
Inheritance Act, 197
Isholhot. *See* Cayuse Five
Isiaasheluckas, 64, 172
Isqúulktpe' iyíwewiy, 11
Istikus, 23
ititámat, also time ball, 25

Jacobs, Melville, 14
James, Edward, 88
James, Gary, 223
Jefferson Peace Medal, 39–41, 62, 73, 112, 137
Jefferson, Thomas, 35, 52, 54, 69, 111
Jim, Howard, 13
Joe, Tom, 140
John Day River, 26, 27, 33, 43, 131, 160
Johnny, Martha, 25
Johnson Creek, , 27, 131, 169
Johnson Creek Restoration Area, 110
Johnson, Annie, 140
Johnson, Charlie, 112, 155
Johnson, Joseph, 112
Johnson, Leslie, 180
Johnson, Lyndon B., 194, 239
Johnson Ridge, 119, 128
Johnson, Tom (Paaxit Tuhmootsut), 118
Jones, Elizabeth, 194
Jones, Jesse, 199

Jones, Linda, 222
Joseph band, 83, 88
Joseph, Chief, 81, 83, 84
Joseph, Old Chief, 23, 50, 76, 78, 83, 88
Joseph, Oregon, 164
Josephy, Alvin M., Jr., xiii
Joshua, Billy, 137
July Grounds, 128, 140, 141, 170, 195

Kah–Nee–Tah Resort, 209
Kamiakin, 82
Kanine, Chief Jim, 112, 135
Kanine Ridge, 119
Kash Kash, James 137
Kash Kash, Sam, 153–5, 193–5, 197, 221
Katz, Vera, 242
kaush, 123, 126
KCUW, 242
Kelly, Col. James, 83
Kelly, Lawrence, 106
Kennewick Man, 225
Kettle Falls, 29
Kiamasumkin, 172
Kilkenney, Mike, 210
King, Miller, Anderson, Nash, 171
Kipsootspaouyeen, 33
Kitzhaber, John, 213
Klamath Tribes, 157, 158, 177, 186
Klikitat language, 14, 29
Koots Koots Wapta, 33
kusi, 31. *See also* horses

La Grande, Oregon, 132, 182, 225
LaCourse, Del, 180
Lake Hume-Ti-Pin. *See* Indian Lake
Lake Wallula, 242
Land Consolidation Act, 197
Land Project Policy Statement, 199
Lane, Joseph, 172
latitlatit, 123
Lavadour, Arnold, 170
Lavadour, James, 250
Law and Order Committee, 182
Lawyer, 62, 75, 88
Lee, Jason, 48, 49
Lee's Encampment, 168
Lewis and Clark Expedition, 35–41, 61, 62, 72, 73, 74, 84–86, 96, 135, 137, 166, 242, 246

Liberty, David, 170
Lloyd, Lee, 120
Lloyd, Mitchell, 140
Lloyd, Dorothy, 120
Lloyd, Mose, 120
Lloyd Raymond, 120
Long Hair, Louise, 80, 140
longhouse, 15, 72, 73, 124, 128, 142, 196, 212, 222, 241, 245, 249
Looking Glass, Chief, 48, 62, 74, 75, 76
Looking Glass Creek, 27
Louisiana Purchase, 40, 54
Lower Monument Dam, 234
Lowry, Chief Elijah, 114
Luce, Charles F. (White Eagle), 159, 169, 175, 178, 180
Luls, 114
Luton, Sam, 155

Magers, Dale, 196
Malheur River, 28
Manifest Destiny, 72, 74, 76, 81, 94, 248
Manpower Consortium, 195, 197
Martinez, Julia, 184
McBean, John, 114
McClanahan, Mark C., 171
McCloud, Edith, 17, 246
McCloud, Mike, 233
McFarland, Louis, 154, 161, 163, 170
McFatridge, Arthur E., 155
McIntyre, Roy, 181
McKay Creek, 26, 119, 123, 134, 168, 194. *See also* Háwtmi Creek
McKenzie, Donald, 45, 46
McLaughlin, Joe, 210
McLoughlin, Dr. John, 48, 49, 62, 173
McNary Dam, 240, 241
McNaught, Craig, 210
Meacham, Oregon, 132, 168
Meacham, A.B., 102
Meanatete, Head Chief (Pierre), 137
Medicine Dance, 123
medicine doctor. *See tewat*
membership laws. *See* blood quantum
Meriam Report, 119, 152
Métis Indians, 44, 46, 53
Mill Creek, 28
Miller, Joe, 133

mimimiyóoxat tu'ynú'suusiin, 87
Minam River, 27
Minthorn, Antone , 87, 181, 195, 205, 212, 221, 231
Minthorn, Armand, 196, 224
Minthorn, Bill, 134, 167, 181, 193, 194
Minthorn, Douglas, 87, 199
Minthorn, Leslie, 194, 196, 216, 217
Minthorn, Wilfred, 140
Mission, Oregon, 72, 81, 123, 132, 194, 195, 239
missions and missionaries, 48–52, 60, 62, 64, 72, 83, 249
Mitchell Act, 218
Monroe Doctrine, 94
Moorhouse, Maj, Lee, 95, 114, 130, 134
Moses, John, 15
Motanic, Dan, 140
Motet Springs, 131
Mt. Adams, 131
Mt. Hood, 34
Multnomah Indians, 34
myth, 6, 9

Nancy Oden Luce Trust, 171
Nash, Doug, 171, 196
Natíitayt (Natítaytma, Netíitelwit), 5, 9, 17, 23, 26, 53, 77, 78, 245
Native American Graves Protection and Repatriation Act (NAGPRA), 217, 225
Native American Journalists Association, 241
nay'mosha (náymuma, himyúume), 24
Nch'I–Wana. *See* Columbia River
New Zealand, 226
Nez Perce Tribe and Reservation, 28, 29, 35, 40, 50, 65, 67, 68, 70, 73, 74, 75, 76, 77, 83, 88, 101, 113, 124, 129, 135, 158, 162, 164, 169, 182, 219, 239
Nixon, Richard M., 187
Nixyáawii Community High School, 249
Nixyáawii Golden Eagles, 251
North West Company, 41, 42, 44–46, 166
Northern Paiute Indians, 32, 82
Northwest Coast Indians, 94
Northwest Power Planning Council, 222, 240
No-Shirt, Chief, 112, 137
nusux, 180
Nuumíipuu (Nuumiipuutímt), 5, 9, 11, 14, 17, 61

Ococtuin, 31
O'Donnell, Terence, 68, 101

Ogden, Peter Skene, 39, 47, 48
O'Rourke, Larry, 210
Old Agency Cemetery, 239
Old Umatilla Townsite, 239
Old Barn, 130, 132, 170
Ollokʷot, 43, 81
Ordway, John, 37
Oregon City, Oregon, 64, 65, 75, 172, 173, 207
Oregon Electric Cooperative, 153, 154
Oregon Game Commission, 158, 159, 239
Oregon Trail, 48, 51, 52, 63, 93, 98, 105, 132, 166, 206, 207, 240
Oregon Trail Advisory Council, 207
Oregon Commission on Indian Services, 213
Oregon Department of Fish and Wildlife (ODFW), 223, 234
Oregon Game Commission, 158, 239
Oregon State Lottery Commission, 207
Oregon Water Resources Department, 234
Oregonian, 209
Overall Economic Development Plan (OEDP), 195, 199, 204

Paaxit Tuhmootsut (Five Ridges, Tom Johnson), 118
Pacific Fur Company, 41–44, 46, 52
Pacific Power Act, 222
Pacific Salmon Treaty, 223
Palmer, Joel, 23, 66–69, 71, 75–81, 84, 87, 98
Palouse Cemetery, 234
Palouse Indians, 28, 82
Pambrun, Pierre, 48, 50
papuu song, 141
Parker, Samuel, 49
Pataha Valley, 29
Patawa, Allen, 112
Patawa, Woody, 194, 209, 210, 212
Patrick, Ike, 140, 155
Patrick, Lawrence 10, 14
Patrick, Mrs. Ada, 11
pelúutspuu, 5, 17
Pendleton Chamber of Commerce, 212
Pendleton, Oregon, 42, 102, 103, 121, 132, 134, 152-165, 185, 205, 209, 213, 215, 216, 228, 232, 235, 250
Pendleton Flour Mills, 202
Pendleton Round-Up, 119, 124, 128, 131–5, 141, 197, 227

Pendleton Woolen Mills, 133
Peo, Chief, 114, 137
PeoPeoMoxMox (Yellow Bird), 52, 69, 71, 74, 79, 80, 81, 83, 111, 112
Picard, Marvin, 181
Pi–Em–Nat Enterprises, 232
Pierce, Franklin, 69
piish, 51
pipe ceremony, 81
piyaxi, 123
Plains Indians, 28, 85
Planning Committee, 195, 198
Plateau country, 6, 7, 23, 24, 27, 29, 32, 33, 36, 39, 41, 43, 44, 46, 72, 78, 89, 123, 137
Poker Jim, 112
Pond, Chief Amos, 112, 114, 134, 137
Pond, Jane Wilkinsen, 140
Powder River, 26, 27
Powwow, 125
Pratt, Judge O.C., 172, 173
Progressive Association, 181
prophecy, 26, 72
Public Law 280, 94, 158, 178, 179, 184–7, 196, 197, 216

Quaempts, Elias, 159, 161, 167, 170
Quill-Quills-Tuck-a-Pesten, 43

Ray, Dr. Verne F. 159, 166
Rayley, Roy, 133
Reagan, Ronald, 240
Red Coat Warriors, 64
Red Elk Canyon, 118
Red Hawk, Chief George, 112, 137
Red Moccasin Tops, 64, 81
Red Power movement, 187, 228, 246
Red River Anglican School, 52
Relocation Program, 177, 178, 194
repatriation, 217, 225, 226, 227
reservation. *See* Umatilla Indian Reservation
retrocession, 173, 184, 185, 187, 197
Reves, Inez Spino, 16
Rez Watch Community Drug Curtailment Project, 250
Rhodes, Willard, 15
Richards, Kent, 54
Richland, Washington, 225
Roberts, Barbara, 210
Rochow, Walter, 159

Roe Cloud, Henry, 121, 152, 154–6
Root Feast, 132
roots, 76, 79, 147, 182
Ross, Alexander, 42–46
Round–Up City Development Corporation, 212, 213
Ruby, Dr. Robert, xiii

Sacagawea, 37, 39
Sahaptian, 5, 6, 24, 152, 128, 135, 152, 155, 166, 242, 241, 247
Sahaptin, 5, 6, 12, 13, 17, 31, 77, 120, 214, 239
Sahaptin Language Consortium, 239
Salish, 24
salmon, 14, 23, 24, 29, 36, 43, 76, 93, 122, 152, 157–9, 161–3, 167, 169, 180, 182, 218, 229, 232, 239, 240, 250
salmon restoration, 217, 219, 221–3, 229-30, 231-2, 235, 250, 250-2
salmon (coho), 234
salmon (fall chinook), 234
salmon (spring chinook), 221, 232, 234, 250, 250
salmon (steelhead), 240, 250
Salmon River, 27, 29
Sampson, Chief Carl, 201
Sampson, Carrie, 249
Sampson, Donald, 210, 223
Sams, Susan, 194
Sand Hollow, 82
Santa Clara Pueblo v. Martinez (1978), 184
scaffolds (fishing), 161
Schuster, Helen, 134,
Schwarzenegger, Arnold, 179
Searcey, Mildred, 102
self–determination, 151, 176, 185–7, 215, 235, 236, 247
Seven Drum religion, 72, 94, 96, 137. See also Dreamer religion
seventh generation, 251
Shaker religion, 15
Sharp, Bryon A., 155
She-Ca-Yah (Chief Five Crows), 78
Sheoships, Joe, 161, 163, 193, 194, 197
Sheoships, Sam, 197
Shishnimishpa, 129, 134
Shoshone-Bannocks. See Bannock Indians
Shoshone Tribe, 32, 42, 46
Showaway, Chief, 114

Siletz Tribe, 186
Silvies, Oregon, 28
Simpson, George, 47, 48
Sisáawipam, 33
Skookum House, 172
Slater, James H., 105
Slater Act. See Umatilla Allotment Act
slavery, 32
Small Business Administration, 196
Small Business Center, 212
Smithsonian Institution, 234
Smohalla, 72, 74, 75, 245
Snake Indians, 32, 47
Snake River, 26, 28, 37, 41, 43, 45, 48, 61, 72, 73, 225, 226
Snake River country, 29, 36, 44, 46, 48, 49, 96, 236
Sohappy, Dominique, 230
Sohappy, Rose, 245
Sohappy, Van, 230
Sohon, Gustav, 65, 71
Solomon, Judge Gus J., 157–9
sovereignty, 62, 71, 86, 93, 121, 135, 139, 156, 171, 172, 174, 176, 180, 181, 183–5, 187, 188, 197, 217, 236, 239
Spalding, Henry and Eliza, 49, 50, 62
spilyáy. See coyote.
Spino, George, 112, 123, 140
Spino, Lillian, 241
Spokane Indians, 82, 101
Spokane River, 29, 49
Spout Springs, 131
St. Andrews Mission, 124, 128, 228, 249
St. Anne's Mission, 81
Steptoe, Maj. Edward, 82
Stern, Dr. Theodore, xiii, 39, 80
Stevens, Isaac, 69, 71, 75–80, 84, 87, 162, 169
Stick Indian, 13
Stikus, Chief, 78
Stuart, David, 42
šúkwat, 5, 10, 14, 142
Sumpkin, Captain, 112, 137
Suphan, Robert, 159
Supreme Law of the Land, 229, 231
suyápo, 73, 173–5, 177
Suyápotimki, 173
Swartzlander, Edward L., 155
sweathouse, 131, 133, 137, 142

Swindell Survey, 220
Talton v. Mayes, 183
talwáskt, 12
tamáapaykt, 12, 13
tamánwit, tamálwit, 3, 17, 23, 73, 77–79, 88, 224, 245, 248, 249
támapaykša, 12
Tamástslikt Cultural Institute, 15, 194, 207, 212–14, 236, 242, 249, 252
Tamatapam, 40, 43, 45, 46, 49
Tanánma, 5, 17
Tandy, Col. F.S., 165
Tawatoy, 48
teekash, 118
Tekajute. *See* Cayuse Five
Telephone Ridge, 118–20
Telokite. *See* Cayuse Five
Tenino Indians, 28, 82
Tetoharsky, 36
termination policy, 86, 92, 94, 95, 113, 117, 121, 139, 148, 160, 175, 177, 178, 191, 216, 246
tewat (tewatat), 122, 123, 137
tewyelenewéet, 87
The Dalles (fort), 42, 65
The Dalles, Oregon, 160, 161, 172, 173, 206
The Dalles Dam, 160, 162, 164, 165, 168, 180, 218
Thompson, Cecil I., 181
Thompson, David, 41–43
Thompson, Joe, 140
Thompson, Rose, 125
Thornhollow, Oregon, 83, 132
1000 Friends of Oregon, 236
Three Mile Dam, 241
Tiloukaikt, 64, 172
time ball. *See* ititámat
Timine Development Corporation, 251
Timothy, 23, 50
Tiwíiteq'is. *See* Old Chief Joseph
timnanáχt, 6, 12
titwatityáaya, 5, 9
Tomahas, 64, 172
Tonquin, 42
Tooholholzote, Chief, 76
Totus, Lee, 118
Totus, Raymond, 118
Touchet River, 27, 28, 76
Towatoy, Cornelius, 81, 83
Townsend, John Kirk, 48

Toy Toy, Charlie, 123
trade, 31–35, 41–48, 53, 62, 63
Trafzer, Clifford, 77
trails, 26–29, 32, 33, 35, 42, 48, 63, 132
Treaty of 1855, 23, 62, 65–78, 62, 81, 84, 86, 87, 88, 93–96, 98, 100, 101, 110, 111, 136, 138, 141, 142, 149, 159, 162, 165, 169, 172, 174, 182, 187, 188, 191, 218, 221, 227, 229, 231, 234, 239, 241, 240, 242, 247, 251
Tribal Credit Program, 170
Tribal Development Office (TDO), 185, 194, 196, 198, 216, 217
Tribal Employment Rights Office, 202, 205
Tribal Farm Enterprise, 170
Tribal Gaming Commission, 211
Tribal Stream Zone Alteration Regulation, 216
Tribal Tax Code, 241
Tucannon River, 27, 28, 76
Tutuilla. *See* Shishnimishpa
Tutuilla Presbyterian church, 124, 126, 128, 129, 130. *See also* Shishnimishpa
Twisted Hair, 36
Tygh Indians, 28

Ukiah, Oregon, 28
Umapine, Chief, 81, 84, 137
Umatilla Allotment Act, 104, 105, 107, 108, 174
Umatilla Agency, 100, 102, 103, 108, 113, 122, 128, 132, 152, 175, 203
Umatilla Basin Project. *See* Umatilla River Basin Salmon Recovery Project
Umatilla Indian Reservation, 15, 33, 39, 61, 65, 67–74, 81, 82, 84, 86, 89, 93–98, 102, 103, 105, 106, 108, 110, 113, 115, 117, 121, 123, 125, 126, 131, 138, 141, 151, 157, 158, 160, 167, 168, 170, 171, 175, 181, 185, 187, 188, 193–5, 201, 206, 207, 211, 215–17, 226, 227, 240, 242, 247, 249, 250
Umatilla Inheritance Act, 240
Umatilla National Forest, 239
Umatilla River and Basin, 27, 28, 33, 37, 40, 42, 43, 48, 51, 63, 81, 102, 103, 122, 123, 128, 130, 132, 133, 160, 165, 167, 218, 220, 229-236, 241, 247, 248, 250
Umatilla River Basin Salmon Recovery Project, 197, 229-36, 248, 252
Umatilla Tribal Housing Authority, 170, 201
Umatilla Indians, 5, 17, 24, 26-28, 31, 33-35, 37, 40, 42-44, 46, 51-54, 62, 65-69, 73-75, 78-79, 81, 84-

87, 89, 93-95, 97, 99, 103, 108, 111, 113-15, 117, 120, 125, 135-7, 141, 155, 157-60, 162-6, 169, 166-8, 170-2, 174, 176, 181, 185-8, 214, 225, 226, 234, 239-40, 249, 252

Union, Oregon, 233

United States government, 33, 40, 46, 48, 61, 65, 67, 68, 71–73, 75, 78, 81, 84, 93–96, 99, 117, 121, 134, 136, 147–9, 159, 167, 168, 172, 173, 175, 182, 184, 187, 191, 218, 246, 247

Upward Bound, 239

U.S. Army Corps of Engineers, 161, 164, 165, 180, 218, 227, 239, 250

U.S. Department of Fish and Wildlife, 218, 220

U.S. v. Oregon, 182, 219–1, 239

U.S. v. Washington, 220

Ut'an'may, 10, 32, 33

Van Cleave, Dean Richard, 159

Vancouver, George, 34

Vancouver Island, 33

VISTA, 239

Wáashat, 15, 72, 196, 239, 245. *See also* Dreamer religion

Waíiletpu, 27, 31, 49, 50, 52, 64, 83, 87, 171, 173

Walamatkin, 40. *See also* Old Chief Joseph

Walla Walla Indians, 5, 17, 23-24, 26-29, 34-37, 39-41, 43-49, 51, 53, 54, 62, 65, 66-69, 73-75, 78, 79, 71, 85, 86, 87, 89, 81-82, 84, 93-97, 99, 101, 103, 111, 112-15, 117, 125, 136-7, 141, 154, 160, 162, 165-6, 169, 172, 173, 176, 188, 214, 226, 234, 240, 251

Walla Walla River and Basin, 27, 28, 39, 43, 45, 49, 62, 72, 160, 219, 229, 235, 249, 250

Walla Walla, Washington, 29, 65, 71, 84, 165, 169, 172

Walla Walla language, 214

Wallowa Mountains, 26, 27, 33, 83, 119, 128

Wallowa–Whitman National Forest, 239

Wallula Gap, 61, 72, 240, 242

Wallula Stone, 241, 240, 242

walptáaykt, 14

wálsakt, 5, 9

Walúulapam, 5, 17, 40

Wanaket Wildlife Refuge, 240

Wanako, 137

Wánapam, 5, 17, 28, 72

Wannasay, Anna, 169, 170

Wéeptes Tehey, 88

war, 60, 81, 82, 91: Bannock War, 81, 84, 85; Big Hole, battle of, 64; Cayuse War, 63–65, 74, 75, 81, 82, 83; Couer d'Alene War, 82; Nez Perce War, 64, 83, 96, 141; Spokane Plains, battle of, 83; Steptoe Butte, battle of, 82; Yakama War, 82; warriors and raids, 33

war dance, 83, 132

War on Poverty, 188, 194, 228, 239

War memorial, 241

Warm Springs Reservation and Tribes, 94, 121, 153, 156, 158, 162, 164, 171, 175, 178, 179, 182, 186, 195, 209, 219, 239

Warne, William E., 156

water rights, 103, 110, 179, 197, 216, 217, 223, 229, 234, 240

Wascopam Band, 82

Wayám. *See* Celilo Falls

Wayam band, 28

Wayám Village, 13

Wayampam, 29

we'nípt, 14, 15

Webb, Amy, 125, 140

Webb, Sol, 15

Wellness Center, 250

Wenaha, 27

Wenap-snoot, 65

Weyatenatemany (Young Chief), 65, 71, 75–79, 89, 114, 251

wéyekin, 83, 142

Weyíiletpuu (Líksiyu), 5, 6, 17, 40, 49, 50

Wheeler-Howard Act. *See* Indian Reorganization Act

whipman, whipwoman, 83, 118, 133, 140, 186

Whirlwind, Charley, Sr. (Shaplish), 7, 8, 137

Whitely, Deborah, 196

White, Dr. Elijah, 52,

White's Law of the Nez Perce, 52

White-Wilkinson, Margaret, 140

Whitman, Dr. Marcus, 49, 51, 63, 64, 85, 86, 172

Whitman incident, 63–65, 74, 81, 172, 173

Whitman Mission. *See* Waíiletpu

Whitman party, 50, 62, 64, 65, 82

Wildhorse Creek, 168

Wildhorse Resort and Casino, 198, 204, 208, 211, 215, 236, 239, 241

wildlife program, 217

Wilkes, Cr. Charles, 29, 50, 52

Wilkinson, Charles, 94

Willamette River and Valley, 49, 52, 63, 64
Williams, Bob, 118
Williams, Gertrude, 125
Williams, Glenn "Denny," 7
Williams, Ethel "Tessie," 18, 194
Willow Creek, 27, 28, 43
wing dress, 129, 125, 126
Winters v. United States (Winters doctrine), 110
Wishxam Indians, 28, 29
wiyánawi, 13
wiyekúutpeme tamtáyn, 12
Wocatsie, Chief Willie, 112, 135
Wocatsie, Viola, 169
Wolf, Chief, 114
Work, John, 48
Wooldridge, Earl, 156, 157

Wyeth, Nathaniel, 48
Yakama Reservation and Tribe, 28, 29, 66, 67, 70, 73, 74, 82, 124, 153, 156, 158, 162, 164, 169, 182, 219, 239
Yakima River, 28, 36
Yelépt, Chief, 37–41, 43, 62, 73
Yellow Bird, Chief, 62
Yellow Bull, 64
Yellowhawk Clinic, 196, 209
Yellowhawk Fun Run, 250
Yellowstone, 29, 35
Young Chief. *See* Weyatenatemany
Young Joseph. *See* Chief Joseph

Zimmerman, William, 121

Photographs and Credits

Page ii — Cayuse Sisters, Lee Robinson, photographer, courtesy of Tamástslikt Cultural Institute Archives

Page 2 — Charlie Shaplish Whirlwind, Sr. in front of Elephant Rock, courtesy of Jerry Gildemeister, photographer

Page 20 — Trade items, including wool, iron, beads, dice, tea bricks, sugar cones, and tobacco, with a reflection of a photograph of a man in trade blanket capote, which hands on the opposite wall. Exhibit, Tamástslikt Cultural Institute, Dallas D. Dick, photographer

Page 58 — Toni Minthorn Cordell, Joe Marek, and Fermore Craig, Sr., at Veterans' Memorial, Fourth of July procession, Dallas D. Dick, photographer, courtesy of Tamástslikt Cultural Institute

Page 90 — Young women in buckskin, photographed by Lee Moorhouse, Courtesy of Special Collections and University Archives, University of Oregon Libraries

Page 146 — Celilo Falls, Herb Alden, photographer, *Oregon Journal*, OHS neg., CN007237

Page 190 — Balloons fly over the Living Culture Village at Tamástslikt Cultural Institute, with a saucer-shaped pithouse in front of a steep-walled pithouse in the foreground, Dallas D. Dick, photographer, courtesy of Tamástslikt Cultural Institute

Page 244 — Viola Minthorn and Jessica Norvell work on cooked moss with elder Inez Spino Reves in Naami Nishaycht Living Culture Village, Dallas D. Dick, photographer, courtesy of Tamástslikt Cultural Institute

NOTE: Most of Lee Moorhouse's photographs that appear in this book were taken between the 1890s and 1920s. He did not put specific dates on the photos, except for special events such as Round-Up and the Fourth of July.